FK 18

AK1107

RESTAURANT PLANNING & DESIGN

RESTAURANT PLANNING & DESIGN

by Fred Lawson

Architectural Press

ISBN 0 85139 115 X
© Fred Lawson 1973
First published 1973 by Architectural Press Ltd.
Filmset and printed in Great Britain by
BAS Printers Limited, Wallop, Hampshire

PREFACE

Restaurant design can be expressed in a number of different ways—by showing photographs and illustrations, by describing selected schemes or by providing a basis of technical information.

In preparing this book, a combination of all of these various approaches has been adopted. Business and functional aspects —on which management policy may depend — have been considered as well as the practical details of construction and furnishings which are required by the architect and interior designer.

Photographs and drawings have been chosen to illustrate particular features but also to provide practical examples of complete schemes since restaurant design is very much a question of this total effect rather than of components viewed in isolation. Not least in importance, a large part of the text has been devoted to technical information— which is so often lacking in studies of this kind. Dual units, in SI and Imperial dimensions, have been quoted throughout for easy identification and reference and a Briefing Guide has been included to show, step by step, the stages in design procedure.

This balance of detail and practical application has been selected deliberately not only to meet the needs of architects and designers but also to provide technical information in a convenient form which will be of value to managers of catering establishments.

For further reading a companion book on the principles of catering design covers, in depth, the more specialised subjects of food storage, preparation and cooking and reference is made to other related studies.

The photographs and details shown on the plans have been furnished by many hotel companies and architects and designers whose work has been prominent in the field of restaurant design. Among these I feel obliged to mention in particular the valuable help given by Mr G. Fowler, project manager, Trust Houses Forte Ltd; Mr A. K. Knight, property manager, Berni Inns Ltd; the management of Centre Hotels Ltd, Crest Hotels Ltd, the London Hilton, and North Hotels Ltd; R. F. Macdonnell, architect, Dublin; W. H. McAlister and Partners, architects; Lucas Mellinger, architect; Stephenson, Gibney & Associates, architects; the Plessey Co Ltd; Oliver Toms (Catering Equipment) Co Ltd; James Stott & Co (Engineers) Ltd, and Concorde Catering Equipment Ltd. I am indebted to Tielman and Roselyne Nicolopoulos for their assistance in preparing drawings for publication.

F. R. Lawson.

CONTENTS

SYMBOLS USED ON PLANS

Number Symbol Equipment

A STORAGE AREAS

1 Shelving

2 Vegetable racks

3 Vegetable bins

4 Storage bins

5 Weighing machine

6 Mobile racks

7 Trolleys

B PREPARATION AREAS

8 Work table or bench

9 Work bench with cupboards/drawers

10 Work bench with waste bin

11 Worktop with shelves

12 Single sink with drainer

13 Double sink unit

14 Mobile sink

15 Wash-hand basin

16 Marble-topped bench

17 Vegetable rack

18 Salad preparation unit

19 Pot rack

20 Trolley

21 Mobile tray racks

22 Refrigerator

23 Mobile refrigerator/refrigerated trolley

24 Deep freezer

25 Potato peeler

26 Chipping machine

27 Mixing machine

28 Slicing machine

29 Chopping block

30 Cutting board

COOKING AREA

31 Proving oven

32 General purpose oven

33 Pastry oven or pizza oven

34 Forced-air convection oven

35 Steaming oven

36 Microwave oven

37 Boiling top—general

8

38	Boiling top with open top burners	66	Tray stand
39	Boiling top with solid top	67	Ice cream conservator
40	Bratt pan	68	Cutlery stand
41	Oven range with boiling top	69	Tray rail
42	Griller or salamander	70	Cashier's desk
43	Deep fat fryer		
44	Boiling pan—rectangular type		

WASH-UP AREA

45	Boiling pan—circular	71	Receiving table for soiled dishes
46	Open well bain-marie	72	Stacking table for clean dishes
47	Extraction hood over equipment	73	Dishwashing machine—semi-automatic
48	Griddle plate	74	Dishwashing machine—'flight' type
49	Toaster	75	Clearing trolley

SERVING AREA

		76	Waste-disposal unit or scraping point
50	Plate lowerator or dispenser	77	Water boiler
51	Hot cupboard unit	78	Water softening equipment
52	Hot cupboard with bain-marie top	79	Refuse bins
53	Bench type bain-marie unit		
54	Pass-through unit—heated		

BAR AREA

55	Pass-through unit—cold	80	Wine refrigerator
56	Refrigerated under-cupboard	81	Ice-making machine
57	Refrigerated cupboard with doleplate	82	Bottle storage racking
58	Refrigerated display cabinet	83	Glass storage racking
59	Milk dispenser	84	Beer engine or dispense points
60	Beverage unit	85	Glass-washing machine
61	Coffee unit	89	Chilled water dispenser
62	Counter unit—unheated		

DINING AREAS

63	Counter unit—with infra red lamps above	90	Beverage vending unit
64	Counter display cabinet	91	Food vending unit
65	Compressor or boiler under counter	92	Waiter/waitress serving station

Technical Standards

At the end of each section and where otherwise applicable, a list of related British Standard Specifications is provided as a source of reference for detailed technical information. Such standards are intended primarily for British practice but the basic functional requirements are generally relevant on an international scale. Further details regarding the Specifications may be obtained from the

British Standards Institute,
Park Lane, London W1A 2BS.

Similar provisions, regulating quality and practice in their respective countries, are made through standards published by other national agencies including the following:

American National Standards Institute Inc., (ANSI)
1430 Broadway,
New York, N.Y. 10018, USA.

American Society for Testing Materials (ASTM)
1916 Race St.,
Philadelphia 3, PA, USA.

Association Française de Normalisation (AFNOR)
Tour Europe,
92, Courbevoie, Paris.

Deutscher Normenausschuss (DNA)
1000 Berlin 30,
Burgrafenstrasse 4–7.

INTRODUCTION

Catering is now in a transitional stage poised ready for change. In the same way as the corner shop has given way to the supermarket, the catering industry is beginning to undergo a process of rationalisation. More and more people are eating out and buying meals to take home; the average customer has greater freedom of choice through increasing affluence and mobility. Equally, the customer is tending to exercise greater discrimination in his search for good food, service and surroundings and in assessing value for money. Through education and travel, he is able to draw comparisons, and may wish to experiment with greater variety of choice. Most of all the customer is aware of hygiene and food quality and the enforcement of higher standards—legally or commercially—which will do much to set the pattern for the future.

At the same time, many caterers are finding it increasingly difficult to show a reasonable return on the capital invested. Costs of labour, food and rents are rising fast, and traditional kitchens are often too large and complex to be operated at an economic level. Also, with traditional methods of food preparation, the productivity of staff is usually low and erratic, and there is often great difficulty in recruiting and retaining adequate and competent staff. From the designer's point of view, the emphasis in restaurant design has previously tended to be heavily weighted towards the expensive and perhaps extravagant décor of the high class establishment. More and more attention however is now being given to the design of the ordinary restaurant, the cafeteria and canteen as customers and employees alike become aware of the need for functionally attractive surroundings as part of their enjoyment of a meal, and this book has been written with this in view.

The future in catering is therefore one of rationalisation, and the successful caterer will be the one who can appreciate the need for change and grasp the opportunities this will afford.

1 RESTAURANT DESIGN

1.01 All aspects of restaurant design are necessarily influenced by four fundamental considerations which are, to a large extent, interrelated:

(a) *Business*—in particular the need to market the establishment and its products in order to attract custom;

(b) *Financial*—the investment costs which will allow a financially viable operation;

(c) *Functional*—the operation of the particular type of catering and the creation of the desired 'atmosphere' in the restaurant;

(d) *Practical*—the features of construction, contents and services which will enable the business to function satisfactorily.

The first three aspects are considered in outline in this chapter as a preliminary to examining their interpretation in the subsequent chapters dealing with practical features of design and construction.

1 BUSINESS CONSIDERATIONS

Marketing.

1.02 The design of a restaurant or other type of catering establishment is not a matter which can be pursued in isolation. Together with decisions on the size and style of operation, range of menu, standard of service and other aspects of policy, it must aim to satisfy a particular market need. Thus, as a basic requirement for design, it is necessary to have some knowledge of the types of customers who are likely to patronize the establishment, their likes and dislikes and the circumstances which might influence their choice. Such information is obtained by carrying out market surveys to assess the potential demand for various types of restaurant facilities and, from this, the feasibility of investing in a particular premises can be properly evaluated.

1.03 *The customer.* Characteristics such as age, social interests, occupation, status and income level will all have expression in preferences for different kinds of restaurants. To try do identify these relationships some form of customer classification may be adopted—for example, the Institute of Practitioners in Advertising (IPA) system of grouping a consumer population into 5 social grades, A B C1 C2 D and E according to occupational and social status. A parallel approach is to try to ascertain National and local public attitudes towards food and eating out.

1.04 *The circumstances.* Apart from personal attitudes, the particular circumstances in which a meal is required must often affect the choice of restaurant, for instance—

• *The situation*—whether at home, at work, travelling, on holiday, out shopping or sightseeing.

• *The occasion*—in seeking entertainment, social company, business, escapism, seclusion, or quiet relaxation; and

• *The need*—for economy, speed, convenience, rest or stimulation, diet or sustenance.

Deliberate selection usually requires some prior knowledge of the eating establishment either as a result of previous experience or through advertisement, recommendation or observation and is generally decided well in advance of the occasion.

When a decision is taken on impulse, the restaurant or cafeteria may also be known, or of a type which is familiar to the intending customer, or may be chosen simply because of its location and apparent suitability for the purpose. In these circumstances, the convenience of location and the prominence and external appeal of the premises play a large part in attracting passers-by, but the selection still depends, ultimately, on the personal interests and circumstances of the would-be customer. The young extrovert will probably be attracted to a bright cafeteria with large windows which reveal a lively—even noisy and crowded—interior; a tired shopper will no doubt seek a convenient, quiet coffee shop with a select but informal atmosphere, while a busy executive might look for an exclusive secluded restaurant as a necessary extension to his working environment.

Employee catering

1.05 The same considerations of customer preferences might equally apply in employee catering. The operator used to working in large factory production areas will probably feel more at ease in a large canteen than isolated into small groups, while the reverse situation is likely to be preferred by administrative staff. In the case of senior executives, the opportunity afforded during lunch to discuss business and to entertain visitors may warrant a high degree of privacy and sophistication in the design of catering facilities.

Evening meals

1.06 Circumstances change during the course of the day and the type of dining facilities sought in the evening are usually completely different from those required, say, at lunch time. The mood and needs of the customer are changed; it is the pleasurable experience of dining out which is often as important as the meal itself, and eating

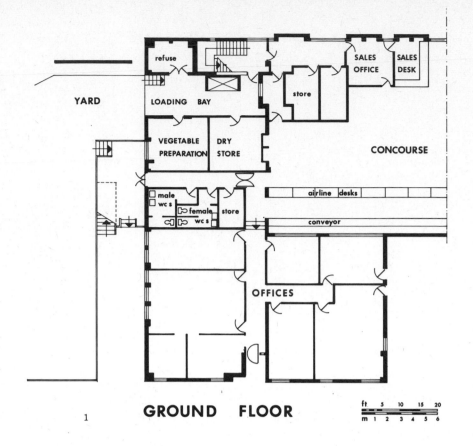

refuse

YARD

LOADING BAY

store

SALES OFFICE

SALES DESK

VEGETABLE PREPARATION

DRY STORE

CONCOURSE

male wc s

female wc s

store

airline desks

conveyor

OFFICES

1 **GROUND FLOOR**

ft 5 10 15 20
m 1 2 3 4 5 6

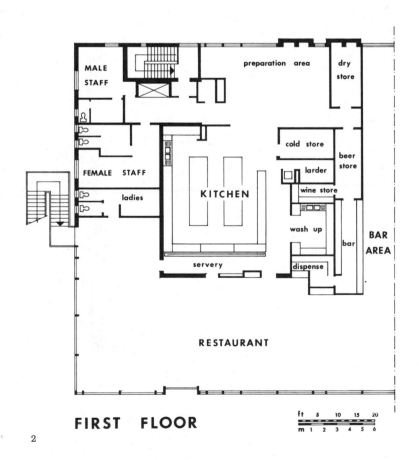

MALE STAFF

preparation area

dry store

FEMALE STAFF

ladies

KITCHEN

cold store

larder

beer store

wine store

wash up

bar

BAR AREA

servery

dispense

RESTAURANT

FIRST FLOOR

ft 5 10 15 20
m 1 2 3 4 5 6

2

Aldergrove Airport, Belfast. Architects—W. H. McAlister and Partners.
Plans of the ground floor servicing area[1] from which food and other goods are transported by lift to the first floor kitchen which is located adjacent to the restaurant.[2]

14

3

4

The main bar serves the area adjacent to the departure lounge based on an open plan arrangement[3]. To one side of the lounge, with a view over the aircraft embarkation/disembarkation area, is the restaurant which seats 120 and a Function room which can be separated by a folding partition and provides seating for a further 80 diners. The restaurant is designed on conventional lines, utilising the airport activity as a focal point of interest beyond the tables[4].

Rapid self-service meals are provided in the buffet situated on the other side of the lounge area which also forms part of the open plan design[5].

5

6
Post House, Swindon. Trust Houses Forte Ltd.
Artist's sketch showing view of the restaurant as seen from the
adjacent road. During the last few years Trust Houses Forte
have constructed a network of Post Houses strategically
positioned along main motor routes and near important centres
of commerce and tourism.

7
Mercedes Benz (Agam), Utrecht, Holland. Catering design—
A. W. Hanfrey for Sutcliffe Catering Co Ltd.
External view of new offices and showrooms with the staff
restaurant on the second floor of the block in the foreground.
The area is serviced by 2 hoists from the first floor kitchen and
self service counters are centrally positioned so that the
maximum number of diners can have window seats.

8

9

*Entrance to the self service area with menu clearly displayed[8].
A view behind the service counter, which is of modular construction, shows the small call order units and hoist for servicing the counter with food from the kitchen[9]. Another hoist
faces into the dirty crockery pre-wash area—on the reverse
side—and is used to return crockery to a first floor dish washing area. From the end of the counter, the dining area extends
across the room with planted containers to provide screening
and direct circulation movement[10].*

10

and drinking are often prolonged to a leisurely pace. For this purpose, selection of a restaurant is usually a much more deliberate process; the atmosphere in which the meal is to be enjoyed assumes a significant part of this choice. Questions of distance and convenience may be relatively insignificant and the market area for a restaurant of high reputation may be extensive.

Market Research

1.07 Fundamental to the success of any restaurant enterprise is the need to identify, quantify and subsequently develop the market which the establishment is intended to serve. In part the market demand may be in existence but it may also be created by displacing other businesses or by attracting wider interest.

Identification

1.08 As part of the promotion of business it is necessary to introduce and develop a particular type of image which is compatible with the price and standards of meal and service offered. This image may be created, in part, by the choice of name. A name appropriate for this purpose may be associated with the type of food, the style of meal, the area or building if prestigious, or a personality if well known. To establish a sense of permanency, a name with historical or traditional links may be adopted or, if an impression of modernity is desired, an appropriately recognisable word may be created.

Having established the name, it is important to project this at every opportunity either directly by repetition or by suggestion and association. Frequently, the theme of design is framed around the title of the restaurant and

this association is then used to develop the particular atmosphere which is desired. Thus one may find the Fleece Bar in Bradford; the Angus Steak House; Duke's in Duke Street; and the Rice Bowl which, needless to say, serves Chinese food.

12

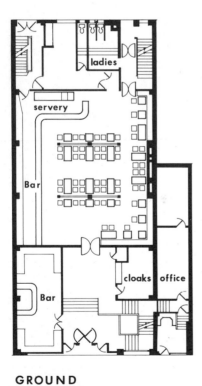
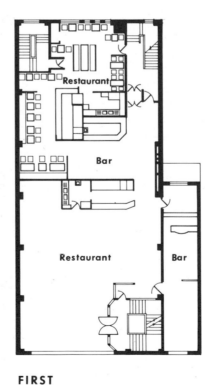
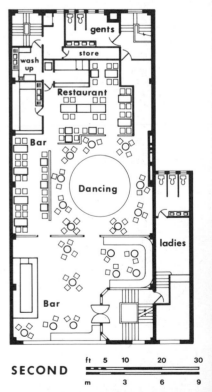

GROUND   FIRST   SECOND

11

The Café Royal, Manchester. Berni Inns Ltd, Property and Planning Department.

The Berni Inn concept is based on the small licensed restaurant which has its own aperitif bar and is served by a grill unit cooking food to order in front of the customer. Within a premises there are usually several restaurant units, each with a slightly different menu, grouped around a courtyard or stairwell.

A conventional kitchen is not required and here this has been converted to a restaurant unit of 48 seats. The theme of the restaurant reflects the local interests of the nearby Hallé Orchestra with portraits of composers. Seats are upholstered in velvet and deeply pinned while the exposed joinery work is in mahogany.

18

Operation

1.09 By itself, the title or even the carefully designed interior will do no more than set the stage for the meal. The image of the restaurant and the reputation of the operating company will, in the long term, depend on whether the operation measures up the the expectations of the customers.

Thus, design must be identified with the operation. A restaurant which relies for its reputation on quick service must be primarily designed to facilitate speed and convenience and other features play a minor role. Similarly a reputation of quiet, almost leisurely sophistication in the dining room will be made possible only by super efficient and highly organised service from the kitchens to ensure that everything is in its proper place at the time it is needed. If there is any failure in communication, or delay in service, the image is immediately lost regardless of the elegance of the surroundings.

The reputation for variety demands careful planning of the kitchen and selection of equipment to ensure that a sufficiently varied choice of food is available at all times. Quality food is often cooked or grilled in front of the customer and, for this purpose, it is necessary to provide visual cooking facilities. Often this is extended to allow the customer to select the particular item of fish or meat, such as steak, before its preparation and, in this case, suitably displayed refrigerated counters will be required and must be in some way incorporated into the overall design of the restaurant.

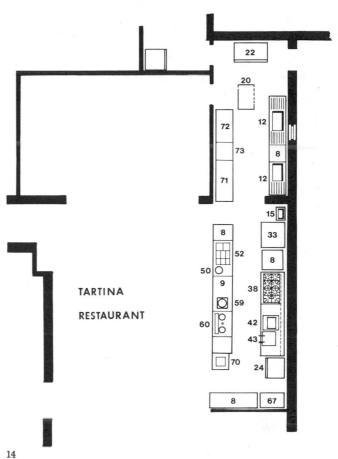

14

Equipment by Oliver Toms Ltd.
Details of the kitchen facilities serving the Tartina Restaurant.

13

The Tartina Restaurant, Portsmouth Centre Hotel. Centre Hotels Ltd.

An attractive display of visual cooking of Continental style meals in a modern functional setting.

15

Call order Units. Stotts of Oldham.
Modern call-order grill unit designed to blend with the elegant
decor of a Manchester club.

Integration

1.10 It is this aspect of design which is often neglected. A dining area, whether in an expensive restaurant or a simple snack bar, must be a unified whole, not a collection of different ideas. The interior design must incorporate the facilities necessary for its proper and efficient use and these should, where possible, form a vital part of the scheme. For example, a display counter—where required—should be designed as a focal point of interest. The counter front, back-bar and canopy can be arranged, decorated and illuminated in a way which creates an appropriate level of sophistication and 'taste'.

In order that suitable provision is made for operational needs, it is better to determine and define these from the beginning rather than to introduce the catering policy after the design scheme is formulated.

Promotion

1.11 A company with several catering outlets may wish to adopt a general brand image which can be applied equally to all their establishments. Such arrangements allow for economy in promotion and advertising since the brand name identifies all the catering premises simultaneously. The repetition of the name implants it in the public's mind and also helps promotion.

When a company earns a good reputation, the name tends to become synonymous with this standard of service and quality. Equally, in some circumstances, the reputation or status of the users may generate interest and further custom. With this prior knowledge or expectation, the choice of restaurant is often made deliberately and a traveller or visitor will seek out the address simply because he or she is assured of obtaining the particular type of meal and surroundings which are identified with the brand image.

Such methods of promotion are used in franchising and in the creation of chains of restaurants and hotels in London and provincial towns and even on an international basis.

Standards

1.12 One of the limitations imposed by brand identification is the uniformity of standards and—to a certain extent—design, which is necessary to ensure that the various premises are recognised to be of a comparable level. If a customer is dissatisfied by one he will tend to regard all other catering establishments in the group in the same light. Hence it is essential that in none of the premises must the standards be allowed to fall below a certain level. On the other hand there must also be an upper limit to the standards of design, food or service, not only to regulate cost and investment but also to avoid disappointment when one experience of a meal is not so good as a previous one.

1.13 If it is desired to operate at different levels in different establishments the simplest answer is to adopt different brand images. Thus a company may run a cafeteria serving fast economical meals under one title and another with expensive personal service under another. Different restaurants can often conveniently operate under the same roof and even be served by the same kitchen. In this way the market is broadened to include a whole range of customers with widely differing needs and tastes.

16

Post House, Coventry. Trust Houses Forte Ltd.
One of the latest Post Houses, completed 1971, the Coventry
Post House has 200 bedrooms, a main restaurant seating 110
and a buttery which can accommodate up to 80. The exterior
is illustrated by an artist's sketch.

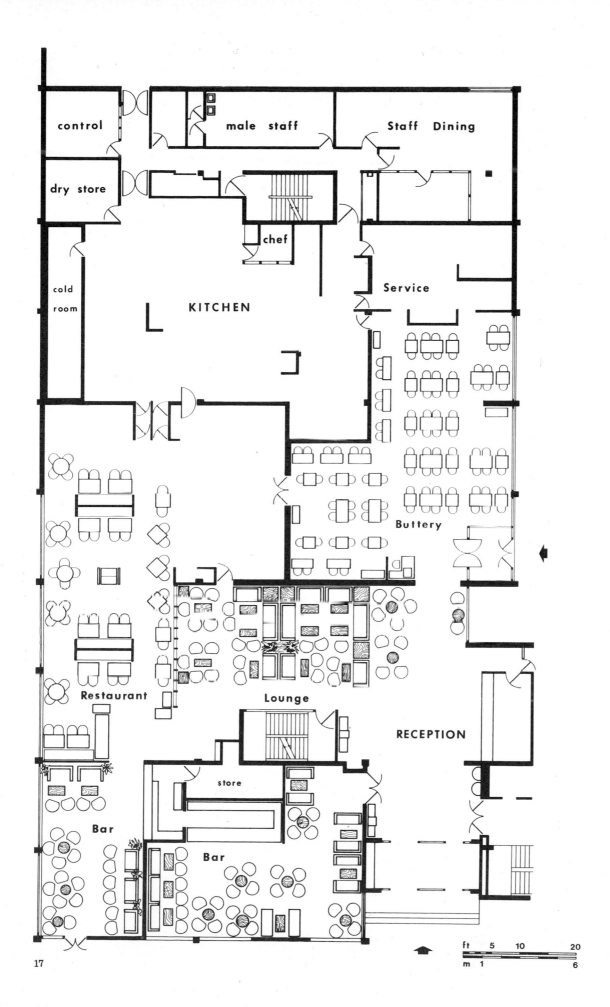

control

male staff

Staff Dining

dry store

chef

cold room

KITCHEN

Service

Buttery

Restaurant

Lounge

RECEPTION

store

Bar

Bar

17

ft 5 10 20
m 1 6

Plans showing the layouts of the restaurants, bars, lounges
and other catering facilities.

Hotel restaurant design

1.14 In the case of a group hotel the limitations on restaurant design are not so stringent since it is the overall quality and service in the hotel generally which establishes the initial relationship with the customer. Hence hotel restaurants may be designed around a selected theme, for example on historical or local association; or to complement a particular speciality of food or to identify a particular mode of service, such as a buttery bar.

1.15 With hotel restaurants, in particular, there is often a need to attract and promote non-residential trade. As a typical illustration of the use of a city-centre hotel restaurant by residents the occupancy figures could be: breakfast up to 100 per cent; lunch less than 10 per cent; dinner 20 to 30 per cent.

The demand at lunch time will depend very much on the type of guest using the hotel, and its location. It will also be affected by the provision of facilities such as conference and meeting rooms which enable business to be conducted in or from the hotel rather than outside. Similarly the take-up of evening meals by residents will be affected by the hotel location and entertainment facilities but also, to some extent, by the 'appeal' of the dining area. In the more relaxed mood of the evening, the design and 'atmosphere' of the surroundings tend to assume greater significance and the resident who has already experienced meals in the restaurant during the day may wish to experiment by eating out elsewhere in the evening.

1.16 One solution to this wide fluctuation in demand is to reduce the size of the restaurant to an economic level by providing room service as an alternative for breakfast and carried to the extreme, the hotel garni—the 'bed and breakfast' hotel—may have no restaurant at all, relying entirely on service in rooms.

A second approach is to provide more than one place for meals but on a much smaller scale than the large tradi-

18
The London Hilton, Park Lane, London. Architects: Lewis Solomon, Kaye & Partners.
Exterior view of the London Hilton which rises twenty-eight storeys and has a total of five restaurants and five bars at basement, first floor, second floor and roof levels. In addition, there are excellent facilities for banquets, business meetings and conventions.

19
The Roof Restaurant and Bar.
The restaurant and bar have been redecorated by the American designer David Williams with emphasis on warmth and colour using rich apricot amber and aubergine against a background of gold.

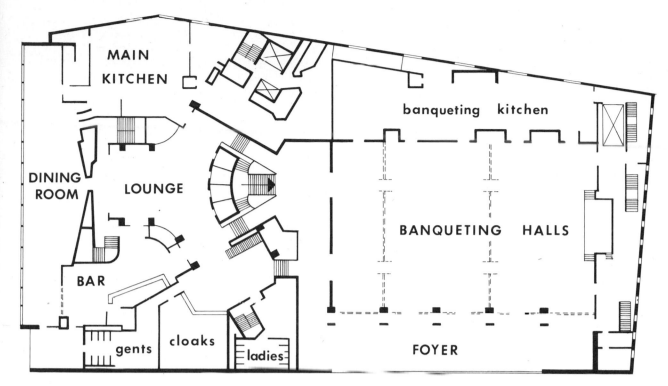

MAIN KITCHEN

DINING ROOM

LOUNGE

BAR

banqueting kitchen

BANQUETING HALLS

gents   cloaks   ladies

FOYER

FIRST FLOOR

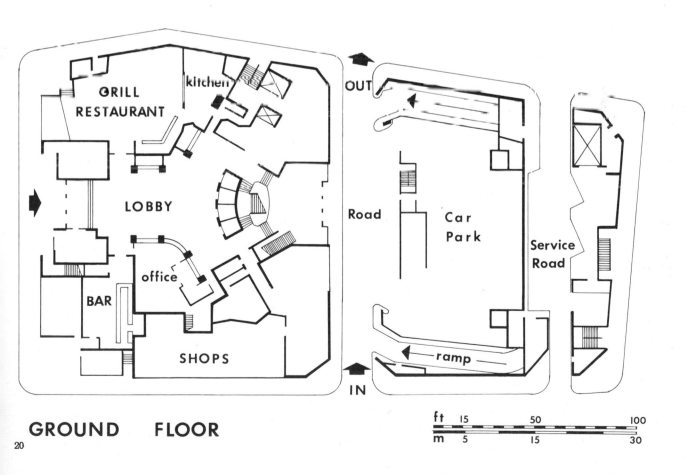

GRILL RESTAURANT   kitchen

LOBBY

BAR

office

SHOPS

OUT

Road

Car Park

Service Road

ramp

IN

ft 15   50   100

m 5   15   30

GROUND FLOOR

The London Hilton, Park Lane, London.
Plans showing the layout of the ground floor Grill Restaurant
and adjacent kitchen and of the dining room, banqueting halls
and their associated kitchens on the first floor.

tional restaurant. A coffee shop, buttery or grill bar may be used to meet the need for quick, light but high quality meals. Evening leisure dining and entertainment at other meals may be provided by a speciality restaurant or by a restaurant suitably located—say, in the basement or at roof level—and designed to create an interesting environment.

1.17 In most cases, hotel restaurants must also attract non-residential trade in order to operate economically and the merchandising requirements which apply to a commercial restaurant apply equally to an hotel. The potential customer must be made aware of the existence of the restaurant and its facilities; the location of the entrance and convenience of direct access to the dining room are critical features in design and the style of décor and meal must be able to compete with other restaurants in the same market. Bearing these requirements in mind it may be advantageous to create in the restaurant an identity separate from that of the hotel and to operate it on a more or less independent basis.

2 FINANCIAL CONSIDERATIONS

Evaluation

2.01 Assessment of value for money as judged by customers is difficult to quantify and is usually most clearly shown by a progressive increase or gradual decrease in numbers. Such factors as convenience, prompt service, good food, attractive surroundings and hygiene may each play a part. Theoretically, it should be possible to determine the relative value of each contributory factor in order to assess the effects of change. If, for example, there is a substitution of inferior food or a reduction in service, what effect will this have on numbers of customers and at what lower price structure will the balance of customer satisfaction be restored? Certain components will obviously have more value than others and the question which must be considered, in deciding the style and cost of a particular design, is how to evaluate the attraction of atmosphere. Would, for instance, the use of inexpensive simple furniture materially affect the response of the customer or are specially designed furnishings necessary to create an atmosphere of exclusive good taste?

Substitution

2.02 There is also the possibility of substitution to compensate for inadequacy or failings in other features. Good, interesting creative design can, in many instances, raise the appreciation of ordinary food by stimulating the senses and providing the optimum conditions for enjoyment—the conditions which can only be described as 'atmosphere'. On the other hand good quality food, well presented, can create such interest and enjoyment in itself that the surroundings become insignificant. Speed and convenience may also be rated highly when the time available for a meal is at a premium.

Profitability

2.03 Thus in assessing an investment, the restaurateur is faced with a number of decisions but, in total, the successful establishment and expansion of his business will depend on its value being assessed higher by the customer than the prices charged. His margin of profit, however, will depend on the prices which are charged being higher than the total costs (food, service and physical facilities) incurred in operating the business. It is this margin which, of course, represents the return on the capital investment

and the entrepreneurial risk involved.

The inter-unit comparison surveys conducted annually by the University of Strathclyde provide details of the financial statistics of restaurant operations and the summary shown in table 1 (i) indicates the specific costs and various levels of profit expressed as a percentage of total sales.

2.04 Where catering is considered on a non-commercial basis, the significance of profit as an indicator of successful operation is not always clearly evident. However, in every case there is a need for accountability which may be shown by comparisons of costs and other features between similar types of operations. In Britain, the annual reports of the Industrial Society are a valuable source of information and similar guidance is provided by the Department of Health in relation to hospitals and the Department of Education for school meals catering.

Table 1 (i) Summary of specific costs and various levels of profit expressed as a percentage of total sales.

| | Total sample | | |
	Median %	Lower Quartic %	Upper Quartic %
SALES	100·0	100·0	100·0
Less: COST OF GOODS USED	42·9	37·2	49·9
Less Total Staff Feeding Cost	2·2	1·6	2·8
GROSS PROFIT	40·8 / 59·2	34·7 / 52·3	47·7 / 65·5
Less: DIRECT WAGES	21·9	18·4	25·5
Plus Direct Staff Feeding Cost	2·2	1·5	2·5
	23·7 / 35·3	20·3 / 27·8	27·9 / 39·2
Less: MANAGEMENT AND ADMIN WAGES including Feeding Cost	4·6 / 29·1	3·3 / 25·7	6·2 / 35·4
Less: EXPENSES OPERATING EXPENSES:			
Uniforms	0·1	0·1	0·2
Laundry	0·7	0·3	1·5
Linen and Linen Hire	0·4	0·1	0·6
China and Glassware	0·4	0·2	0·8
Silverware	0·2	0·1	0·3
Kitchen Utensils	0·3	0·2	0·4
Heat, Light and Power	2·3	1·9	3·3
Paper Supplies	0·4	0·2	0·7
Menus	0·2	0·2	0·3
Contract Cleaning	0·2	0·1	0·3
Flowers and Decorating	0·3	0·2	0·4
Miscellaneous	2·3	0·7	2·9
TOTAL OPERATING EXPENSES	7·5	6·4	9·3
ADMIN AND GENERAL EXPENSES:			
Office Printing, Stationery & Postage	0·4	0·1	0·6
Telephone	0·2	0·1	0·3
Trade Subscriptions	0·1	0·0	0·1
Insurance	0·4	0·3	0·5
Commissions	0·7	0·4	1·0
Bad Debts	0·2	0·1	0·2
Professional Fees	0·4	0·3	0·6
Miscellaneous	0·7	0·3	2·0
TOTAL ADMIN AND GENERAL EXPENSES	2·4	1·7	3·7
Advertising and Promotion	0·7	0·3	1·0
Music and Entertainment	0·2	0·1	0·3
Rent	3·8	3·0	5·5
Rates	1·3	0·9	2·2
Depreciation	2·2	1·3	2·6
TOTAL EXPENSES	17·8	15·1	22·5
PROFIT	13·3	7·2	16·5
PROFIT before charging Rent, Rates & Depreciation	18·7	14·0	23·5

Based on the Inter-unit Comparison Survey, University of Strathclyde.

3 FUNCTIONAL CONSIDERATIONS

Life of a restaurant

3.01 As with most forms of business investment the profitable life of a restaurant, snack bar, canteen or any other type of catering facility is limited. In some cases the location of the premises may be such that the injection of new capital in order to redesign and modernise the facilities will attract new custom and provide a further lease of commercial life. The rundown of business may, however, have nothing to do with the suitability or otherwise of the premises or of the good value for money provided. It may be the result of the market moving elsewhere—for example the gradual decline of an area or the closure of local places of employment or entertainment. In considering whether further investment is worth-while, regard must be given to these secondary influences which are outside the control of the business.

Assuming there are no major changes in the market potential, the design life of a catering facility may eventually be determined by four main factors:—
· Changes in fashion and attitudes;
· Obsolescence or wear and tear;
· The effects of competition
· Changes in management policy

(a) Changes in fashion

3.02 Fashion changes in restaurant design occur regularly over cycles of time, the cycle being determined partly by external pressures and competition in commerce, and in part by the frequency of replacement normally found necessary or desirable to maintain a particular standard of appearance. In a modern affluent society the increasing appetite of the consumer for new domestic products and for changes in style to match has produced a greater awareness of fashion. Interior furnishings, fittings and décor quickly become recognisably 'dated' and this is particularly the case when a person dining out anticipates a standard of surroundings different from what he would normally enjoy at home.

Hence, a restaurant which relies on a modern impressive design and décor to attract custom may have a life cycle of only three to five years. On average, five to seven years would be a reasonable basis for the operation of most catering facilities, while a restaurant designed in formal traditional style and serving meals of high quality may require no dramatic change in design for seven to ten years or more.

Apart from fashions in design represented by changes in the style of furniture and décor there is also an underlying trend towards greater sophistication in environmental control. The user is now accustomed to, and expects, a comfortable ambient temperature and humidity; the air must be free from unwanted cooking smells; the lighting must be appropriate for his mood and, if he is seeking relaxation or seclusion, noise is likely to be an irritant. These standards of discrimination apply also to hygiene and to the quality of toilets and cloakroom facilities.

21

The Buttery, Staffordshire Post House, Newcastle-under-Lyme. Trust Houses Forte Ltd.
Constructed in 1966–67, the simple décor and furniture of one of the original Post House buttery restaurants illustrate the advancing sophistication of restaurant design over the last five years. The Buttery, seating 72, has orange coloured polypropylene chairs and pedestal type tables with ash wood tops.

22

The Buttery, Washington Post House, Tyneside. Trust Houses
Forte Ltd.
In one of the latest Post Houses, completed 1971, the buttery
of the Washington Post House is based on John Masefield's
poem 'Cargoes' illustrated by murals in alcoves along the wall.
The Buttery, which is licensed, serves light meals throughout
the day until late evening and has seating for 80.

23

Plan of the buttery layout.

ft   5   10   20

m   3   6

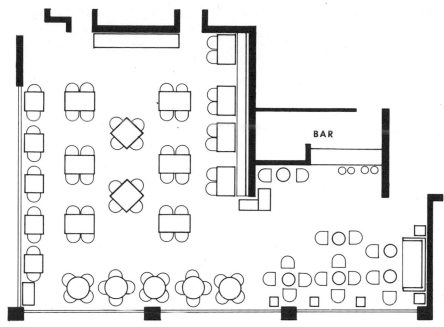

24

Plan of the restaurant layout, Washington Post House.

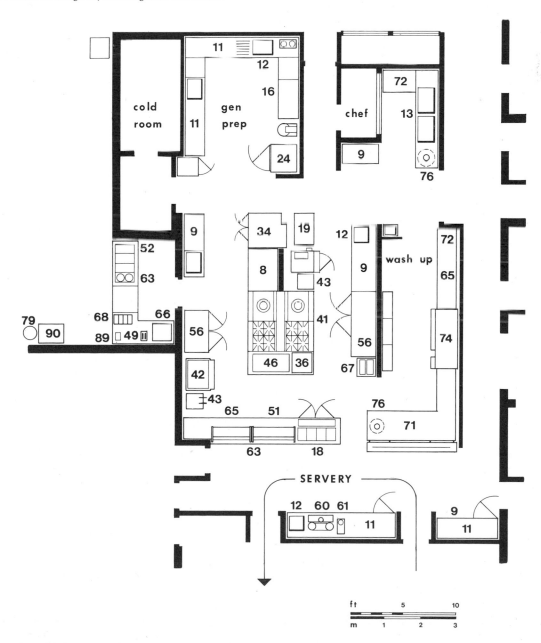

25

Plan of the main kitchen.

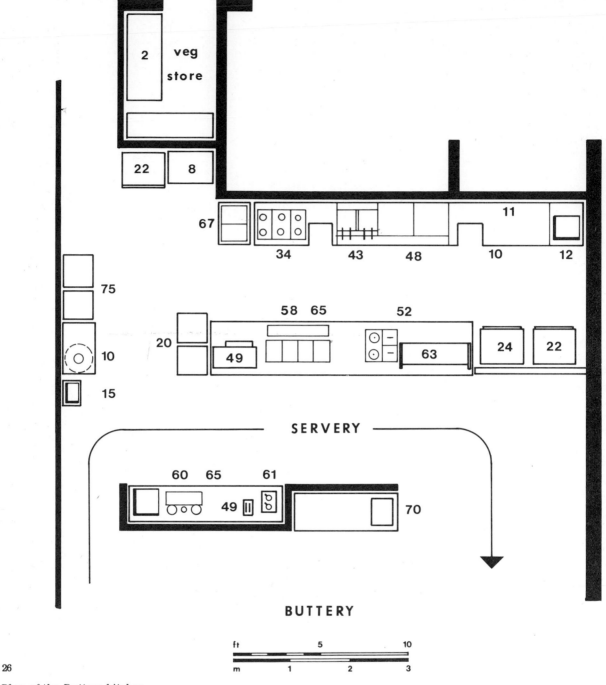

SERVERY

BUTTERY

ft   5   10

m   1   2   3

26

Plan of the Buttery kitchen.

Changes in attitude towards meals

Choice

3.03 In general, the consumer public enjoys greater freedom of choice now than ever before. There is greater mobility and opportunity to travel, more time is available for leisure, and more people have the means to enjoy dining out. However, the pace of life is also tending to be accelerated, time during the working day is often at a premium, and formality—necessitating a change of clothes—is increasingly waived.

Changes in attitude are reflected in the preference of the à la carte menu to a set meal; the tendency to take meals, in the form of snacks, outside conventional meal periods and by the use of self-service, or even self-catering, rather than waitress service. It is also shown by the patronage of restaurants which have character and 'atmosphere' in preference to those of nondescript style although there

may be an appreciate price difference. Even with a semi-captive market such as in employee catering, individual choice may be expressed by the percentage of employees who take up the meals provided and this will be an indicator of the suitability or otherwise of the catering service.

Time

3.04 Pressures on time often have a significant if not over-ruling influence on choice of meal. Breakfast is more likely than not in simple Continental style. Informality at dinner suggests a small intimate restaurant rather than one which is large with conspicuous seating. At lunch time the demand for hurried meals is shown by the preference for self-service rather than the risk of having to wait to be served at the table, and by the development of improved systems of self-service—such as the 'free-flow' system—which enable large numbers to be served with the minimum of waiting or queuing.

28

Duration

3.05 Meals are also tending to be shorter. A restaurant meal is now more commonly two courses than three and the attitude towards traditional cooked meals is also changing. The sweet is more likely than not pre-packaged or tinned and served cold; the growth of the sandwich bar concept indicates the popularity of food ready prepared for immediate consumption; and the development of visual and accelerated cooking equipment is in response to the demand for light grilled and fried meals prepared quickly to order.

(b) Obsolescence, wear and tear

Furniture and decoration

3.06 The useful life of different components in a catering establishment will vary from item to item. It may be necessary, for example, to redecorate the paintwork of a restaurant and its approaches once a year to maintain a bright attractive appearance. On the other hand expensive wall coverings such as screens and panelling may need to last as long as the concept—three to seven years or more. Similarly, the use of purpose-designed and fitted furniture will normally be based on the projected life of the restaurant and in this case the covers and those parts which are liable to soiling or damage must be renewable. In other cases, where standard furniture is selected, the life expectancy may be determined over a shorter period particularly if the furniture concerned is liable to become 'dated'.

Carpets are subject to considerable soiling, staining, wear and tear, and even with a good commercial quality carpet renewal may be necessary after three to five years. To localise the excesses of wear, carpets may be laid in strips or tiles with the facility of replacing only the parts necessary.

Catering equipment

3.07 In the kitchen, the functional life of cooking equipment, preparation benching and serving counters is generally well over ten years. However, while the equipment may still be serviceable, the cost of replacing burnt-out elements and switches and other components may reach a level which justifies change. Further, with electrical, gas-burning and mechanical equipment there is the problem of obsolescence. With modern design, equipment tends to become less obtrusive and awkward to use, controls provide greater sophistication of modulation and self-adjustment and efficiencies are higher. Hence there comes a time when it is desirable to introduce changes and for most purposes eight to ten years is a realistic period.

(c) The effects of competition

Competition

3.08 In entering into competition with another catering establishment, one objective is to attract the customers known to be using the other premises, ie to obtain business by displacement. At the same time, the fact that there is more than one restaurant or similar facility in an area tends to generate more trade because of this association. In addition, customers who would not normally eat out will, perhaps, begin to use the facilities and expand the market.

Provided the market is large enough, competition may be no more than a stimulus to better management and service. It is perhaps because of this lack of real competition that canteen facilities serving a captive or semi-captive market are frequently unimaginative and out of date.

In other situations, competition may cause the demise of a restaurant simply because the return on operating costs reduces to an uneconomic level. It may be that, with a restricted market, neither of two competing businesses can show a profit and both could exhaust their resources in trying to increase the value to the customer of the meals, service and surroundings without charging adequate prices to cover the real costs incurred.

Imitation

3.09 In entering into competition, the most effective way of revealing better value for money to the customer is to copy and improve on the facilities available elsewhere. Copying is also common where it is seen that similar facilities in another area—not in competition—are particularly successful and can be applied in a new scheme with or without modification.

Innovation and the introduction of new ideas into catering design and operation involve a greater risk and warrant a

27
Kitchen evolution
An hotel kitchen designed twelve years ago showing the apparently unplanned array of equipment and services. The use of wood surfaced preparation tables is now prohibited.

28
Staff Catering facilities, British Steel Corporation. Equipment by Stotts of Oldham.
A modern range unit of four ovens with matching bain-marie/ hot cupboard and two gas heated grillers.

careful appraisal of trends and fashions in addition to market surveys. A concept which is too far in advance of its time is just as likely to fail as one which is obsolescent. Equally a design may be impracticable or uneconomic at the particular level of market for which the business is catering.

It is the speed of innovation and copying which, to a large extent, determines the life of a restaurant rather than the durability of its components.

(d) *Changes in management policy*
3.10 Apart from external influences and competition, changes are introduced within the organisation, either to bring about savings or improvements in operation or to produce a better image. Such changes often stem from ambitious management and can generate greater trade and improved profitability over the long or short term. However, it is important to consider the total cost and timing of alterations.

The most economical way of introducing changes during the life of a concept is to utilise the opportunities afforded through normal replacement of decoration, carpets, linen, tableware and other items. By co-ordinating the timing of replacements which are necessary through obsolescence or wear and tear, with other desirable changes in styling and menu, it is possible to achieve dramatic improvements without necessarily alienating the original customers. However, to obtain the maximum benefit from redecora-

tion and replacements, it is essential that the mainten-ance programme is planned from the start and suitable schedules drawn up well in advance of the work so that the relationships and whole cost can be viewed in perspective. Accelerated obsolescence may also be brought about by innovations in equipment and facilities which warrant a change in the original concept or policy; for instance, the introduction of more economical, efficient or sophisti-cated appliances, or a change in the availability and cost of food materials in different forms. Similarly, changes may also be necessary because of operational problems particularly in respect of labour difficulties and costs.

4 CHARACTERISTICS OF CATERING FACILITIES
4.01 The range of facilities provided in catering for meal requirements is extremely wide, being determined by market demand and varying with size, price, occasions of use and other conditions. To establish design require-ments it is useful to classify restaurants into different types and, in this context, the most important distinc-tions are:
(a) methods of serving food.
(b) emphasis given to particular features.
Using this classification, restaurants can be broadly—although not exclusively—grouped into eleven types which also tend to reflect the degree of personal attention and sophistication provided. To some extent, this will show a correlation with the type and length of meals served

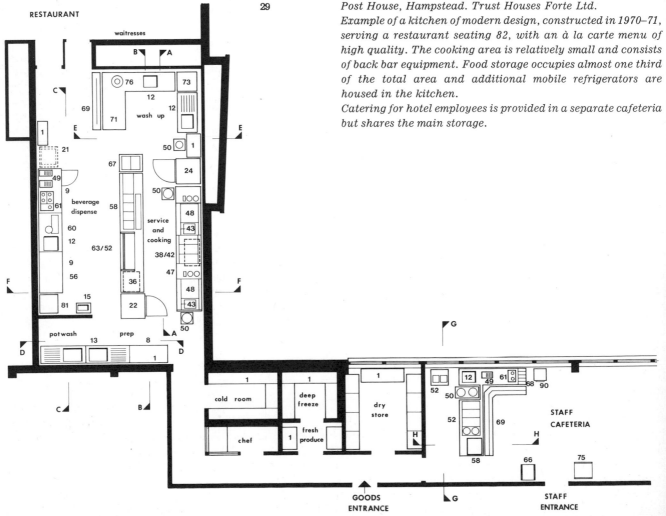

Post House, Hampstead. Trust Houses Forte Ltd.
Example of a kitchen of modern design, constructed in 1970–71, serving a restaurant seating 82, with an à la carte menu of high quality. The cooking area is relatively small and consists of back bar equipment. Food storage occupies almost one third of the total area and additional mobile refrigerators are housed in the kitchen.
Catering for hotel employees is provided in a separate cafeteria but shares the main storage.

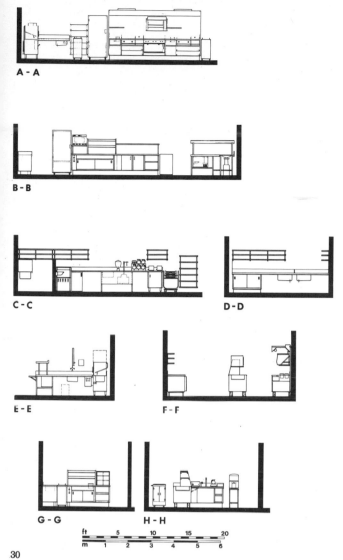

A - A

B - B

C - C   D - D

E - E   F - F

G - G   H - H

ft   5   10   15   20
m   1   2   3   4   5   6

30

Sections through the kitchen showing relative positions and heights of equipment

and the prices charged. The following summary outlines some of the features which are commonly associated with each type of catering facility.

Snackbar service

4.01 This is usually restricted to light meals and refreshments selected from a display or prepared to order and eaten at the counter or taken by the customer to a table. Emphasis must be given to economy of space and staff and the choice of call-order items is limited to a small number of popular dishes which can be easily prepared on simple equipment.

Food is normally cooked within the counter area in view of the customer and the basic equipment might include a small bain-marie, griddle plate and griller or toaster. A deep fat fryer and microwave oven may also be installed but the benefits of extending the menu range must be weighed against the extra costs of the equipment and its operation.

The food ingredients may be supplied ready prepared on a daily basis or be prepared on the premises in a separate small kitchen which is also used for sandwich making and washing up. Essential equipment for this purpose includes a refrigerator for storage of perishable food and a sink with hot and cold water. In common with other small premises, sanitary accommodation for staff may need

to be shared but must include hand washing facilities. As with all catering facilities, the location is critical and a small snack bar is often provided in a shop room or other premises adapted for this purpose. In this case, the designer may be faced with the problems created by a narrow frontage and other limitations on space, particularly in providing service access for delivery of food and installation of engineering equipment such as ventilating plant. To allow maximum use of the restricted space it is common for the minimum sizes of fixed furniture—including counter seating—and aisle spacing to be adopted. In addition, the area must be designed on strictly functional lines to facilitate cleaning and maintenance while the desired social 'atmosphere' may be created by the use of bright colours, modern fittings and features of interest, such as posters and murals. Music—to the customers' selection—is generally provided.

The spending rate per occupant is often low but, in a suitable location, the seat turnover tends to be high with a continuous occupancy extending beyond normal meal periods throughout the day and evening.

Variations of the snack bar concept which have been adapted to different situations include:

(a) *Public bar catering*—to provide sandwiches and simple hot meals during part of the day but with the minimum of alteration to the premises and capital expenditure.

(b) *Sandwich bar catering*—with specialisation in sandwich varieties and cold sweets, to eliminate the need for cooking equipment: the space utilisation is generally very high.

(c) *Coffee bars*—to supplement the main restaurant service in employee and residential catering. A separate beverage area may also serve as a counter-attraction to encourage customers to vacate the main restaurant after a meal, thereby increasing the seat turnover rate.

Café service

4.02 A café is usually designed along traditional lines and has a kitchen separate from the dining room. Waitress service may be provided for convenience although the meals are often ordered and collected when ready from a small service counter in the dining room. Choice on the menu is usually limited to two or three dishes and the main meals are plated in the kitchen although cakes and similar made-up items may be selected from a counter display.

Space in the kitchen and dining room is frequently restricted and these two areas may need to be at different levels, served by a food hoist or lift in order to utilise a basement or upper floor.

For economy in space and capital investment, the cooking equipment in the kitchen is usually kept to the minimum, based on a short menu of the most popular dishes, perhaps with one or two speciality items. If necessary, menu choice may be extended by the use of convenience foods, such as frozen prepared food and 'boil-in-the-bag' products.

The layout of furniture in the dining room must be designed for maximum use of the area and space allowances of 0·83m² (9 sq ft) per person or less are usually adopted. Furniture may be fixed or freestanding, selected from a standard manufactured range for economy and functional durability. Similarly, the interior décor is normally designed on strictly practical lines to facilitate cleaning and maintenance. In this area of catering, the market tends to be very price-conscious and trade is usually reliant on regular customers. To promote this relationship, features of domesticity may be included—eg gay curtains and occasional table decorations.

Self-service cafeteria

4.03 Self-service provides a number of advantages in that:
(a) the staff required for serving meals can be reduced;
(b) service of food to large numbers of customers arriving at the same time can be accelerated;
(c) choice of food items is facilitated and the serving counter acts as a display area to promote sales.

The main disadvantage lies in the amount of space occupied by the counter and its approaches and circulation areas. Typical space allowances for cafeteria service are in the order of 1·4 to 1·7m² (15 to 18 sq ft) per person. A long single counter, double counter or multiple short counters may be used, positioned within or preceding the dining areas. Essential features, common to all self-service arrangements, are simplicity of layout and ease of circulation to and from the service counters.

The kitchen area must be adjacent to or within a convenient distance of the servery. Pass-through units may be provided where there are dividing walls; otherwise mobile trolleys—preferably heated or refrigerated—may be required to transport food to distant counters. Kitchen equipment must be selected to meet the peak period of demand and a detailed assessment of meal requirements compared with appliance capacities must be made in order to install equipment of adequate size and versatility.

Self-service is often chosen for speed and convenience and the seat turnover rate is usually high, on average being occupied two to three times during each main meal period. The period of use may, however, be restricted to one main meal, as is often the case in employee catering.

In the dining area, the furniture and internal finishes must be selected to withstand heavy usage while retaining a

31

32

33

34

Staff Catering, Texas Instruments Ltd., Bedford. Equipment by Oliver Toms Ltd.
Free flow food hall with echelon units arranged in separate bays[31]. *Behind the service counters are pass through cup-* *boards supplied from the kitchen*[32]. *A salad counter is to one side of the main circulation*[33]. *Also illustrated are mobile cashier desks, the positions of which can be modified as required*[34].

good appearance with the minimum of attention and cleaning. To allow flexibility of use, it may be desirable for the furniture to be stackable and interchangeable in unit sizes.

Arrangements for clearance of tableware and the cleaning of tables are essential considerations which must be decided at an early stage in the briefing.

Variations of self-service include:

(a) *Vending installations* in which food is obtained from an automatic machine and heated, if required, by operating an automatically controlled oven.

(b) Prepared meals and other food items may be served for consumption off the premises. 'Take-away' arrangements vary considerably in the type and scale of operation and may be provided as an adjunct to normal catering facilities or as an exclusive system.

Counter service

4.04 The principle of counter service is similar to that of a snack bar but offers a wider range of selection of more expensive food items which are mainly prepared to order in view of the customer. To provide maximum seating, the counter is usually extensive and is often supplemented by waitress service to tables. For counter service the space occupied per diner varies between 1·4 and 1·9m² (15 and 20 sq ft).

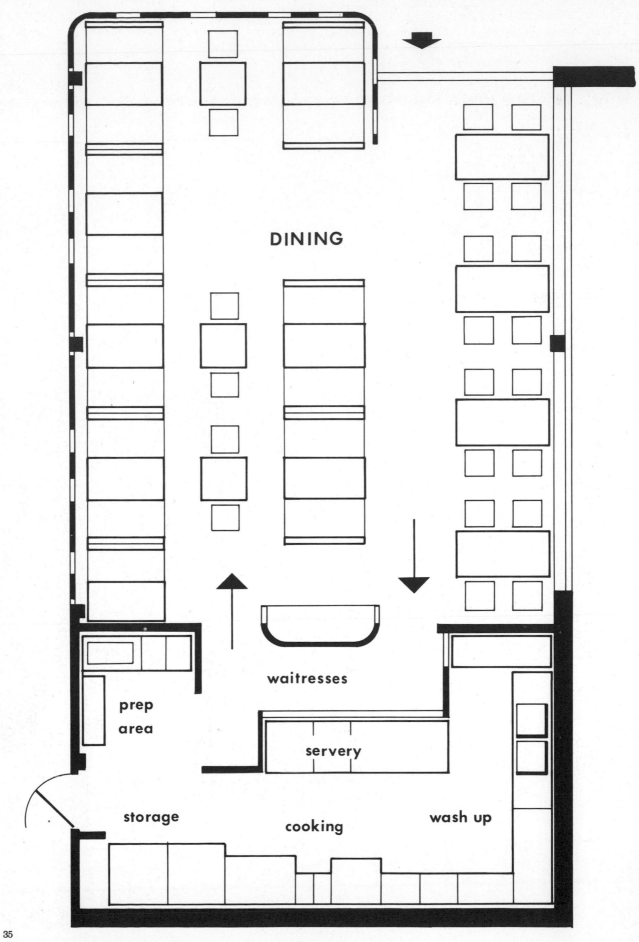

DINING

waitresses

prep
area

servery

storage

cooking

wash up

35

Coffee Shop, The Hull Crest Motel. Crest Hotels Ltd.
The Coffee shop constructed in 1971 overlooks the Humber
estuary and is characterised by features and furniture resem-
bling those of a ship[36].

As a rule, the counter fittings and equipment are designed and selected to give an appearance of sophistication. Cooking appliances are normally of modern modular design, mounted as back-bar units under a ventilation canopy. The latter is often designed as a decorative feature and, similarly, the design of the counter usually combines functional requirements with distinctive styling.

Preliminary food preparation and part-cooking is often carried out in a separate kitchen although the tendency is to minimise this work—and the size of the kitchen—by the use of pre-prepared food. Adequate provision must, however, be made for refrigerated storage and space for dishwashing equipment.

The furniture, including counter units, is generally constructed in situ or manufactured to specific design.

Counter service includes a variety of modified arrangements designed to improve service and/or utilise space.

These include the *tunnel system* in which tables or counters are arranged around parallel service passages, thus separating the customers from waiting staff.

Coffee shop service

4.05 A typical modern coffee shop provides waitress service to tables with a choice of refreshments and light meals selected from a menu. Sweets and gateaux may be displayed on a trolley or in an attractive showcase.

The styling of such a restaurant is usually modern but with emphasis on quiet informality and good taste. Subdued relaxing colours are mainly employed in the décor with simply styled but distinctive furniture. Fabrics are used to a greater extent than plastic upholstery.

The size and equipment for the kitchen can be kept to a minimum and will normally include facilities for accelerated cooking—such as a microwave or convection oven—and conventional call-order equipment.

Buttery bar service

4.06 This is a development of the counter service concept, catering for the modern tendency towards shorter meals of one or two courses taken at varying times of the day and evening. In a buttery bar, meals may be taken at the counter but are more commonly served at the table; some visual cooking may be provided but meals are mainly prepared in a separate kitchen—using similar back-bar equipment.

The design of a buttery bar is usually distinctive, often based on a theme and incorporating special features of styling and representation. Furniture is normally manufactured to special design, providing a balanced arrangement of freestanding chairs and tables and banquette seating. To allow almost continuous use over long periods, the design must facilitate easy cleaning and maintenance. Tables are invariably left uncovered except for place mats and the floor may be carpeted or—more commonly—finished with an attractive and durable flooring surface.

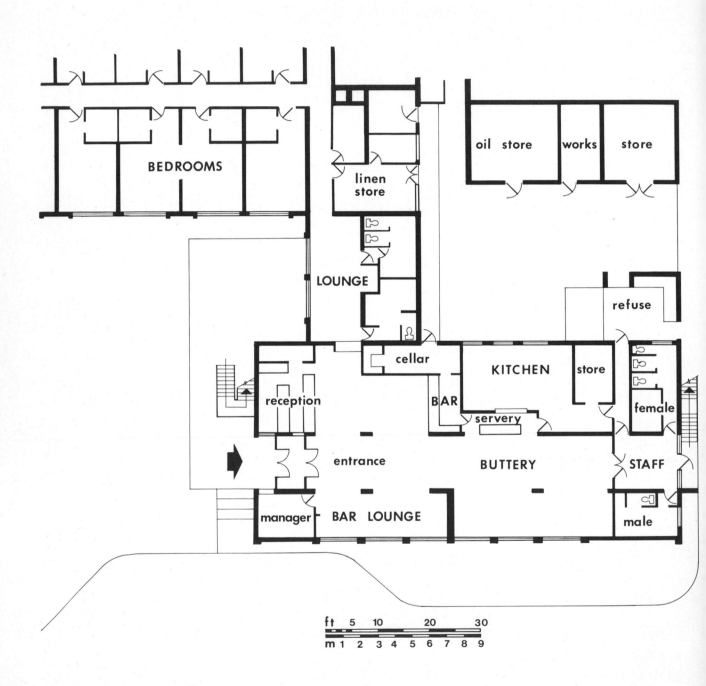

37
Post House, Sherborne. Trust Houses Forte Ltd.
Plan showing the lounge, buttery, kitchen and store areas.
Bedrooms are to the left of the hall lounge, separated from the public rooms.

38

The Buttery

Styling of the buttery, which seats 70, is deliberately severe with exposed brick walls, timber ceiling joists and brick flooring. This hardness is relieved by leather upholstered chairs and curtaining and by the use of pictures and ornaments to create focal points of interest.

39

The Bar and entrance to the Buttery.

Separation of the bar has been achieved by means of a dwarf partition enclosure lined with bench seating. The wall of the bar area is decorated by a wall mural and the ceiling in this part has been lowered to create the appearance of intimacy within the enclosure in addition to housing ventilation plant.

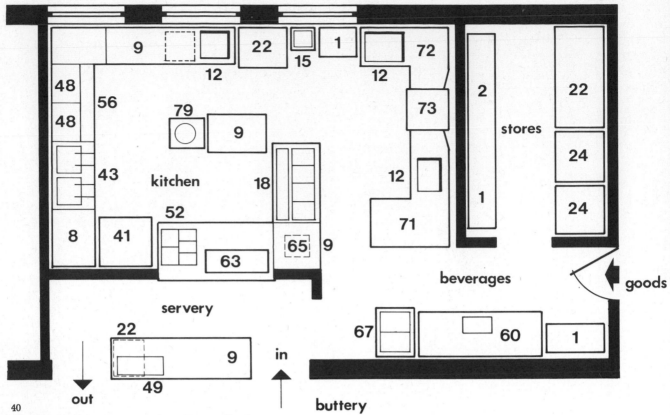

48 56
48
43 kitchen
8   41
52
63
9
22 12
79 9
18
65 9
22
72 12
73
12 71
2 1
stores
22
24
24
goods
beverages
67 60 1
servery
22 9
49
in
out
buttery

40

Plan of the kitchen layout, Post House, Sherborne.

Speciality restaurants

4.07 In a speciality restaurant emphasis is placed:

(a) on the style of food preparation and presentation as characterised by Chinese, Indian, Italian and other nationality restaurants, or

(b) by specialisation in particular food dishes—beef, fish, chicken, and so on.

The level of sophistication and prices varies widely from one restaurant to another but, in each case, the design, décor and fittings must complement the speciality and are usually specifically commissioned. Where possible, authentic decorations and fittings should be incorporated into the design.

Cooking is usually done on specialised equipment or equipment which has been adapted for the purpose, but conventional cooking facilities are also provided to allow variety in the choice of meals. In designing a speciality restaurant, it is desirable to carry out detailed research into recipes and methods of preparation as a preliminary to kitchen planning.

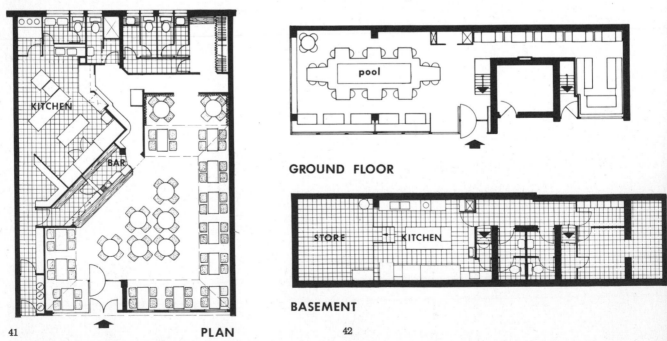

KITCHEN
BAR

41 PLAN

pool

GROUND FLOOR

STORE KITCHEN

BASEMENT

42

The Rice Bowl, Croydon. Architect: Lucas Mellinger.
Located in two new shop-units, the design provides the widest restaurant frontage, allowing a tradesmen's entrance on one side. The décor can be readily transformed – by wall-blinds and lighting effects – for evening use.

The Rice Bowl Edgware Road, London. Architect: Lucas Mellinger Associated with K. A. Short.
Designed as a Chinese restaurant of distinctive character, the main tables are grouped around an illuminated copper-lined pool with banquette seating along the perimeter wall.

The Yin-Yan motif shown on the entrance is repeated on the menu folders.

Traditional restaurants

4.08 Typically, the meals in a traditional restaurant are served from dishes at the table by a waiter or waitress. The tables are widely spaced and generously proportioned

Decorations include cane lamp shades, traditional Chinese articulated brass fishes and a tree rooted in the floor void.

with placings for two, four and larger groups as required. White or coloured table cloths and serviettes are provided and the tableware is usually of good quality china and silverware or stainless steel. Space allowances of 1·1 to

43

Parador nacional Casa del Corregidor. Spanish National Tourist Office.
An example of one of the state run paradors or hotels provided in restored castles, palaces and mansions by the Spanish

Ministry of Information and Tourism. In reconstructing the interiors careful attention has been paid to detail and authenticity.

44

Shiruko Restaurant, Kyoto, Japan.
The entrance to a traditional Japanese restaurant serving a popular choice of local dishes.

1·4m² (12 to 15 sq ft) per diner are usual.

The décor of a restaurant is generally restrained with emphasis on quality of carpeting, wall coverings and furniture. Floral arrangements, selected paintings and decorative features may be introduced as discreet focal points of interest and the effects of lighting and mirrors are often employed to heighten the impression of space and quality. The highest levels of cuisine are often served in surroundings of elegant simplicity with the minimum of detraction from the table. In this case emphasis is given to personal attention and the presentation of food, and facilities must be provided for cooking at the table.

As a rule, the range of choice offered on the menu is extensive and the kitchen tends to be disproportionately large, although economies can be made by rationalising the methods of food preparation and the selection of equipment.

Entertainment dining

4.09 This covers a broad spectrum of catering facilities in clubs and in those restaurants used for social and leisure dining. Emphasis in interior design is usually placed on creating the correct 'atmosphere' using a combination of seating arrangements, lighting, colours, surface effects and decorative features to produce the desired impression. Furniture is usually specifically designed for this purpose and is often arranged in alcoves and small groupings for privacy. This may be emphasised by the use of sunken or mezzanine floor areas. Thick carpeting and sound absorbent surfaces are usually necessary and the furniture is upholstered for luxury and comfort. The illumination is generally provided by local lighting points at the tables

45

Shores and Tamarisk, Old Brompton Road, London. Architect: Lucas Mellinger Associated with Peter Young.
Tamarisk is a Middle Eastern cabaret/restaurant situated on the first floor of these premises which also incorporate a speciality fish restaurant—Shores—in the basement. Both restaurants have separate entrances, bars and kitchens but

may share a common ground floor lounge and cloakroom area as required.
The design of Tamarisk includes a dining gallery to increase the number of tables in close proximity to the acting area[45]. The walls are hung with tapestries and the ceilings are formed from louvres vaulted over the area[46].

46

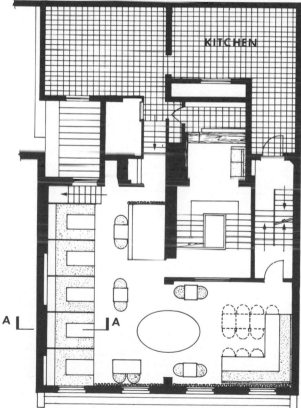

KITCHEN

A | | A

FIRST FLOOR

47   **SECTION A_A**

supplemented by regulated background lighting. Cloak-room, bar and lounge facilities are essential and a wide selection of drinks is usually served at the table.

Provision may be required for entertainment—including a stage area and/or dance floor—and this will influence the layout of tables and seating, service and ancillary facilities. Removable carpeting and furniture may be used to allow flexibility in the use of this area.

The choice of menu is often extensive but is usually based on meals which are easily and quickly prepared to order on fast-cooking equipment. To economise in kitchen space, food may be delivered partly or fully prepared ready for cooking.

Banquet service

4.10 In the design of banquet facilities the main features are usually:

(a) flexibility in the layout of the dining areas;

(b) ability to cope with large numbers of customers arriving and requiring service at the same time at cloakrooms, bars and in the banquet room;

(c) good acoustics, lighting, air-conditioning and internal communication services to allow for variations in use; and

(d) special provisions for cooking and for holding and conveying food and drink to facilitate rapid service.

To allow flexibility, a large area is often divided by movable partitions designed to prevent sound transmission. The furniture must be stackable and of interchangeable units which can be easily linked together. Where the floor is also to be used for dancing, the carpet must be removable and facilities provided for storage of the displaced furniture. The ceiling and wall surfaces should be selected to reduce distortion and reverberation of sound and the design must incorporate lighting, ventilation, internal communication and other engineering services outlets.

The entrance foyer, cloakrooms, toilets, bars and other ancillary facilities require careful planning in relation to the main routes of circulation and to the possibility of sub-division in the banquet room. The sizes of such facilities must be based on peak demands.

Similar provisions apply to the planning of the kitchen and service arrangements. The location of the kitchen, means of transport of food and drink and travel routes of waiting staff are important factors in maintaining good service. If the main kitchen is distant, a service kitchen may be provided; heated and chilled trolleys or mobile cupboards are also used for transporting and serving meals. Within the kitchen, the equipment usually includes convection ovens, boiling pans and steam ovens. Considerable chilled storage is necessary for cold sweets and ices.

48

The Dringhouses Room, York Post House. Trust Houses Forte Ltd.
The Dringhouses room provides facilities for private groups and meetings, seating up to 90 theatre-style or 65 for private parties and banquets. It is easily divisible into two sections each seating 40 theatre-style. The end wall is lined with cork tiles for sound absorption and textured effect.

49
Nine Kings Suite, Royal Lancaster Hotel, London.
A view of the banquet room having a layout of circular tables.

Remote catering services

4.11 Several areas of catering are involved with the service of meals taken to or by the customer outside a normal dining room. These extend over a wide variety of situations and circumstances, as indicated by the following:

(a) *Take-away restaurants* operate like ordinary shops, supplying meals—which are selected from a menu—over the counter for consumption off the premises.

(b) *Meals-on-wheels* and similar welfare services supply hot meals from heated and insulated containers to various homes and centres.

(c) *Hospital catering*—includes distribution of individual meals to patients over a widespread area of the hospital complex.

(d) *Vending outlets* may be supplied with chilled or frozen prepared meals from a central kitchen ready for end-cooking in the vending unit when required.

(e) *Room service* in hotels and residential institutions enables meals to be provided in the guest's individual rooms from a central or local kitchen.

(f) *In-transit catering*—by air, rail or sea-ferry—is often affected by limitations in space and journey time which necessitate the use of meals prepared, and often prepacked, in advance.

In each case meals are prepared in a kitchen which is remote from the place where the meal is eaten and precautions must be taken to avoid any deterioration in the condition of the food. Where distance and time allow, the meal may be transported hot for immediate serving either in bulk containers or ready portioned on individual plates. In other circumstances, food must be immediately cooled to a temperature which will inhibit spoilage and food poisoning organisms during storage and transport. Only in the final stage is re-heating allowed and this is carried out immediately prior to consumption at the distribution outlet.

The design of kitchen facilities for the purpose of remote meal supplies is often simplified when the meals are prepared in advance of requirements and independent of meal times. With this greater flexibility kitchen equipment and staff can be more continuously used throughout the working day and the efficiency and output is generally higher. At the end of the cooking or preparation process the food is either quick-frozen or chilled depending on the storage life required and stored at this lower temperature until needed. This process, usually described as the 'Cook-freeze' system, is the origin of many of the 'convenience foods' used in catering.

In the case of meals which are distributed hot, special provision must be made for retention of heat and rapid transportation and a number of specific catering systems have been introduced to meet these requirements, particularly in the field of hospital catering.

Where remote sales of meals are involved, dining facilities are not usually required since the food is either taken away from the place of purchase or eaten in an area which is, at other times, normally used for another purpose. In all situations where food is supplied, hygienic requirements must be observed. The equipment in which food is transported and served must have non-absorbent linings that can easily be cleaned and suitable washing facilities need to be provided for this purpose at the place of supply. Walls, floors and other surfaces in the vicinity of a vending outlet or service counter must also be designed to allow easy cleaning and maintenance.

When meals are pre-packed prior to distribution, the container forms an important consideration both in providing protection and separation for the food items and, subsequently, in serving as an eating surface or utensil. At the point of use provision must be made for collection and disposal of the container and packing material.

2 EXTERNAL FEATURES

THE EXTERIOR

1.01 Apart from meeting structural and functional requirements the external façade of a restaurant, snack bar or other catering unit serves to disclose the nature of the business and to attract customers. To do this effectively the exterior must:

· make passers-by aware of the type of facilities available,
· convey a correct impression of the quality of the interior, and
· be in harmony with the surroundings.

Location

1.02 To a large extent the location will determine the main market and, hence, the type of establishment required. The importance of local characteristics in selecting a site and mode of operation is revealed by carrying out market surveys in the area.

Allied to this is the need to consider the surroundings. The aim of attracting custom need not clash with the desirability of maintaining harmony with surrounding buildings and landscape. Usually it will be found that aesthetic considerations and business objectives are complementary. The type of customer who patronises a particular area is generally one who appreciates the character and attractions of that locality whether these are sedate and exclusive or lively and cosmopolitan.

1

Miyaka Hotel, Kyoto, Japan.
The Japanese wing of the hotel enclosing a courtyard with a sand and moss garden.

1.03 In the case of employee catering facilities the approach is basically the same. One of the primary considerations must be the location of a canteen or restaurant in a convenient position of access relative to areas of employment; for instance, the directors' dining area, if provided, should be conveniently accessible to the board-room; the works canteen should be positioned so that the entrance is near the factory, preferably with cloakroom and toilet facilities adjacent.

View

1.04 The relative importance of a view will depend very much on the type of restaurant, its main period of use, and the extent to which interest and attraction is provided within the interior of the room itself. Generally speaking, when a view from a restaurant is outstanding this aspect should be emphasised in the position, shape and design of the room and in the layout of the tables.

A view may be natural or created artificially by landscaping and ornamentation work. Specifically, in certain localities the windows may look out over the sea or surrounding hills, valleys and rural environs. In an urban setting, the scope for a so-called 'natural' aspect is limited but would include such features as a park, river or garden. This is, however, not the only outlook which may be interesting. The view of an urban skyline—particularly from a high level—is often full of variety and fascination during the day and night. Even the urban scene, motorway traffic, aircraft and other features may provide a suitable aspect when viewed from a vantage point.

Within the premises an animated view can be created artificially by projecting photographs or silhouettes on to

2

Mayflower Post House, Plymouth. Trust Houses Forte Ltd. Completed in May, 1970, this hotel occupies a fine site high up on Plymouth Hoe and the restaurants, which form an octagonal annexe to the main bedroom block, are designed to take advantage of the views over Plymouth Sound.

4

The restaurant provides self-service buffet luncheons and an à la carte menu for dinner, accommodating up to 80 for each meal with some banquette seating but mainly individual chairs arranged to take advantage of the view. The furnishings comprise a warm mixture of orange, gold and dark aubergine, with a carpet patterned in similar colours. To soften the large area of glass, windows are curtained in fine silk in a brilliant orange and gold stripe.

Along the back wall is an abstract mural composition in perspex (as illustrated) by David Colwell, RCA. The restaurant bar is divided from the main restaurant area on one side by a perspex screen and on the other by camellia trees.

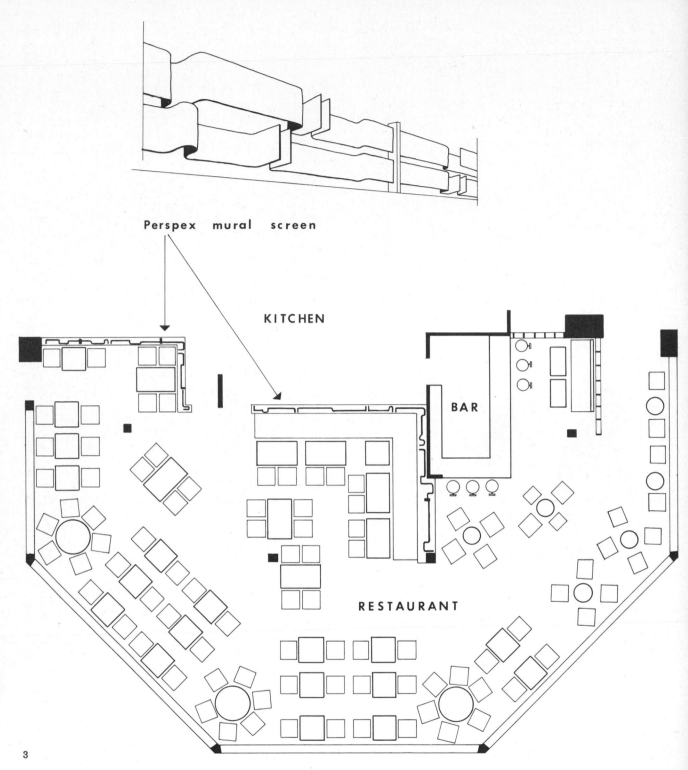

Perspex mural screen

KITCHEN

BAR

RESTAURANT

3

Plan of restaurant and adjacent bar areas, Mayflower Post House.

5

Dining Room, Sceilig Hotel, Dingle Co. Kerry, Ireland. Architects: Stephenson Gibney & Associates.
An unusual design of an hotel restaurant with views over the sea, adjacent sand and sky. A warm sand coloured carpet covers the floor and the circular timber chairs are stained bright orange with small orange and red upholstery. The drapes are a specially woven mixture of deep natural linen and wool.

a screen. The designer may also introduce a focal point of interest and the whole theme of the interior may be developed around this feature. It is also important to remember that, in the right social setting, the presence of people may generate interest and 'atmosphere'

Visibility

1.05 Potential customers must be made aware of the existence of the establishment either by the prominence and distinctive features of the premises or by signs and directions. The display of advertisements and notices is restricted by planning legislation and, with few exceptions, is generally limited to built-up commercial areas. Similarly, in areas of special control there may be limitations imposed on the size and style of name display on the premises. In considering the visibility of the restaurant, there are essentially three ranges of view involved: pedestrians in a town centre or other area; slow moving traffic in a town street; and fast moving traffic along a highway. The market for trade is generally not distinct but may be made up of pedestrians and urban traffic or both fast and slow moving traffic.

A pedestrian will usually have the opportunity to stop and consider the appearance of the exterior, to check any menu which may be displayed, and to judge the suitability of the premises from glimpses of the interior through the windows and entrance before deciding whether to enter.

1.06 Depending on traffic conditions and the speed he is travelling, a motorist will normally have to make an instant decision, based on the appearance of the building from some distance away. He will possibly be attracted by the impressive size and elegance of a restaurant or, if he seeks informality, by the bright flamboyant styling of a snack bar. In pursuing this interest, other factors will also play a part—the availability of car-parking, the number of cars already there, the difficulty of crossing the road and the appearance of the premises on closer viewing. Having stopped deliberately, the customer is then in a semi-captive condition. Although the premises may not measure up to his expectations he may be reluctant to move on elsewhere because of the extra inconvenience this could cause.

With faster traffic the view ahead is extended and the correct location and visibility of a restaurant or café become even more important. Under these conditions it is the side view of the premises, as seen from a very acute angle, which is initially the most conspicuous, and a building is usually more easily visible if it is set well back from the road. To improve awareness, it may be an advantage to locate a group of premises—restaurants, snack bars, filling stations and other services—together and the competition between alternative catering facilities may be more than outweighed by the mutual benefit of attracting greater attention. This is particularly necessary if passing traffic is to be diverted from a main highway or motorway to an adjacent secondary road.

External façade

1.07 The exterior of a catering premises is usually an important feature of merchandising and should be used to promote the business either directly by advertising or more discreetly by suggesting the type of meals and service available. In order to perform this function, the design of the visible exterior should aim to:

· create an awareness;
· generate interest;
· suggest the interior and
· indicate the standard.

Although these needs can be considered individually they are essentially interrelated since part of the attraction to the premises is provided by an interest in what is inside. For high quality dining, the exterior may be calm with a traditional façade and a relatively modest sign. The emphasis here could be on elegance and simplicity suggesting an interior of good taste and exclusive quality. Windows will probably be draped to provide privacy rather than publicity, and the main feature of awareness is usually an impressive entrance.

A restaurant catering for a less formal market may well have large feature windows for the specific purpose of revealing the style and character of the interior, and also to some extent the occupants. This is particularly important for the type of coffee shop or snack bar operation in which the social atmosphere is an important feature of attraction. The façade will vary from one establishment to the next but one factor common to all design considerations is the need to make the exterior conspicuous enough to arouse interest.

Characterization and colour

1.08 The design should also be in character with the interior. A Chinese restaurant may, for instance, be shown by suggestions of canework, pagodas and screens, and by oriental signs and pictures; Continental meals are often indicated by representative styles of national architecture with features such as whitewashed walls to emphasise traditional simplicity, and the restaurants which form part of a group usually adopt a particular branded style of design and insignia to enable them to be easily recognised.

1.09 Colour can be used to draw attention, to provide a hygienic clean impression, and to imply standards of quality. Employed in small quantities in detail work, gold, purple and wine red tend to suggest expensiveness and luxury. A white background is often associated with cleanliness and efficient management—but only if the paintwork is properly maintained. Pastel and tinted colours may also achieve the same effect but a dense colouring or chroma should be used only in small areas. The colours used in external paintwork should, where possible, be sharp, clear and fresh. The dull grey and brown ranges are often not a sufficient contrast with a background of brick or stonework.

Landscaping

1.10 External colour and contrast may also be provided by landscaping. In a suburban or rural setting trees, shrubs and lawns may be used to create variations in outline, texture and shade which enhance the appearance and impressiveness of the building, in addition to providing a

6

The Cedar restaurant.
The sunken hexagonal restaurant has been designed to give an impression of spaciousness and to take advantage of the mature garden surroundings.

7

Post House, York. Trust Houses Forte Ltd.
Opened in September, 1971, the York Post House has 104
rooms, a buttery for up to 60 diners and the Cedar restaurant
also seating up to 60. The restaurants are located in a single
storey building separated from the accommodation block and
trees on the site have been retained to provide an attractive
mature landscape.

view from the interior. Colour can be provided by flower beds, window and wall boxes and by climbing plants which are also useful for screening. Landscaping is by no means limited to vegetation. Similar effects of contrast and variety are achieved by decorative paving, ornamental and natural stone walling, by the use of pools, fountains and other features of interest. Often these can serve functional as well as decorative purposes. Walling and ornamental fencing may be used to delineate boundaries; cobble stones and various forms of raised paving can be employed to discourage cars and people from crossing certain areas, natural and reconstructed paving slabs may be used in the construction of a terrace or patio to form an outdoor or covered extension to a restaurant.

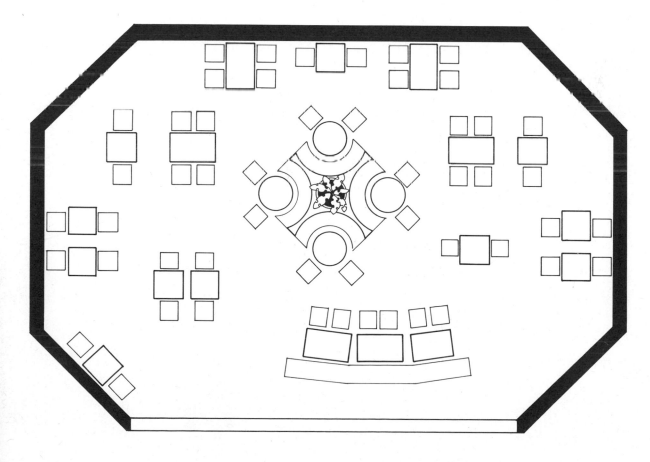

8

Plan of the restaurant seating arrangement.

9

10

11

Jury's Hotel, Westport, Ireland

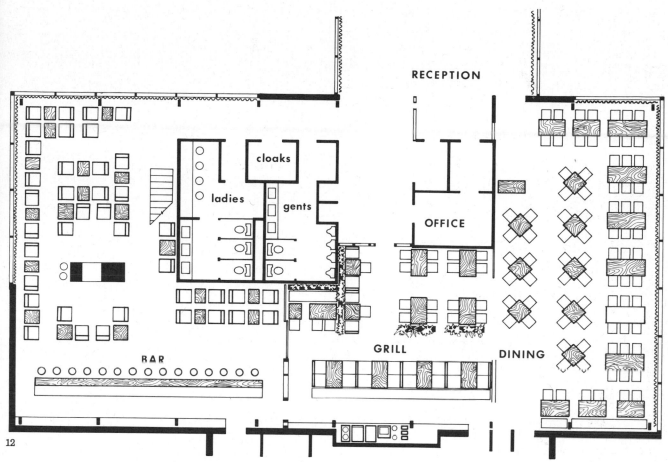

RECEPTION

cloaks

ladies   gents

OFFICE

BAR   GRILL   DINING

12

Jury's Hotel, Westport, Ireland. Architects: Kidney Burke.
Situated in an attractive landscape of trees, the design of the
single storey restaurant features exposed roof boarding and
timber screens. The dining room is divided into small group
seating areas by low partition walls.

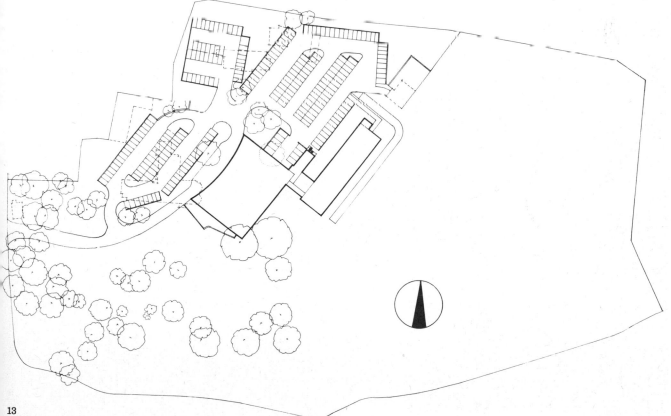

13
Site plan showing the layout of buildings and car parking
area for the Leeds/Bradford Post House.

14
The Post House near Leeds and Bradford. Trust Houses
Forte Ltd.
An artist's impression of the Post House constructed in 1971
showing the separation of the public rooms from the taller
block which accommodates 120 bedrooms. Public areas include
a restaurant seating 100, buttery with 70 seats, lounges and
conference facilities.

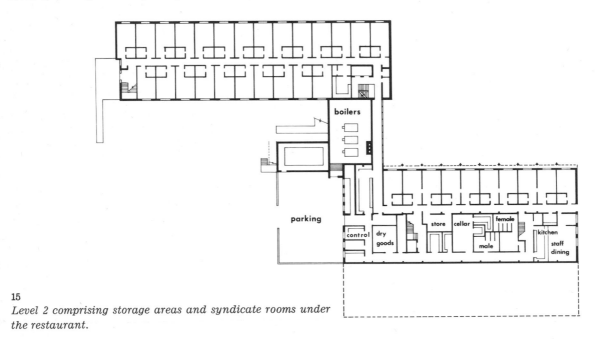

15
Level 2 comprising storage areas and syndicate rooms under
the restaurant.

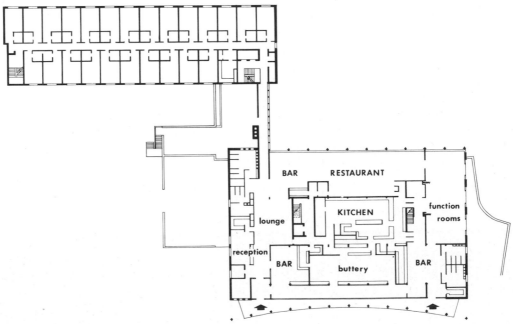

16
Level 3 showing positions of the restaurant, bar, buttery and
kitchen areas.

External lighting

1.11 Lighting in various forms, is used to make premises sufficiently conspicuous at night to attract potential customers and, in this sense, is also a design tool. Obviously when a restaurant closes in the evening external lighting is not essential except perhaps in the interests of safety and security. However, where the premises adjoin a path or place used by the public there may be some publicity advantage in having part illumination and display of information.

Most restaurants which remain open long hours cater for an entirely different market in the evening to that using the restaurant during the day. For example, the change-over may be from business luncheons to leisure dining, or from customers requiring fast service at lunch time to those seeking a more sociable background in the evening. This change in emphasis and atmosphere can be helped by careful use of lighting to create the illusions desired.

Lighting can be used in many ways to illuminate and show off the premises effectively without being a blatant form of advertising. Examples of lighting schemes include:
· Illumination of windows to reveal the elegance of draped curtains;
· Concealed lights to show off the building features in relief,
· Floodlighting to display the façade and imposing appearance of the building,
· Directional lights to illuminate signs and information,
· Space lighting in the car-parking and entrance areas; and
· Glass panelled doors to reveal a bright inviting interior.
In town centre sites, the effect of simple outside illumination may be counteracted by the higher background level of lighting from street lamps, shop windows, vehicles, and other sources. Under these conditions of competition some form of direct advertising may also be desirable to draw attention to the restaurant and might include the use of self-illuminated signs, distinctive colours or moving lights. Large windows also help in providing a shop front effect to show off the interior and are equally effective whether this is brightly lit or alluringly shadowed.

17

Shores and Tamarisk. Architect: Lucas Mellinger.
Exterior view of two restaurants, which occupy one building, showing the illumination of signs and menus.

2 THE ENTRANCE

2.01 The position and arrangement of the entrance require careful consideration. Factors to be taken into account are:
· Position relative to the external flow patterns of traffic;
· Conspicuousness and proportions in relation to the frontage,
· Shelter provided—by recess, canopy or lobby,
· Type of doorway, size, glazing and furniture,
· Access for other purposes and for other users,
· Attendance and security,
· Lighting in the entrance area,
· Display of menus and information,
· Regulation of heating and ventilation,
· Fire regulations and means of escape from premises in event of fire,
· Access for goods and services,
· Design of approaches—if required, and
· Relationship between entrance and interior layout.

Steps

2.02 In many cases the restaurant may be located on a different level from that of the entrance, involving negotiation of stairs or lifts. The effect of this separation on the use of the restaurant will vary from one situation to another, but it is often found to be a deterrent partly because of the extra effort needed to reach the dining room and the inconvenience this may cause and perhaps partly because the customer is not sure what he will find when he arrives there. An exception applies when there are adequate compensations from the particular location such as a view over the surroundings. In addition, steps leading down to a basement restaurant used for, say, leisure dining may create an impression of mystery and suspense which can be employed to advantage. Where it is necessary, because of site conditions or costs, to provide the dining room at first floor level it is important to make a sufficiently attractive feature of the entrance and staircase to offset their limitations.

Provisions for safety and fire

2.03 Single steps and low flights of wide stairs to accommodate changes in level within the restaurant area are liable to cause accidents and should, where possible, be avoided in the main routes of circulation. Otherwise, steps must be:
· Deliberately positioned in areas where divisions occur between rooms and passages and where steps might reasonably be anticipated;
· Provided with an adequate landing space, clear of the door swing, before or after any doorway;
· Clearly indicated by a change in type of flooring or by contrasting strips along the edges of the treads; and
· Well illuminated—if the lighting in the adjacent area is subdued, by recessed lights fitted in the sides at floor level.

2.04 Staircases are also subject to specific constructional standards in order to meet safety and fire escape requirements. These would include:
(a) *Width*—determined by the maximum number of persons likely to occupy the premises and use the staircase as a means of escape in case of fire. Preferably, widths of 1100 mm (3ft 6in) allowing two people at a time, or 2000mm (6ft 6in) for up to four persons, should be adopted for this purpose.
(b) *Inclination*—the treads and risers should be comfortably proportioned and for most purposes a 150mm (6in) rise for 300mm (1ft) going is appropriate. Each flight of stairs should have no more than sixteen risers between

landings.

(c) *Hand rails* must be provided on both sides. A staircase 2000mm (6ft 6in) wide or more must also have a handrail in the centre. The height and security of handrails and balustrades to stairs and landings are important considerations.

(d) *Headroom*—the clearance above the staircase should be at least 2100mm (7ft) vertically and at least. 1500mm (5ft) at right angles to the pitch line.

(e) *Fire*—provision must be made for adequate resistance and protection against fire either in the construction and/or by provision of sprinkler or drencher systems. Appropriate precautions must also be taken to prevent smoke and fire spreading to other areas along the staircase and corridors.

(f) *Exit*—where a staircase is to be used as a fire escape route, it must lead to a safe exit from the building. All exits must be clearly marked as required by Fire Regulations.

(g) *Lighting* The minimum standard of lighting in staircases and corridors is 100 lux (9 lumens/sq ft) and the lighting points must be positioned to avoid strong shadows and shielded against glare.

(h) *Construction*—a variety of methods and materials may be used in stair construction, mainly reinforced concrete, natural or artificial stone or—subject to Fire Regulations —wood. Concrete, with selected aggregates, may be left as an exposed surface and be polished or treated to give a marble-like effect (eg terrazzo); to avoid slipperiness, strips of carborundum and similar rough materials are set into the treads. Finishes applied on a concrete base include quarry tiles, mosaics, resilient tiles and carpeting. In each case, the edges of the treads or nosings need treatment to prevent breakage and slipperiness in use. It must also be easy to distinguish the edges of the steps under the prevailing light conditions.

3 EMPLOYEE CATERING FACILITIES

3.01 The requirements for merchandising which apply to commercial restaurants are not so important in catering for a semi-captive market such as in employee catering. None the less, many aspects such as the need to promote the catering service and to provide an attractive environment both within and around the dining areas still apply. In this case it is the social benefits rather than the commercial considerations which promote an interest in design. Catering facilities, whether self-supporting or subsidised, must also be run on a sound financial basis and this is often reflected in the appreciation of the quality of the accommodation provided.

Landscaping is frequently used to introduce relief from the monotony of buildings and impermeable surfaces. External lighting is invariably provided in the interests of safety and security, and entrances need to be carefully planned to allow for the large numbers of employees who may use the catering facilities over a relatively short period of time. The disadvantages of steps are still relevant but mainly on account of the danger of congestion occurring during rush periods. Provisions with regard to safety and provision of adequate means of escape in case of fire are particularly important in view of the large numbers of employees likely to be involved.

3 FOOD AND DRINK SERVICE

Considerations

1.01 Fundamental design requirements, such as the arrangements to be used for serving meals and clearing the tables, must be decided at the initial stage of restaurant planning since these will dictate the relationship between the restaurant and service areas and may also affect the layout and spacing of furniture within the dining area.

Depending on the system which is employed, the space allocated to food service can occupy a section of the kitchen, extend into the dining room or form a separate area —as in the design of food halls. Direct access to the kitchen is typical of waiter or waitress service but may also be used, where appropriate, for self-service cafeteria. In each case, the serving counter normally acts as a line of demarcation between the kitchen proper and the corridor used for collecting meals. One of the advantages of this arrangement is the facility it provides for economically isolating both the kitchen and the servery from the dining room, thus reducing noise transference and the disturbance of seated customers by others waiting to be served.

In contrast, for counter dining, snack bar and most self-service cafeteria arrangements, the service counter becomes an integral feature of the restaurant. This also applies where, to allow cooking of food within view of the customer, the servery is open to the dining room. In both cases the counter displays are often designed distinctly to attract attention and interest.

Food service halls are, relatively, a new development, which introduces the 'supermarket' approach to food service. The 'free flow' system is typical of this arrangement and is designed to facilitate rapid service of meals for large numbers of diners with the minimum of waiting.

The method of food service which is most appropriate for any particular catering establishment will depend on a number of considerations but these can generally be reduced to three main headings:

(a) Customer preferences

1.02 Market surveys should reveal the potential demand for various types of restaurant facility. Depending on the situation and circumstances, the primary need may be for the personal attention conferred by service at the table. In other cases, the greater independence allowed by self-service may be preferable or, as a third alternative, the most popular demand may be for dining at the counter or snack bar facilities. Within each of these main methods of service, there are different levels of sophistication in the way meals are presented to the diner and reference should be made to Chapter 1 (4.0) for a further classification.

Where the market is sufficiently large it may be advantageous to provide different restaurant facilities within the same establishment in order to cater for a variety of needs. Thus, in an industrial situation, a canteen may be available for fast self-service meals at economical prices, an executive dining room with waitress service and vending machines for use outside the main meal periods. Similarly, an hotel may operate a coffee shop or buttery in addition to its main restaurant in order to extend the range of customers.

(b) Operating conditions

1.03 In deciding the type of service, consideration must also be given to the conditions under which the restaurant is likely to be operated. Where catering is for large numbers or involves a high incidence of simultaneous use, speed and organisation are essential requisites of efficient operation. Economy of staff, particularly when meals are taken outside normal work shifts, may also be an important factor in providing simple self-catering or automatic vending facilities.

The increasing popularity of 'take-away' meals for consumption off the premises must influence the planning of future restaurants in which multiple facilities are to be provided.

(c) Physical limitations

1.04 Regardless of other considerations, the location of a restaurant may, by virtue of its high value or conversion costs, short lease, small size or other, physical or financial limitations, channel the scope of investment to a narrow band of choice.

2 FOOD SERVICE ARRANGEMENTS

2.01 The meals in a restaurant may be served by:
(a) Self service;
(b) Waiter or waitress service to tables;
(c) Counter service;
(d) Automatic vending;

Design requirements for waiter or waitress service and self-service by the customer are, essentially, similar since the needs for organised flow routes and fast service are the same in both cases. The main distinctions arise from the need to provide the self-service customer with more direc-

1

Staff catering, The Plessey Co Ltd, Ilford.
Details of the trays used for self-service showing raised rims for dishes and utensils and the angular shape which is particularly suitable for negotiating internal turns in the counter line. The shape of the trays is designed to fit neatly on the tables.

tion and assistance in selecting items of food and the opportunity which then arises, to use the service counter for salesmanship to generate impulse buying by attractively setting out the items on display. In the case of waiter or waitress service, part of the work involved in serving food or beverages from the counter can be transferred to them and the service counter and fittings can thus be simplified and modified—e.g. by providing a still room—to facilitate this dual role.

Counter service differs in that the diner although stationary is seated at, or adjacent to, the service counter and is thereby able to select items from food on display or in course of preparation. This type of operation tends to specialise in quick informal service with a limited menu of popular dishes prepared on back bar equipment within view of the customer. To extend the dining area, tables may also be provided served by waitresses or used by customers served from the counter. There is a wide variation in counter systems ranging from snack and sandwich bars to speciality grills providing high quality meals to call order.

Automatic vending is based on the use of machines which are operated by coin or key to provide individual hot or cold meals or various kinds of beverages. Vending machines may be used to augment a counter service or to serve as a self-sufficient catering unit.

3 DESIGN FEATURES

3.01 The various arrangements for self-service of meals can be grouped into two main categories each with many variations to suit particular requirements.

(a) *The cafeteria system*—consisting of a number of units arranged in series to form a continuous counter along which the customer travels with a tray to select various items of the meal which are paid for at the end of the counter line.

(b) *The free flow system*—based on several separate counters which are approached in parallel, the customer using any one of the counters which are free to obtain the particular meal required. Payment is made on leaving the area at any one of several cash desks.

2

Staff catering, The Plessey Co Ltd, Ilford. Equipment by Oliver Toms Ltd.
An example of the free flow system of self-service designed to *cater for 1500 to 2000 meals over a period of 1½ hours. Meals can be obtained with the minimum of queuing at any one of the echelon units, at the cold buffet or at the grill bar according to choice.*

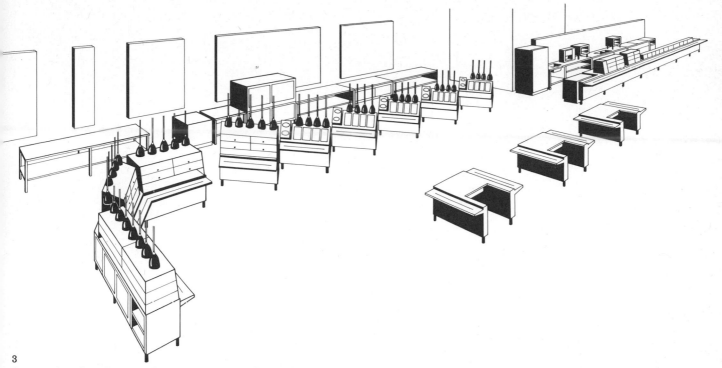

3
Perspective drawing of the servery area illustrating the arrangement of the echelon units designed for a free-flow system of self-service.

4
Example of a small servery counter.

Clearance of tables

3.02 With all forms of self-service a degree of organisation and direction is necessary and this is even more emphasised when self-clearance of tables is involved. Generally, self-clearance of used tableware is not readily accepted by the customer and is difficult to operate satisfactorily in competitive catering because of irregular use and varied degrees of co-operation. Self clearance of tables is commonly used for school meals and in certain forms of resi-

dential and employee catering but, in all cases, the arrangements must be simple and convenient if they are to be effective.

Where self service of meals is operated it is necessary to make deliberate provision for the clearance of used tableware by trolley or direct to a collection point and adequate access between tables must be allowed for this purpose.

4 THE CAFETERIA SYSTEM

4.01 The simplest cafeteria arrangement is a single straight counter with various sections for cold service, hot dishes, sweets and beverages. For large numbers the counter lines may be doubled or trebled; on plan, counters may be straight, curved, extend round internal corners or around the outside of an island service area. Specialist sections at one end of the line may be used for grills, salads or snack items, and by-pass arrangements provided. A variety of alternatives are employed for serving beverages and for payment.

5

6

7

The Carnival cafeteria; Express Restaurants.

A gay simple restaurant with self-service counter. Carnival motifs are used throughout on menu boards, trays and decorations. Of particular interest is the self-service cutlery and sauce stand[7].

Position

4.02 The cafeteria layout needs careful planning to ensure efficient use, bearing in mind that the self-service will often be operated by customers of different ages, sizes and aptitudes, many of whom may be unfamiliar with the arrangements. To enable food to be easily transferred to the service counter this should be close—preferably adjacent—to the production area with heated and refrigerated pass-through cabinets between. Satellite counter systems supplied with prepared food from a central commissary are more adaptable in location and can be designed in island arrangements.

The counter must be conveniently placed in relation to the traffic routes followed by the customers entering the restaurant, but should be sufficiently set back from the entrance to avoid congestion and confusion when groups of customers wait in this area. It is also necessary to arrange the layout in a way which will minimise the risk of collision—particularly when trays are being carried—and avoid disturbing people who are dining. This is achieved by planning flow routes for customers to approach directly to the serving area without crossing or meeting those who are leaving.

Space can be saved if movements to and from the serving counter are confined to distinct passages and, depending on the shape and size of the space available, it may be advantageous to site the serving counter in a separate room with individual 'in' and 'out' openings. This room may form the entrance hall to the restaurant proper or be fully or partly partitioned off from the dining area. Other advantages which derive from screening the counter include improved appearance and privacy in the dining area, less noise transmission and easier control. Such screens may be decorative as well as functional or may merely suggest a division by providing a break in the continuity of the space—such as with portable plant troughs or ornamental iron work.

In dining rooms which are for multi-purpose use, for example in schools and institutional canteens, it is usually necessary to provide shutters or doors to close off the serving counter when it is not required. Under these conditions a separate counter for beverages and, perhaps, snack items is desirable to allow flexibility in the use of the room.

Speed of service

4.03 The rate at which customers can pass along a serving counter is affected by many things—the meal served, design and layout of the counter and slowness and indecision on the part of the customer. A steady flow can be facilitated by minimising the congestion in those areas which are potential bottlenecks.

(a) *Menu selection*

The menu and price list of individual items must be clearly visible well in advance to minimise hesitancy in selection and must also be within view at the counter.

(b) *Serving*

Delays are most likely to occur where customers are unable to serve themselves. These areas are usually in the hot service and beverage counters and at the cash desk.

For most cafeteria counters offering a choice of meals a typical customer flow rate is between six and nine per minute for a single line and one cash desk and increases to ten to fourteen per minute with some by-pass facilities and double cash desks. Increased flow rates may be achieved by duplicating the counter lines. In peak conditions a space of about 600mm (2ft) is taken up by each person in line.

Counter design

4.04 A straight counter is usually adopted for simplicity in layout and operation and to allow economy with the use of standard counter sections and interchangeable units. Counters may have to be arranged to fit the space available but counters extending around external corners are liable to cause tray spillage and negotiation of internal corners tends to slow down movement. Where changes in direction are necessary these are best accommodated in a slow curve if possible.

The length of a counter depends on the types of meals and range of choice offered and may vary from 6m to 15m (20ft to 50ft) although the trend is towards the use of shorter counters supplemented where necessary by separate beverage service. Details of counter dimensions and fittings are described in the book *Principles of Catering Design*.

Lighting

4.05 Lighting in the area of food service needs to be at a high level of intensity, particularly around the cash desk area. In the servery area generally, 400 lux (37 lumens/sq ft) would be appropriate, with 600 lux (56 lumens/sq ft) for the service counter, cash desk and where price lists and menu details are displayed.

Careful colour selection of lighting fittings is also essential. With fluorescent lighting, a light rich in the red colours of the spectrum is most suitable for display purposes —for example the British Standard colour 'De luxe natural' (55) which produces a soft light emphasising the redness of meat and other food.

Lighting fittings positioned low over the counter area must have sufficient screening so that the light source is not directly visible and liable to cause glare. This can be achieved by using deep individual shades for light bulbs, or by mounting such fittings as fluorescent tubes behind a fascia. In the former type of fitting quartz lamps provide the dual function of illumination and warming.

Ventilation of the servery

4.06 Some form of local ventilation is usually required in the servery to prevent the accumulation and condensation of steam and fumes from food which is being served and also to reduce the build-up of heat from the exposed surfaces of the bain-marie counters, hot cupboards and other equipment and from the large numbers of people who may congregate in this area.

In many cases, where the servery is open to the kitchen, the extraction system in the latter will provide an adequate air flow over the counters but some form of balancing is desirable by providing plenum air inlets at strategic points. Where the servery is separated from the kitchen, local extraction must be provided in or over the counter and also over any back-bar or cooking equipment. Cooking smells and fumes from the latter must be confined and removed from the source using extraction hoods to prevent staining on adjacent walls and ceiling.

To balance the air being extracted and avoid excessive smoke and odours being drawn into the servery, plenum air inlets are often also provided around the ceiling or canopy perimeter. As with all ventilation systems, careful regulation and balancing of the air distribution is necessary.

Cutlery and condiments, etc

4.07 To reduce congestion in the vicinity of the service counter cutlery should generally be provided in conspicuous display stands situated to one side of the flow route followed by customers leaving the cash desk. The stand must include a well supported rest area for trays and suitably shaped compartments for cutlery pieces which will allow their easy removal by the handles. This area can create as much obstruction to the flow as the service counter itself and is possibly more liable to produce accidents while trays are being balanced. Careful positioning and adequacy of size and number of alternative points are, therefore, important considerations.

Where the menu is fixed or choice limited, cutlery may be collected before the meal. In this case the tendency is to take up more pieces than are required and it is better to pre-wrap the cutlery items in napkins and place them in a shallow container next to the tray stand.

Water glasses should be available on the tables or on a trolley stand next to a water supply point. The latter must have a sink and drainage outlet and is usually supplied through refrigerated water cooling apparatus.

Salt, pepper, mustard and sauce containers are usually provided on the tables and sugar may also be available in a dispensing container or pre-wrapped in portions.

From the counter to the dining area

4.08 When customers leave the counter area carrying trays their concentration is usually divided, mainly on balancing the tray and its contents without spilling and partly on looking for a suitable table or other destination. They are thus more vulnerable to accidents, collisions, and errors of judgment in distance and position, and the exit route must not be obstructed, particularly by low objects; there must be no steps nor changes in level; the slipperiness of the floor must not increase; and there must be sufficient width to allow passing but not to encourage crossing over.

In establishments catering mainly for shoppers, or with a high proportion of older customers, there are many advantages in providing staff to carry the customers' trays from the cash point to the tables.

5 FREE FLOW SYSTEMS

5.01 The main disadvantage of the cafeteria counter arrangement is the way in which customers have to pass in line along the whole length of the counter in order to select the particular meal required. Any delay in the flow is liable to hold up the whole line and a certain amount of queueing is almost inevitable during peak periods. The efficiency of a continuous counter can be improved by providing by-pass facilities and this principle is extended in the free-flow or multi-point system. This may be described as the supermarket approach to meal service and may take several forms depending on type of establishment and space available.

5.02 Customers entering the food hall may select their meals from a number of service counters each offering a particular choice of course. Depending on the type of meal and size of establishment there may be three for the main course, two for sweets and one for sundries such as ice-cream, confectionery and so on. A separate chilled counter is provided for salads and cold meats, otherwise the counters are adaptable to allow flexibility in operation, for example if there is a heavy demand for a particular dish this may be served from more than one counter. Each counter serving the main course would include an entrée, two vegetables and gravy or sauce as required.

By distributing the service over a number of counters, a large number of customers can be served in a short time and this arrangement is particularly suitable for large-

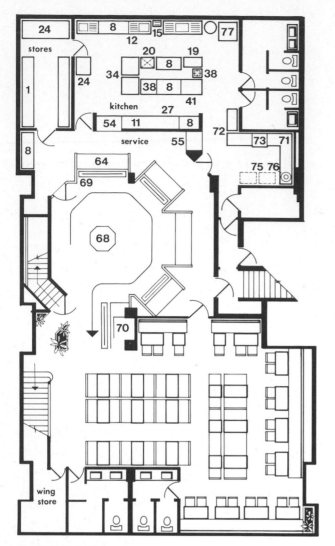

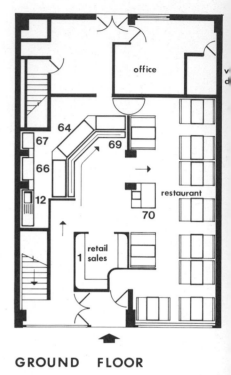

GROUND FLOOR

BASEMENT

8

Anna's Kitchen. Equipment by Oliver Toms Ltd.
Entrance and ground floor of a small restaurant with separate
self-service counters for hot meals, cold dishes, coffee and
drinks arranged octagonally around the circulation area.

10

11

12

A small basement kitchen with a central island including a convection oven and oven range. The area is fully mechanically ventilated with plenum inlets along perimeter walls to balance air extracted through the central canopy.

scale employee catering where the number served per meal is more than about 600.

Payment for the meal is made on leaving the food service hall before entering the dining area and the same free-flow principle is applied by providing a number of cash desks, thereby enabling several customers to pay at the same time.

Planning

5.03 The individual counters may be arranged in a line along one side of the room but must be seen to be separated into distinctive meal sections to ensure effective use of the system. An alternative arrangement which promotes better distribution is to offset the sections so as to produce a staggered layout. Salads and cold dishes, appropriate for quick service, are usually kept to a separate section at one side of the main flow to encourage bypassing. Similarly, the beverage counter should be next to the exit to minimise the length of carry. A call-order bar specialising in grills and other individually prepared dishes may be provided but should be located to one side of the main serving area in order to minimise congestion. The counters are often arranged in the form of a U-shape to allow maximum use of the perimeter of a room for service, and other combinations of counter systems are possible including part cafeteria style counters to provide, for example, a wider choice of salads, cold dishes and pastries.

5.04 In view of the risk of cross traffic and possibility of collisions between customers moving across the food hall, some form of control by guided routing is desirable, using deliberately positioned islands. It is also necessary to ensure adequate spacing and numbers of serving counters to avoid congestion and the total area occupied in serving, say 800 to 1000 meals in one period is about 186m² (2000sq ft). Successful operation of the free-flow system is dependent on the customer being familiar with the arrangement. With this objective, menus must be clearly displayed and counters easily identified, so that the customer can easily locate the courses served. Stands for trays and cutlery must be conveniently positioned near the entrance and exit, respectively, to the service area and, where directions are required, they should be prominent and precise. The operational and environmental considerations which apply to cafeteria service are also relevant to this area.

Variations
5.05 On a smaller scale, the free-flow principle of self-selection may be introduced as a modified version of the snack and sandwich bar. In this case a choice of sandwiches, pastries and ices, which may be pre-packed for self-service or served by counter staff, is available at a number of display counters around the perimeter or on one or more sides of a service area.

Beverages are also provided but from a position near the cashier to minimise the length of carry to the dining area. In addition, a section may be devoted to short-order items prepared as required on equipment behind the counter.

The service hall may form the entrance area to a dining room or be a partitioned-off section. In each case the design of both the service and dining facilities is based on a need for quick convenient light meals and is capable of a very high and continuous occupancy ratio. It may also be possible to use the service area alone for take-away meals and facilities for this purpose should be provided.

6 WAITER AND WAITRESS SERVICE
The service counter arrangements for waiters and waitresses are similar to those for a cafeteria but are usually separated from the dining area, shorter in length and purely functional in design.

Screening
6.01 In conventional waiter or waitress service the counter is invariably divided from the restaurant to provide screening. Separate 'in' and 'out' swing doors are usually necessary for proper circulation and these must be:
(a) Self-closing with the minimum of noise;
(b) Provided with kicking and finger plates to reduce damage;
(c) Fitted with transparent viewing panels if there is any risk of collisions; and
(d) Preferably screened from the restaurant to reduce noise, draughts and glare disturbing diners at nearby tables.
To prevent congestion in the service corridor a clear width of 1350mm (4ft 6in) should be provided which will allow one person to pass while another is being served.

Counters
6.02 Since the counters have no merchandising value they are kept as simple and functional as possible and are made up from hot and cold cupboards with bain-marie or plain tops. Depending on the type of restaurant, the hot cupboard capacity may have to allow space for large serving platters and dishes, although, usually, less food is pre-plated in advance of orders and the counter and shelf areas can be considerably smaller than those required for cafeteria service.

However, for banquets the temporary storage of plated meals and serving dishes will normally have to be increased because of the quick service demanded. This requirement may be met by using mobile cupboards—both heated and refrigerated—which can be brought into the serving line as needed.

Operational features
6.03 Economy of staff and speed may be promoted by waiters and waitresses serving themselves with certain items, but this advantage must be balanced against the need for accountability and food portion control. A still room is often provided for self-service of tea, coffee and similar beverages and, in hotels particularly, this area is frequently equipped as a supplementary kitchen or pantry for light breakfast and supper service when the main counter is closed.

From an operational viewpoint firm discipline in movement and functions of waiting staff is essential and this must be facilitated by appropriate planning. It is, for example, usually considered necessary to provide some form of barrier—by counters or otherwise—between the waiting area and the kitchen proper. In addition, an efficient system of ordering and identification must be devised which will enable the position to be seen at a glance and relayed to the remote areas of the kitchen as required. Arrangements must be made for used tableware to be deposited on a suitable receiving counter sited conveniently near the entrance to the serving counter. Details of space and functional requirements for the wash-up area are given in the book *Principles of Catering Design*. The procedure for collecting and depositing used tableware also needs precise organisation.

Cutlery and tableware may be collected from the serving area from stands provided near to the counter line. Alternatively, to save journeys and time in attending to the customers' needs, the waiter or waitress may operate from a station in the restaurant with a sideboard for cutlery, table items, and replacement linen to serve a particular number of covers.

7 COUNTER SERVICE
7.01 By taking meals at the counter, the customer can select the meal required without having to carry it away to a table. Such an arrangement lends itself to visual cooking where dishes are prepared to short-order, and grilled or fried as required on back-bar equipment in the view of the customer. It is also used extensively for snack meals selected from display cabinets located around the counter area or described on the menu boards exhibited. Generally, for practical reasons, the range of choice of short-order dishes is limited to two or three of the most popular items which can be easily and quickly prepared on restricted equipment, but this menu may be supplemented by meals cooked in an adjacent finishing kitchen. The latter is also necessary for the preparation work involved in pre-portioning, pre-cooking and plating or packaging of the food, but need be only a relatively small area if convenience foods are mainly used.

7.02 To enable maximum use of the area, the counter needs to be as long as possible commensurate with reasonable

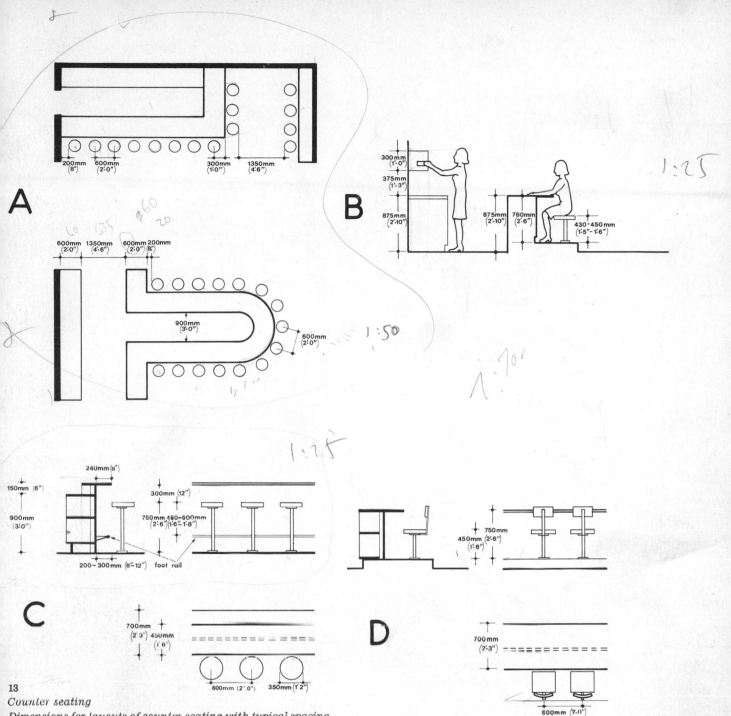

13

Counter seating

Dimensions for layouts of counter seating with typical spacing allowances.

access to both sides, and this is achieved by arranging it in a series of parallel lines, comparable to fingers, with the service corridor extending between counters on each side and one end. The parallel layout is advantageous in that it allows easy and unobstructed access to each counter place for the staff who are able to serve rather more customers than would be possible with a normal waiting system. A further merit from a commercial point of view is the high occupancy ratio of the counter seats, arising partly from the nature of the meals, partly from the fact that customers are more conspicuous at the counter than at a table, and tend to leave immediately they have finished their meals.

To cater for customers who prefer personal company or solitude, it is desirable that part of the area should have conventional tables and chairs, and this is often advantageous in using the spaces in which counter construction might be difficult or uneconomic. For this purpose seats may be individual chairs or of the bench or banquette type, arranged in lines around the perimeter walls, in booths or in island groupings. Service to the tables may be by wait-

ress or self-service from the counter, depending mainly on the nature of the meals and prices charged. For short-order meals waitress service is preferable in view of the delay involved.

Counter design

7.03 In determining the dimensions for counters and stool seating, consideration must be given to anthropometric data, ie representative user sizes, and other ergonomic features. Essentially there are four aspects of measurement which will determine suitability of design:

(a) The average height and forward reach of staff serving behind the counter;

(b) The need of counter space for display, for preparing and serving food, and for dining;

(c) The heights of the counter and dimensions of the associated seating for the comfort of the diner; and

(d) The space needed in front of the counter for access and use.

A suitable height for a working surface—such as a preparation table—is at elbow level and for a short woman this represents a distance of about 900mm (35½in) from the floor. In reaching forward, however, less strain results if the surface is higher, and the front section of the serving counter can be up to 1080mm (42½in) high. To accommodate these two heights the counter may be constructed in two levels or, as an alternative, an intermediate height of about 970mm (38in) may be used for a combined surface top. The maximum forward reach across the counter—which determines the overall counter width—is between 600mm and 700mm (24in and 27in) and the counter top should extend 230mm to 300mm (9in to 12in) over the front to allow knee space when customers are seated. It is an advantage to provide additional space under the counter for a parcel shelf.

7.04 *Counter seats* or stools are normally fixed to the floor to ensure maximum use of counter space and avoid any risk of toppling over under the restricted conditions. The height of the seats must be related to the height of the counter with a clearance of 230mm (9in) or more—based on thigh thickness—between the seat and underside of counter extension, giving an overall difference between the counter and seat surfaces of about 280mm to 300mm (11in to 12in). If a foot support rail is provided the seat of a stool may be up to about 800mm (31in) high, otherwise it must only be a little more than the average length of the lower leg—about 460mm (18in).

To allow adequate space for customers seated at the counter, the width assumed for design requirements is that of a large man which, with space for elbow room, amounts to 600mm (24in). This determines the spacing between centres of stools but if the length is very restricted a lower standard of 550mm (22in)—based on an average man's width—may be adopted. The width of the stool seat is normally limited to about 360mm (14in) to

facilitate access between the places provided.

Constructional features

7.05 Counter fronts or fascias must be functional as well as decorative and in view of the amount of impact, scraping and marking, particularly from shoes, and soiling by spillage and wet clothes, the surfaces must be durable, impervious, easily cleaned and capable of maintaining a good appearance under these working conditions. The same requirements apply to the tops of the counters, and various patterned, grained or mottled designs—which disguise minor scratches—of laminated plastics are appropriate for this purpose. While the vertical surfaces may be brightly coloured and highly decorative, patterns on the horizontal working and eating surfaces must be subdued, and a careful balance must be maintained between the extent of pattern and colour here compared with the surroundings—carpet, wall coverings, curtains and so on.

Most metalwork on counters and fittings is of chrome plated or stainless steel and it is essential that all exposed edges and joints are properly covered to avoid any sharpness or roughness—including the underside of the counter ledge.

7.06 Confectionery and pastry items on display on the counter must be enclosed in appropriately designed cases to avoid mishandling and contamination. Café sets and other beverage-making equipment, and soda fountains if used, may be mounted on the counter but must be far enough from the customers to prevent accidental splashing or other dangers. For economy in counter space these are best located on the back-bar at the remote side of the serving area. Back-bar equipment also includes small conventional ovens, microwave ovens, griddles, deep fat

14
Stotts of Oldham
Back bar grill unit to provide called order dishes for a 100 seat restaurant.

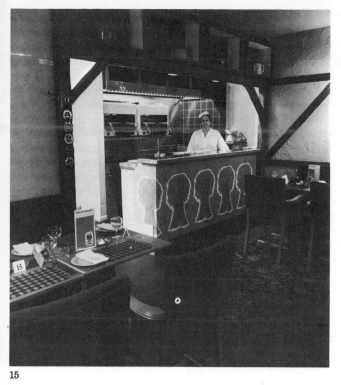

Grill Bars. Berni Inns Ltd.; Property and Planning Department.

One of the main features of Berni Inns is the grill bar providing a short grill menu of popular dishes cooked to order in front of customers. With physical limitations imposed by one unit and the policy of keeping the restaurants small and personal, each inn normally has a number of restaurants each served by a grill bar offering a slightly different range of menu and by a separate aperitif bar. The latter is also used for serving coffee. Cooking units are standardised for each range of menu although they can be built into a variety of surroundings. The illustration shows one of the grill bar units in the Criterion, Shrewsbury.

15

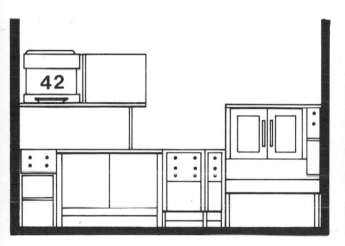

ELEVATION

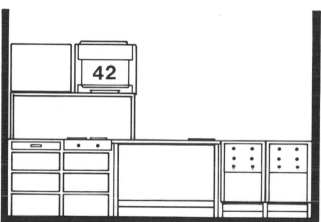

ELEVATION

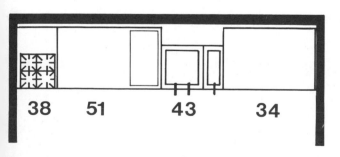

PLAN

ft 1 2 3 4 5
mm 500 1000 1500

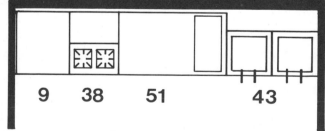

PLAN

ft 1 2 3 4 5
mm 500 1000 1500

16
Plan and elevation of standard Steak and Duck bar.

Standard Steak Bar and Steak and Plaice Bar.

fryers, grillers, toasters, boiling tops, bains-marie and hot cupboards. For speciality dishes small rotating spits or rotisserie and other specific equipment may be used. The amount of equipment installed is normally limited by space and by the cost and impracticability of preparing a wide range of varied dishes within the counter enclosure. In most cases this work is concentrated on a few of the more popular dishes, and the bulk of the initial preparation is done in a separate kitchen.

8 AUTOMATIC VENDING

8.01 There are three main areas in which automatic vending has become widely used:

(a) Providing a meals service at times when the main catering services are closed—for example, for travellers, shift workers and night staff;

(b) Supplementing the main catering area to provide a more efficient and wider ranging service—examples include the use of beverage machines with main counter service to reduce congestion; automatic vending in subsidiary areas as an alternative or extension to the catering facilities; and the use of beverage machines near places of work and traffic routes instead of trolley service;

(c) Completely automatic cafeteria or vending bars may also be provided where the size and situation warrants this as an alternative to personal service. Vending bars may be used as a form of service counter filled directly from a small store room positioned behind the banks of machines. The store room must contain deep freeze and refrigerated storage for reserves of food and may include limited kitchen facilities for preparing sandwiches and snack meals.

Mounting

8.02 Alternative designs may allow for fixing vending equipment to a wall, mounting on the floor or assembling in a group. In deciding the best location and arrangement, consideration must be given to the means of access for refilling, cleaning and servicing. The appearance of vending machines of different sizes, shapes, illumination and features is unattractive and machine groupings should preferably be of the same manufacture and fitted into continuous fascia panelling to form a unified matching frontage. The external finishes may be stove or vitreous enamel, stainless steel, anodised aluminium or laminated plastics, and must be sufficiently robust to withstand repeated usage, risk of pilfering and other damage.

Surroundings

8.03 The area in which vending machines are located should be treated in the same way as a normal servery counter. Flooring must withstand continuous traffic and spillage of grease and water without becoming dangerously slippery or difficult to clean and maintain in a good condition. Vinyl asbestos and composition tiles are commonly used for this purpose. Similarly the adjacent walls must be impervious and easily cleaned, and are often surfaced with mosaic or other forms of glazed tiles to form a decorative and functional background.

Good lighting in this vicinity is essential and, in addition to a general level of lighting equal to 600 lux (56 lumens/sq ft) over the local area, lighting is often provided within compartments of a machine to show the contents. Concealed lighting may also be mounted above and in front

18
Vending equipment. GKN Sankey Ltd.
Vending machines serving hot and cold meals and beverages, grouped into a suite. This is facilitated by use of modular dimensions and matching façades.

19

Bar Unit. Berni Inns Ltd Property and Planning Department. A typical aperitif bar showing the use of good lighting to provide a focal point of attraction in addition to creating good working conditions. This bar is also used to serve coffee after meals.

Points of interest include the posted list of prices and compact arrangement of drinks in storage and on display. The floor in the immediate vicinity of the bar is tiled to avoid damage to the carpet.

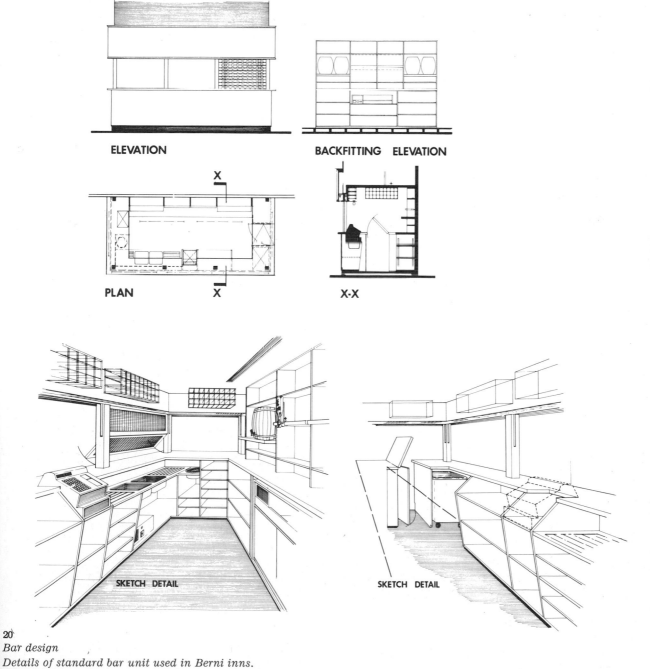

ELEVATION

BACKFITTING ELEVATION

PLAN X

X·X

SKETCH DETAIL

SKETCH DETAIL

20

Bar design
Details of standard bar unit used in Berni inns.

of a range of machines to provide additional local illumination.

9 BAR SERVICE
Licensing
9.01 The sale of alcoholic drink as part of a meal or otherwise is controlled by a system of licensing under the Licensing Acts 1962 and 1964 which apply to England and Wales and by the granting of certificates under similar legislation in Scotland. Licences may be granted only where the premises are suitable for the purpose, and the licensing justices may take into account matters such as safety, means of escape in case of fire, sanitary accommodation and the separation of sections in which drink is sold from other areas. Any structural alterations to licensed premises must be approved by the justices who also have the authority to require alterations to be made before a licence is renewed.

Licences are granted for specific purposes, for example restricting sale of drinks to persons taking a substantial meal at a restaurant, to residents of an hotel and their private friends, to certain times of the day, and for occasional use in other premises when banquets and so on are held. The procedure in seeking a licence is also laid down, and legal advice on this subject is usually necessary before an application is prepared.

Bar design
9.02 A bar counter is often a focal point of attraction and is designed as a feature of interest. In this respect the design is an individual matter and as such dependent on personal attitudes and tastes, but fundamentally it should endeavour to reflect the style and character of the restaurant and to create the right 'atmosphere' for the meal. This subject is examined generally in Chapter 5.

The constructional features and dimensions of the bar to meet functional requirements can be detailed more precisely since they are determined largely by operational and ergonomic considerations. In layout, a bar usually comprises two main counters, the back counter which serves as a display and storage area, and the front counter over which drinks are served and which, when circumstances and situation allow, may also be used by customers drinking at the bar. On plan the counters are usually straight and parallel, separated by the space used for service which is an optimum of 1050mm to 1150mm (3ft 6in to 3ft 9in) wide. In other cases the front counter may be wrapped around an island area or curved to provide a longer and more prominent frontage.

For waiter service a section at the end of the lounge bar may be separated to allow direct access and an unobstructed route to the dining room. Alternatively, a dispense bar may be provided to serve a dining or banquet room exclusively by waiter or waitress service. The latter is designed to facilitate rapid service of bottled and other drinks, and areas which would normally provide display are modified to allow additional bin storage of wines.

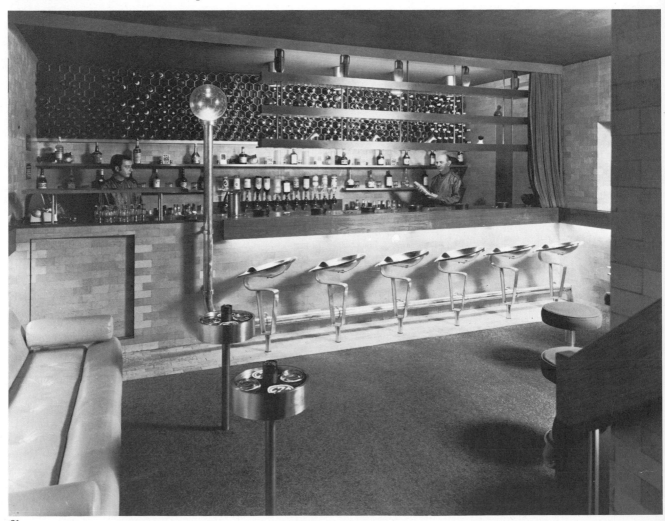

21
Hatchett's, Piccadilly. Architect: Lucas Mellinger Associated with G. Burns.
The Piccadilly bar showing leather tiles, brass plated tractor seats, anodised aluminium honeycomb wine racks and chain mail curtain in front of the bar.

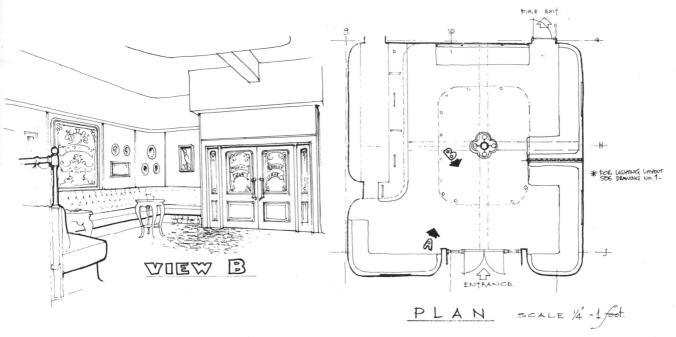

VIEW B

PLAN   SCALE ¼" = 1 foot.

FIRE EXIT

✱ FOR LIGHTING LAYOUT
SEE DRAWING No. 1.

ENTRANCE.

ENTRANCE DOORS.

VIEW A

TAVERN BAR   THE EXCELSIOR HOTEL

22
*Tavern Bar, Excelsior Hotel, London Airport. Trust Houses
Forte Ltd. Architects: Garnett, Cloughley, Blakemore &
Associates.*
Artist's sketch of the interior as a preliminary stage in design.

Location

9.03 Where possible the lounge should be positioned conveniently and conspicuously adjacent to the public circulation route following the optimum sequence of:

cloakrooms and toilets

lounge bar

dining room ◁▷ waiter service

It should not, however, be obligatory to pass through the immediate bar area to reach the dining room although the lounge may be more flexible in shape and extend to include an open corridor with seating space on one or both sides. Where the bar and lounge are supplementary to the restaurant, the areas provided are usually kept to a minimum.

Bar details

9.04 The upper part of the back counter is used for display of spirits and other drinks and also forms a decorative background. A work top—for dispensing—is provided at counter level, and storage shelves below for bottled lagers and beers. The top shelf of this unit should be refrigerated for chilling bottled drinks before service. Space on the back counter should be provided for the cash register which must be in a position visible to the customer, convenient for use, but not obstructive to other servers. Alternatively, where there is enough space the register may be housed in the front counter but this should not be in a remote position.

Front counters are usually a convenient height for leaning on—1000mm to 1150mm (3ft 3in to 3ft 9in) and a foot rail and counter stools may or may not be provided depending mainly on the style of the restaurant. The width of the counter is determined by length of reach and is normally a total of 600mm to 700mm (2ft to 2ft 3in) in two sections, the counter top being 450mm to 550mm (1ft 6in to 1ft 9in) wide and the under-counter work area or sink extending out a further 150mm (6in) to allow easier access.

9.05 In a bar which is subsidiary to a restaurant virtually all sales of drink will be in bottled or canned form, and pumping equipment is rarely installed. It is, however, desirable to have facilities for wine cooling and also an ice making machine should be fitted either under the counter or in the vicinity convenient for use in both bar and restaurant service.

A sink with draining board must be provided in the bar for washing glasses unless alternative provision is made for the glasses to be taken to a central wash-up area. In a large bar a glass washing machine may be installed and built into the counter unit with the necessary plumbing and electrical connections. Provision should also be made for empty bottles, broken glasses and other refuse by providing suitable bins in the bar unit.

To allow access to the bar servery the counter may be fitted with a lift-up flap and hinged door panel. Secondary access for supplies of drink and for the removal of empty bottles usually requires a separate entrance to the side or rear of the servery and provision should be made for isolating and securing the drinks store when it is not under supervised use.

Similarly, when the bar is not functioning, provision should be made for either the whole bar or the back counter—in which the drinks are kept—to be shuttered off for security and several designs of rolling or sliding shutters or grilles are available.

Construction and services

9.06 The bar counter, fittings and shelves should be of hard smooth impervious materials which are easily cleaned; plastics laminates, glass, chrome plated and stainless steel are commonly used. To provide an illusion of depth, sparkle and multiple display the back counter is often fitted with mirrors.

Servery floors must also withstand frequent spillage, washing and traffic, but to allow for standing at the bar in comfort a very hard surface is not desirable. Suitable materials are asphalt thermoplastic, resin-rubber and composition tiles and sheeting, coved at the junctions with the counters. Depending on the extent of use and traffic, similar materials may be used in the area immediately in front of the bar, but for light usage the carpeting of the lounge may be continued up to the bar with provision for replacement of this section when necessary.

Walls in the vicinity of the bar, and the counter front itself, should be covered with durable materials which will resist burning and marking and permit wiping over. The wall surfaces can often be protected by a dado rail or panel at the height most susceptible to damage, and less damage is likely when tables and chairs are in fixed positions.

Over the lounge area generally carpeting is most frequently used as a floor covering and the conditions which apply to the carpeting of restaurants apply equally here (see Chapter 7, para 7.35 to 7.37).

9.07 The engineering services required to create a satisfactory environment include controlled ventilation, heating and lighting. For an internal room or corridor, both plenum (inflow) and extraction ducting must be installed to ensure thorough distribution of air without draughts or discomfort. To allow for smoking a ventilation rate of four to six air changes each hour should be available. Extraction should not be concentrated within the bar area—since this will cause the smoke to collect—but rather distributed in front of the bar canopy. An exception applies when the bar is used for catering, and in this case extraction must be provided to cooking equipment.

Lighting in the lounge is designed partly for decorative reasons but should give an overall level of illumination of about 100 lux (9 lumens/sq ft). In the bar area a much higher illumination is essential—300 to 400 lux (28 to 37 lumens/sq ft)—and care must be taken to screen the bright light sources from view to avoid glare.

The ambient temperature should be maintained at about 18°C (65°F). Initially this will depend on heating—by warm air or otherwise—but when the room becomes heavily occupied, temperature regulation becomes more a function of ventilation and air-conditioning to remove heat.

To facilitate vacuum cleaning and other uses, electrical socket outlets should be provided around the lounge area and electrical connections, suitably protected against the effects of moisture, are necessary in the bar for various items of equipment. Plumbing services are also normally required to the bar counter.

4 INTERNAL ARRANGEMENT

ACCESS

1.01 Access to the dining area may be:
· direct;
· through an intermediary passage or stairway;
· through an ante-space with cloakroom and toilet facilities adjacent;
· through a reception area with lounge and bar service; or
· through a self-service hall for collection of food.

Direct access is the usual arrangement for most small street-frontage premises where the high value of the frontage to the property requires that this is put to maximum use. In this case, the wc and cloakroom facilities—if provided—are sited in any other part where space and engineering services are available. If space at ground level is at a premium, these facilities may be on a different floor.

Where the dining area is separated from the entrance or at another floor level, the route must be clearly identified and made as attractive as possible to compensate for any disadvantage of inconvenience or remoteness.

Relationship

1.02 If space allows, cloakroom and toilet facilities should be available, ideally between the entrance and dining room and conveniently positioned adjacent to the main circulation route to and from the latter. A reception area may be provided to serve as a meeting and gathering place, for service of drinks before and after the meal and perhaps as a general lounge for coffee and light refreshments. The correct location of the bar in relation to the lounge and dining room is important in order to facilitate drinks service, but it should not be necessary to have to pass through the bar area in order to reach the dining room, and part of the lounge should also be separated from this area. This subject is expanded in chapter 3,9 and is illustrated in many of the layout plans.

Self-service of meals, based on the free-flow system, can conveniently be provided in an ante-space between the entrance and dining areas. A number of alternative layouts are possible using through or indirect routes of circulation. Self-service arrangements are described in chapter 3.

Circulation within the dining area

1.03 Within the dining area the circulation of customers must be regulated. In the case of an expensive restaurant, customers will probably be received and taken to their seats by the head waiter but in other circumstances the movements of customers to the serving counter or tables, as the case may be, will need to be guided into definite flow patterns partly for the convenience of the arriving and departing customers, and partly to avoid unnecessary disturbance of others. There should be no need to thread through a maze of tables with the risk of collision with other diners or servers. The aisles from the entrance to the counter, and through the main body of the dining area, must be adequately wide and the main circulation routes, entering and leaving, must not cross.

Table 4 (i) Widths required in dining areas

Requirement	mm	in
Aisles		
Comfortable for 1 person	900	36
Comfortable for 2 people to pass	1350 (1100)*	54 (42)
Comfortable for 3 people to pass	1800 (1500)	72 (60)
Access to tables		
Minimum for direct approach	450	18
Minimum for sideways movement	200	8
Space for manoeuvre in sitting down	300 (200)	12 (8)
Space occupied by diner seated measured outward from table	450 (400)	18 (16)
Customers		
For comfort seated at table	600	24
Under compact conditions, light meals	550	22
Crowded, standing at counter	450	18

* Widths quoted are based on average body dimensions and requirements. Figures in brackets represent absolute minima

Direction of movement

1.04 To ensure that customers follow the routes provided for circulation a variety of techniques may be employed using suggestion, direction or obstruction as a means of guidance. This is particularly important when, in the case of self-service, large numbers of people may be entering and leaving both the restaurant and service counter, and all assessments of space requirements must be based on the peak figures.

For self-service planning, the main considerations are:
· Position of the counter in relation to entrance and dining areas;
· Visibility of the menu and other information;
· Space for assembly, decision and queuing;
· Indication of routes from entrance to counter and to exit;

· Distribution of customers in the dining area; and
· Avoidance of cross traffic or by-passing.

The counter or service area must be conspicuous immediately on entering the restaurant and should preferably be located conveniently near the entrance. Space must, however, be allowed for people waiting or reading the menu and for the queues which may form at the peak times. The space provided must be enough to avoid causing congestion in the entrance, and a linear allowance of 450mm (18in) per person waiting in a queue is usually adopted for calculation purposes.

When the service counter is set well back from the entrance it should preferably be approached through a straight wide aisle, and similar provision should be made for the exit. Typical widths which allow people to pass easily without congestion are quoted in table 4 (i).

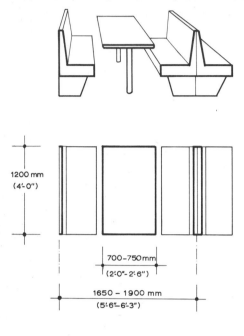

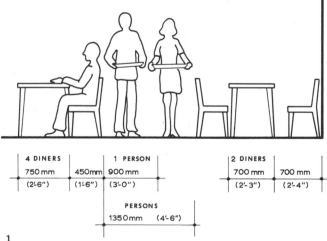

1
Minimum spaces between tables to allow for seating, access and circulation.

If indistinct the routes can be deliberately indicated by signs, and movement may also be regulated by the use of visual and physical barriers or obstacles. These must be sufficiently high and conspicuous to be easily noticeable under possibly crowded conditions, and may be movable to allow re-positioning for varying use of the restaurant. Examples include fixed or demountable barrier rails, permanent or movable screens, floral displays, decorative posts and cables and solid partitions.

Seating and table arrangements

1.05 The arrangement of seating and tables in the dining area is similar whether self-service or waitress/waiter service is used except that, in the former, emphasis will normally be given to practical simplicity with rows or groups of tables separated by wide straight aisles. This also facilitates the use of trolleys for table clearance. With experienced waiter or waitress service at the tables a more flexible layout is possible, allowing greater variations in the style and arrangement of the furniture.

2 TYPES OF FURNITURE

2.01 Various styles of tables used in catering establishments can be considered under four main groups:
· Counters or bars;
· Fitted tables and built-in furniture;
· Freestanding tables with legs or pedestal supports, and
· Adaptable tables with interchangeable units.

Counters are described in detail in chapter 3 and may be arranged in any of three basic layouts, depending on the size and shape of the room; namely, straight, single U-shaped, or multiple U-shaped. Counters are also used with separate tables in order to cater for different customer needs.

The stools for use with counters may be fixed stools with or without backs, movable stools without backs, or normal height chairs.

With high stools some form of footrest is essential either as a continuous rail or step or as an individual fitting forming part of the stool. The use of normal height chairs is limited by the need for the counter top to be at a suitable working height for serving, and by the greater depth of leg room required.

Ergonomic considerations in the design of counters are described in chapter 3, para 7.03, and for fixed seating a space allowance of 550mm to 600mm (1ft 8in to 2ft) is usually adopted, increasing to 600mm to 650mm (3ft to 2ft 2in) where fixed stools with backs are used.

Fitted tables

2.02 The arrangement of fixed seating on opposite, adjacent, or three sides of a table may be used to form a separate booth. Booths with seating on three sides of the enclosure are often used around part of the perimeter or grouped to form an island arrangement in the centre of the dining area. Such enclosures are appropriate for small parties of customers but must normally be balanced by other table arrangements.

Tables with banquette seating on opposite sides are generally arranged in parallel rows across the dining area and this style may be used throughout the restaurant. The fitted table may be fixed, movable or have a fixed base with movable top to allow easier access. Against a wall, the table may be cantilevered clear of the floor or may be partly supported by a leg in addition to the wall bracket. In other situations the table is usually supported by a pedestal rather than legs which may obstruct access. The width across a table with people facing each other should take into account the space occupied by knees under the table, the ease of reach and conversation across the table, and the surface area needed for tableware. In addition, considerations of economy in space must normally be applied. It is usually the knee room requirements which determine the minimum size possible, and to allow for these a table of 600mm (2ft) is the smallest practical width and a width of 750mm (2ft 6in) is recommended for leisure dining.

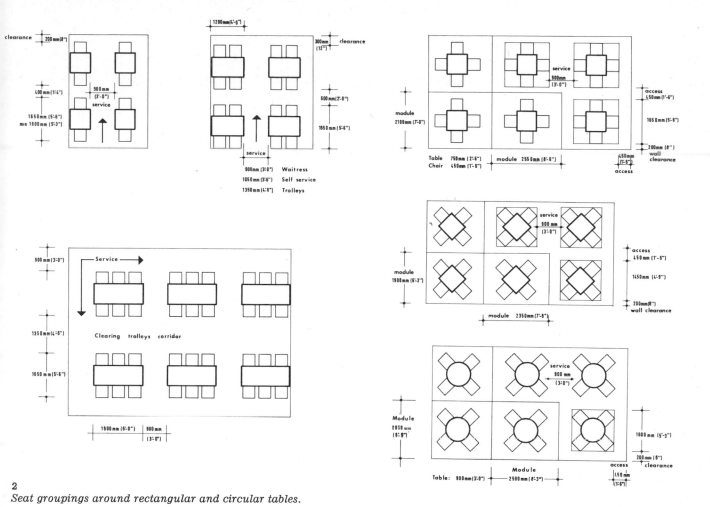

2
Seat groupings around rectangular and circular tables.

Module
1800 mm (6'-0")   1200mm (4'-0)

Module
2100 mm
(7'-0")   1650 mm
                                          (5'-6")

900mm
(2'-0")   ← Service — 900 mm

Module
1900 mm
(6'-3")   1350mm
                    ← Service —   (4'-6")

Module
1900 mm
(6'-3")   1200 mm
                                          (4'-0")

Module
1900mm (6'-3")
min. 1650 mm (5'-6")   **BOOTH SEATING**

3
Banquette seating arrangements and limiting dimensions
including space for access and service.

Table lengths are related to the shoulder width of an average large person, plus an allowance for elbow room, giving a total of 600mm (2ft) per person as a minimum for most purposes. However, if space is restricted, fixed banquette or booth seating may be designed on a minimum width of 1100mm (3ft 6in) for two people. With wall booth arrangements, the maximum length is governed by the length of a waiter's reach in serving to 1200mm (4ft), ie two people side by side.

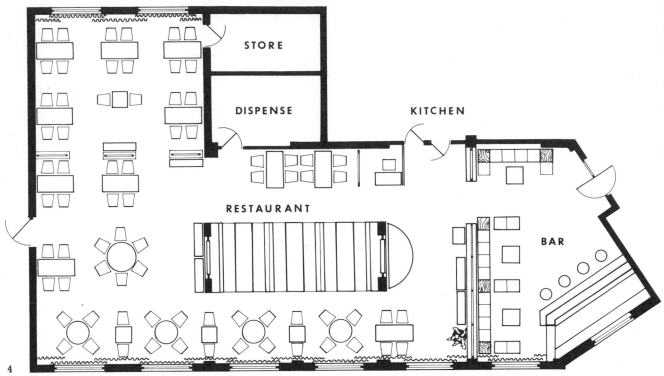

4

Brabazon restaurant, Excelsior Hotel, Birmingham Airport. Trust Houses Forte Ltd. Architects: Garnett Cloughley Blakemore & Associates.
Constructed in 1971, the Brabazon restaurant provides for a total of 100 places of which 24 are accommodated in the central island area of banquette seating.

View showing central area of banquette seating.

Banquette seating

2.03 Fixed banquette seating is normally upholstered for comfort and appearance, and its performance should be considered from three aspects:

· Method of suspension
· Type of filling and
· Covering materials

Modern types of suspension employed in upholstered furniture include steel compression or tension springs, and rubber webbing. The suspension system must be sufficiently stiff and strong to avoid excessive sagging, and a weak point can be the way in which the suspension is fitted to the frame of the seat and back.

The main types of filling materials are rubber latex or polyurethane in the form of foamed moulded shapes. Important features for filling materials include the indentation hardness, density, durability and the loss of hardness when in service. The durability of polyurethane foam tends to vary considerably but shows improvement as the density increases. The relevant British Standard specifications for filling materials are BS 3129: 1959: *Latex foam rubber components for furniture* and BS 3667: 1966: *Flexible polyurethane foam*.

In addition to the foamed materials, stuffing materials are also used to a certain extent either individually, as in cushions, or as a composite layer of wadding over other fillings to provide a soft even base for the covering fabric.

The filling of banquette seating is important since customers have to slide into position from the side. The seat should be relatively firm and flat while the back may be more flexible to conform to the curvature of the spine.

2.04 The covering material must be either easily removable for washing, or suitable for cleaning in situ. In Britain, the Council of Industrial Design has laid down the following basic requirements for upholstery fabrics and these are also applicable internationally:

· adequate strength;
· resistance to abrasive wear;
· resistance to burning;
· resistance to slippage of the component yarns;
· dimensional stability (shrinkage—stretching), and
· colour fastness to light, rubbing and cleaning.

The properties specified should be retained following normal processes of cleaning and use.

In certain fabric materials other features such as the resistance to snagging and pilling can also be significant and, apart from the question of serviceability, regard must also be given to other changes which may produce deterioration in the appearance. These would include the resistance of a pile surface to crushing, the surface dulling of certain smooth fabrics, shading, the permanency of staining and marking, and the effects of various detergents and cleaning agents.

Covering materials used in upholstery work extend over a wide range of choice from natural hides and sheet plastics such as polyvinyl chloride to woven fabrics. The latter include pile fabrics, moquettes, tweeds, brocades and tapestries each with different characteristics and serviceability. To a large extent the wearing properties will also depend on the type of fibre and yarn used in the weave of the fabric.

Table 4 (ii) Characteristics of upholstery materials compared

Material	Use	Main features of comparison
Natural fibres		
Cotton	Used alone or in mixture with other fibres for economy or improvement in properties	Cotton and linen are washable but tend to crush and stain easily. May be modified by treatment
Linen		Linen is extremely durable
Wool		Wool has a high natural resilience and recovery
Synthetic fibres		
Rayon, modified rayon	Used alone or added to other fibres for economy	Rayon has poor durability and resilience. Usually mixed with other fibres
Nylon, Terylene	Used alone or to reinforce other fibres	High abrasion resistance and strength
Acrylic fibres—Acrilan, Dralon, Courtelle	Generally used alone	Properties intermediate between those of wool and nylon. May be used in stretch fabrics
Plastic coated yarns	Used alone	Combine resistance to staining and ease of cleaning with appearance of woven fabric
Sheet materials		
Natural hides	Limited by cost	Expensive. Durable but must be kept supple. Liable to be cold to touch
Polyvinyl chloride	Plain or backed by expandable fabric	Appearance of leather. Should be given a textured or grained surface to reduce points of contact and perspiration. Fabric reinforcement improves resistance to cracking

Dimensions

2.05 Dimensions in seat design must be based on anthropometric considerations. For a seat depth, 430mm to 450mm (17in to 18in) is most appropriate and this should have a slight backward slope of up to 3° to 5° but should not be excessively domed. The Advisory Committee on Hotels and Restaurants' report to the Council of Industrial Design recommended that a standard seat height of 430mm (17in) should be adopted, with a corresponding height of 700mm (28in) for the table top. Again this is a standard applicable internationally.

In low banquette seating, particularly where the seats are arranged back to back with each other, an allowance of 100mm (4in) should be made for the customers' head leaning back. With the various dimensions quoted, the overall distance across a booth will be a minimum of 1600mm (5ft 3in) using a 600mm (2ft) wide table or about 1900mm (6ft 3in) wide for comfort with a table 750mm (2ft 6in) wide.

Legged tables

2.06 Conventional tables normally have four or more legs depending on size. Legged tables are available in a wide range of standard production models or may be manufactured to specific requirements at higher cost.

Materials used in construction of frames include wood and steel. In wooden frameworks, beech and oak are in general stronger than other timbers and should have straight grain for strength with well fitted joints—preferably reinforced. The surfaces, including the underside of the top, must be free from roughness and splinters.

Metal frames are usually formed from tubular steel welded together, and enamelled or chrome plated for protection. The welding is usually an important feature of constructional strength and an indication of the quality—as is the way in which the metal frame is secured to the top.

Table tops may be of a variety of materials including plastics such as acrylics (Perspex) and polypropylene, glass, sheet metals and wood sheeting as solid timber, chipboard, or plywood. The last two are usually surfaced with plastic laminates (melamines) or with selected wood veneers, but the quality of the surface may depend on whether table cloths are to be used. Usually, to allow flexibility, it is desirable to provide for dual purposes.

A surface which is to be left exposed must be impervious to reasonable heat, water, grease and acids. It should not chip, scratch nor discolour with normal use, and should preferably be cleanable with a damp cloth. The finishes used for wooden furniture include oil, wax, French polish, nitrocellulose, melamine, polyurethane, and polyester.

Tests for the resistance of clear wood finishes to heat and liquids are specified in

BS 3667: *Methods of test for clear wood finishes for wooden furniture;*

Part 1: 1965 *Low angle glare*

    2: 1971 *Resistance to wet heat*

    3: 1971 *Resistance to dry heat*

    4: 1970 *Resistance to marking by liquids*

    5: 1972 *Resistance to marking by oils and fats.*

2.07 Dimensions for tables and chairs are based on the same data as outlined for banquette seating (para 2.05). The Advisory Committee on Hotels and Restaurants' report to the CID recommended that a table of 750mm (2ft 6in) square should be used where possible, although in very restricted areas a smaller table size of 700mm (2ft 3in) square may be used for one or two people. Two standard 750mm tables joined together are adequate for six people or for seven if semicircular ends are fitted.

Circular tables of 900mm (3ft) or greater diameter offer advantages in increasing the local density of customers and providing some variety in the layout but cannot be joined together.

In determining the space requirements for tables, allowances must be made for the customer's access to his seat and the space needed for manoeuvre as he sits down, which amount to at least 500mm (1ft 8in) and 200mm (8in) respectively. The latter must be added to the chair dimensions giving a total width of at least 700mm (2ft 4in) for seating around the table. For waiter service and aisle space, a minimum of 900mm (3ft) should be allowed between the seats when in use.

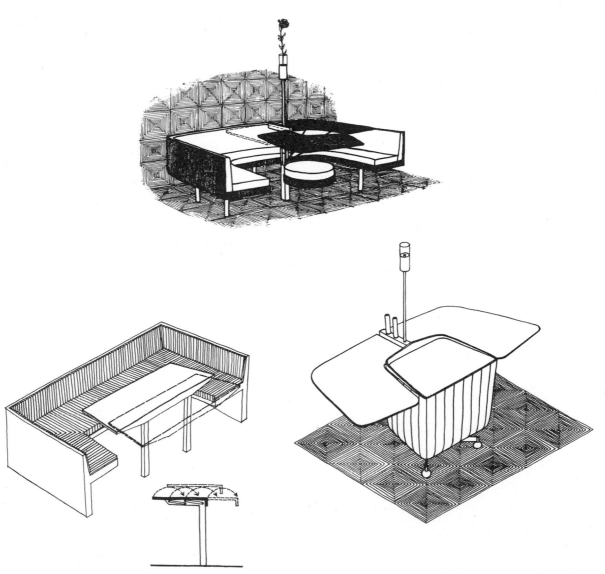

6
Architect: Lucas Mellinger.
Sketches of tables and seating arrangements specifically designed to facilitate access.

Pedestal tables

2.08 Moulded and shaped frames may be used to form pedestals for circular or square tables which are usually fixed in position, but may be freestanding. The pedestal design allows greater flexibility in the positions of the chairs and economy in space, but such tables are generally designed for specific requirements and tend to be more costly than conventional legged tables.

Adaptable tables

2.09 Where possible legged tables should be adaptable to form different layouts and groupings, allow substitution of round or square tops, and permit compact stacking and easy transport.

The first requirement can be met by linkage fittings which join tables together, for example to form rows for banquet or convention use. The method employed in linking tables together must be simple and quick to assemble and remove, and it must not leave any sharp or prominent projections below the underside of the top, nor reduce the space between this and the seating to less than 230mm (9in) clearance.

To permit variations in table shapes, circular or square tops should be removable and interchangeable using a standard frame. Further variations in layout can be provided with semi-circular linkage units or by the use of trapezoidal shapes.

Stacking is facilitated by separating the tops and inter-setting the frames. In some cases a frame may be inverted and fitted with dolly wheels for use in transporting the stacked tops into storage.

To facilitate both interchange of components and storage, modular co-ordination is essential and a module size of 100mm (4in) is recommended.

Flexibility is an important factor in many hotel restaurants which cater for conferences or banquets, and in

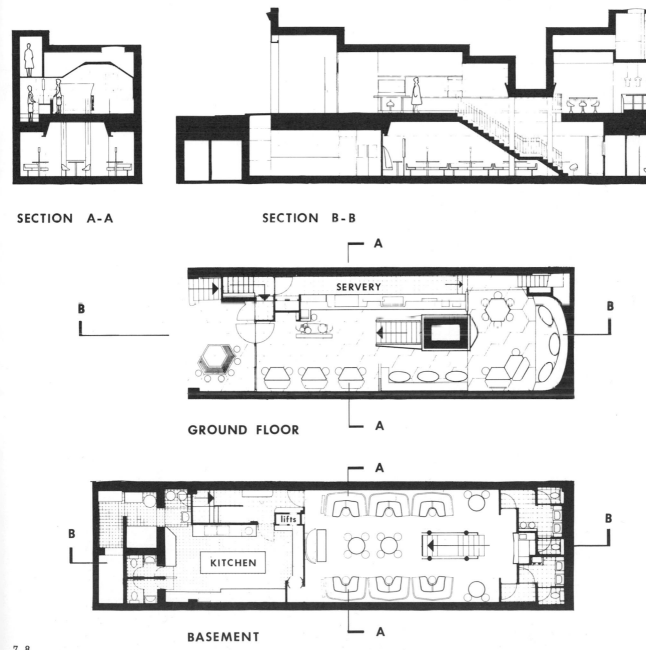

SECTION A-A

SECTION B-B

GROUND FLOOR

BASEMENT

7 8

Sands, New Bond Street, London. Architect: Lucas Mellinger associated with K. A. Short.
Before alterations, the building included numerous obstructions and maximum use of the ground floor and basement has been obtained by incorporating these into the design, in- *creasing the usable floor space by 48 per cent. The ground floor design is based on a hexagonal pattern—as seen in the terrazzo floor panels[9] and tables[10]. The basement restaurant is more formal with purpose made tables and seating. Linings and floor carpeting are designed with a Persian pattern[11].*

9

10

11

school meals, residential or employee catering where the dining room is used for several purposes including social events.

Chairs

2.10 Dining chairs are usually fitted with legs although pedestal designs are available. Chair frames are most commonly made of solid or laminated wood or of tubular steel with a circular or rectangular cross-section. To a minor extent, aluminium and moulded plastic or glass fibre designs may be also used. The seats and backs may also be of moulded plastic (eg polypropylene) or laminated wood shaped to the particular form required either as a continuous sheet or with separate seat and back panels. Wooden chairs based on reproduction or contemporary styles can be obtained in a wide variety of designs chosen from a standard production range or specially made to order. The framework and foundation may be combined with infill woven work (eg wicker work and tapestries) or upholstered with fabric or sheet materials. Details of the method of suspension, type of filling and covering

12
Staff canteen Foster Finance Ltd, Dublin. Architects: Stephenson Gibney & Associates.
An attractive layout of modern restaurant furniture in moulded white Arkana with bright red upholstery.

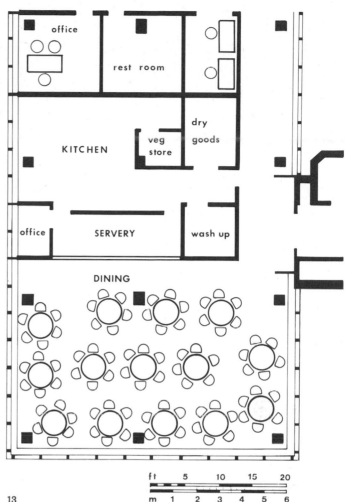

13
Plan of the staff restaurant, situated on the top floor of a five-storey building, which is designed to cater for about 120 lunches between 12.30 and 2.30 pm each day with waitress service.

materials for banquette seating (2.03, 2.04) apply also to upholstered dining chairs and other furniture.

To allow easier access in a restricted space and to limit the width, most dining room chairs do not have arms. However, chairs, whether of production or special design, may be fitted with arms in situations where the need for impressive appearance outweighs the disadvantages of size and weight.

Important features in chair construction include rigidity of joints—although the frame may be flexible—adequate strength, reasonable weight, good balance, freedom from rough or sharp edges, and feet protected against damage to the flooring. Stackability may also be a necessary requirement and, in this case, minimum weight is also an important consideration.

Woodwork must be given a protective finish to enhance the grain and appearance and to reduce marking and staining. The finish must be appropriate to withstand heavy use, and the possible effects of water, grease and cleaning. Steel frames are usually chrome plated or enamelled and a high quality finish is necessary in view of the difficulties of renovation.

Furniture is frequently chosen or reproduced in period styles to create a suitable impression and atmosphere. In adopting a particular style, it is often important to ensure that the whole of the furniture and décor of the restaurant is in keeping with the period represented. A good and inexpensive outline of the historical development of English furniture designs is given in the book *English Furniture at a Glance* by Barbara Jones (Architectural Press, London).

Banquet arrangements

2.11 Various alternative arrangements of furniture are used for banquets depending on the size and shape of the room and the positions of service facilities but the tables

14
The Queens' Hotel, Burton-on-Trent. Berni Inns Ltd, Property and Planning Department.
A forty-two seater restaurant formed out of the previous conventional kitchen. The vaulted ceiling is false but was chosen to obscure partly the main plumbing services in this area. This restaurant is a good example of broken up areas at different levels giving very personal seating layouts. The cellar theme is emphasized by barrel decorations and bottle labels.

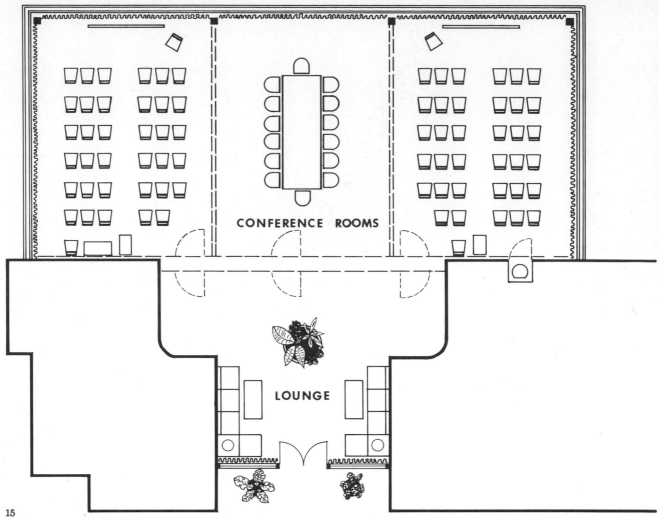

CONFERENCE ROOMS

LOUNGE

15

*Conference Suite, Excelsior Hotel, Birmingham Airport.
Trust Houses Forte Ltd. Architects: Garnett Cloughley,
Blakemore & Associates.*

*This suite, which opened late 1971, has a total internal area
of 17·4m × 8·0m (57′ × 26′) which can be divided into three
smaller conference rooms.*

are usually joined together to form long rows in parallel
linked by a 'head' table at right angles. An average place
width of 600mm (2ft) is allowed, and the absence of separating spaces between the tables enables high local densities
of occupancy to be obtained. To facilitate fast service on
both sides, large aisles should be left between the rows,
preferably about 2000mm (6ft 6in) wide but, as a minimum,
1500mm (5ft) may be adopted.

When a restaurant is rearranged for a banquet it is
possible, with the same total occupancy, to leave a part
of the floor—about half the total—free for social gathering, exhibitions or entertainment.

Stations

2.12 A small sideboard for temporary storage of table and
serving items may be used as a station for waiters or
waitresses. The elaboration of these facilities will depend
on the level of sophistication involved in the meals
served, and the number of stations used will be based on
the number of customers and the extent to which the
tables are isolated from the servery.

As an indication of staffing requirements, average
numbers of seats or placings served by a waiter or waitress
are 12 to 16 where the menu is restricted; 8 to 12 for typical
meals and 4 to 8 placings for à la carte meals offering a
wide choice in each course, the number depending on the
type of restaurant, staffing structure and degree of elaboration used in meal service.

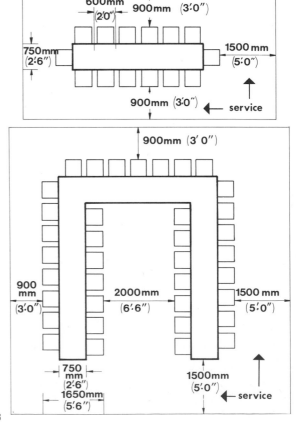

16

Banquet layouts
*Typical layouts of banquet tables with appropriate space
allowances for (a) seating and (b) service access.*

The siting of a station is important in terms of its efficient use and effect on the surroundings. It should be located near the servery, near the wash-up and—for economy—in a space which is otherwise unusable. The minimum distance to the nearest dining table must be at least 1200mm (4ft) and some provision should be made for screening and sound damping to avoid disturbing the near-by diners. To reduce encroaching into the circulation area the depth should be limited to about 500mm (20in) and an optimum working height is about 970mm (38in). Stations positioned in the dining area should be limited in use to assisting service. The main stations for deposit of dirty tableware and other functions should be kept outside the room because of the noise and nuisance which may arise, and serving stations are usually inappropriate in restricted space.

3 DENSITIES

3.01 The density of occupancy which can be obtained in different types of restaurant and dining areas will depend on several factors such as the

· price of meals and standard of accommodation and surroundings expected;
· method of food service and
· types and arrangement of tables and furniture generally.

(a) *Price and duration of meals*

There is, to some extent, a correlation between the space provided and the time taken over a meal, and this tends to be reflected in the price of the meal involved. In situations where dining is a lengthy process—up to 2½ hours in business lunches or leisure dining—an atmosphere of relaxed comfort forms an essential part of the enjoyment. On the other hand where there is a rapid turnover of customers during the meal period, restrictions on space and movement may be tolerable for the short times involved, particularly where there are compensations in convenience and speed of service.

Considered from another aspect, an awareness of the adequacy or otherwise of the dining space will also depend to a large extent on the attitude and expectations of the customer and, in this respect, there is some identification with socio-economic groupings as used in market surveys.

(b) *Method of food service*

The method of food service will have a considerable effect on the overall space requirements. With waiter or waitress service the spacing for access between chairs of adjacent tables can be kept to a minimum of about 900mm (3ft) and practically the whole room can be used as the dining area. Counter service is less economical in the space

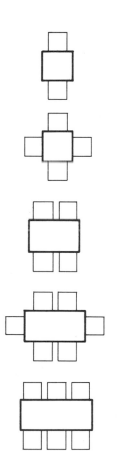

Dining area	Lounge area
TABLE DIAMETERS 900–1000 mm (3'-0"–3'-3") 3 or 4 chairs	4 or 5 chairs
1050 mm (3'-6") 4 or 5 chairs	5 or 6 chairs
1200 mm (4'-0") 6 or 7 chairs	7 or 8 chairs
1500 mm (5'-0") 8 or 9 chairs	9 or 10 chairs
750 mm diam. (2'-6") semicircle increases chair seating by 1	

Dining area	Lounge area
750 x 750 mm (2'-6"x 2'-6") min. 700 x 700mm (2'-3"x 2'-3")	700 x 700 mm (2'-3"x 2'-3")
min. 750x750 mm	750 x 750 mm (2'-6"x 2'-6") min 700 x 700mm (2'-3"x 2'-3")
1200x750 mm (4'-0"x 2'-6")	1200 x 750 mm (4'-0"x 2'-6") min. 1200x700mm (4'-0"x2'-3")
1500x750 mm (5'-0"x 2'-6")	1500 x 750mm (5'-0"x 2'-6")
1800x 750 mm (6'-0"x 2'-6")	1800 x 750mm (6'-0"x 2'-6")

17
Dimensions for various table layouts and local seating densities.

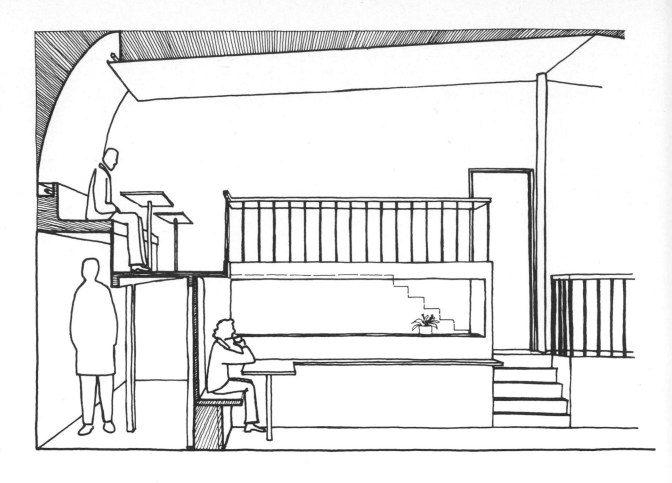

18
Architect: Lucas Mellinger.
Sections showing the use of stepped flooring and balconies to
utilise tall ceiling space in modernisation of conventional
rooms.

occupied, while in self-service arrangements a large part of the area is taken up by the serving counter and the circulation of customers, giving a low overall occupancy. However, against the latter, there are certain savings of space in the kitchen service and plating areas.

(c) *Type and arrangement of furniture*
The third main factor affecting seating densities is the type and arrangement of the tables. For comparison, examples of the local densities of table arrangements are shown in table 4 (iii) and illustrated on page 73.

Table 4 (iii) Space allowances based on average requirements

Type of seating and service	Area per diner	
	m²	sq ft
Table service		
Square tables in rows:		
parallel seating 2	1·7 to 2·0	18 to 22
parallel seating 4	1·3 to 1·7	14 to 18
diagonal seating 4 *	1·0 to 1·2	11 to 13
Rectangular tables in rows:		
seating 4	1·3 to 1·5	13 to 16
seating 6	1·0 to 1·3	11 to 14
Circular tables in rows:		
seating 4 *	0·9 to 1·4	10 to 15
Fixed banquette seating		
In booths seating 4		
waitress service	0·7 to 1·0	8 to 11
including counter for		
self-service	0·9 to 1·4	10 to 15
Counter seating		
Tunnel counters	1·4 to 1·6	15 to 17
Single counters	1·7 to 2·0	18 to 22
Single counters used with		
wall units	1·1 to 1·4	12 to 15
Banquet groupings		
Multiple rows	0·9 to 1·1	10 to 12
Single row	1·0 to 1·3	11 to 14
Self-service (trolley clearance)		
Rectangular tables in rows:		
dining area only		
seating 4	1·4 to 1·6	15 to 17
seating 6	1·1 to 1·3	12 to 14
seating 8	1·0 to 1·2	11 to 13
including counter area		
seating 4	1·7 to 2·0	18 to 21
seating 6	1·3 to 1·8	14 to 19
seating 8	1·2 to 1·6	13 to 17
Self-service (self-clearance)		
Rectangular tables in rows:		
dining area only		
seating 4	1·3 to 1·5	14 to 16
seating 6	1·0 to 1·2	11 to 13
seating 8	0·9 to 1·1	10 to 12
including counter area		
seating 4	1·5 to 1·9	16 to 20
seating 6	1·2 to 1·6	13 to 17
seating 8	1·1 to 1·5	12 to 16

* Economy in space is obtained with tables at 45°

5 ATMOSPHERE AND INTERIOR DESIGN

Influences on enjoyment

1.01 The enjoyment of a meal in a restaurant, snack bar, canteen or any similar situation will depend to a large extent on the meal, the service and the surroundings provided. However, the customer's reaction will also be affected in part by personal attitudes and preferences. Among the components which determine satisfaction

· Time	· Convenience
· Mood	· Atmosphere
· Anticipation	· Impression
· Attitude	· Service
· Valuation	· Charges

Time and convenience

1.02 Concern over time may dominate the customer's attitude towards a meal and, regardless of other considerations, delay and inconvenience may cause extreme irritation. In these circumstances, convenience of location and speed of service will be important components of satisfaction. This situation may arise in the short meal periods provided during the working day, or when travelling.

Mood and atmosphere

1.03 Mood is a complex temporary state of feeling, created by psychological and physiological influences. To a certain extent, mood can be induced or ameliorated by social and environmental conditions and it is this aspect which is considered in relation to the atmosphere in a restaurant. Mood tends to influence choice—often a customer will prefer privacy or company, formality or informality, excitement or relaxation.

Atmosphere is the term used to describe the combined effect on the customer of the surroundings and company. It is made up of many contributing features which will vary in their relative importance from one situation to the next. For instance, an air of formality induced by a large spacious room may be very appropriate as the setting for a conference lunch or banquet but on other occasions the informality of smaller, more personalized, areas will often be preferred. The style of design, choice of decor and furniture arrangement together will tend to create a particular image whether of exclusiveness or any other desired characteristic. The customer's confidence in the efficiency of management will often be reassured by the clean appear-

ance of the premises whilst his enjoyment of the meal experience can be heightened by good quality table appointments and the attractive presentation of food.

Atmosphere may also be introduced by providing a wider horizon of interest through external or internal views, background music, lighting effects and the use of special features in design. However, acceptable levels of congestion, disturbance, noise and brightness will depend very much on the social environment and on individual reactions. Similarly, comfort is an important consideration when a meal is prolonged but may be less so in other circumstances.

In some instances, restaurant design may allow for flexibility in layout and appearance to suit each meal occasion but the high initial cost and the time needed to produce dramatic changes will usually be prohibitive in all but the larger conference and banquet rooms which often have to provide this facility to ensure full utilisation.

To a large extent atmosphere—or an awareness of the atmosphere—can be generated by occupants themselves and by the efficiency and attitude of staff. Indeed an empty room, no matter how well designed, is often devoid of atmosphere except perhaps a sense of exposure. The more crowded a room becomes the less influence the surroundings will tend to exert on the occupants. Under those conditions, the most dominant consideration is whether the customer prefers to eat in company or in a more private setting, and whether the standard of service he or she expects can be maintained.

Atmosphere can be affected dramatically by small things. For instance neglect of maintenance, failure in hygiene, or discomfort due to bad design, all tend to leave a lasting impression more prominent than other influences.

Anticipation and impression

1.04 The customers anticipation may be founded on: the appearance of the premises, recommendations of other customers, or previous experience. In each case the customer builds up an impression of the type of meal, service and surroundings which will be provided. Should any of these not measure up to his expectations, the disappointment may become a source of irritation and dissatisfaction.

To a certain extent this problem can be offset by providing a choice in menu, a moderate—although not excessive—range in prices, and variations in the type of seating and table arrangements which are equally attractive. It is, however, important that the exterior of the premises—including the entrance—should reflect accurately the character and price level of the restaurant.

1.05 Impressions are also determined from several considerations, mainly whether:
- the food, service and physical environment meet expectations;
- the meal and facilities represent good value for money;
- the other customers are socially acceptable.

The impressions formed by a customer will to a large degree be conditioned by experience and intensified by particular points of annoyance or enjoyment.

Attitude and Service

1.06 The attitude towards sociable surroundings and company will vary according to the customer's mood and circumstances, and is one of the factors which will influence his choice of eating place. The bright lights, informality and noise which are appreciated on one occasion could well be an intolerable intrusion at another time.

As a separate issue, the qualitative assessment of company may be an important consideration. The presence of well known personalities, and the social or commercial standing of other customers, may be an attraction through their influence and association.

Good service can, to a large extent, achieve a similar effect by creating within the customer a sense of being important, attractive or interesting.

Valuation and Charges

1.07 This aspect is discussed under financial considerations—Chapter 1, para 2.00—since it is fundamental to the success of a business. In general terms, a customer who values a meal higher than its cost is normally one who is satisfied. In this context, it is not merely the food which determines value but the way it is served, the atmosphere in which it is enjoyed, and the facilities provided for the convenience and comfort of the customer.

2 INTERIOR DESIGN

Integration

2.01 To be fully effective the atmosphere within a restaurant should be created deliberately by design not only of the interior of the room but also of the services and catering components which are necessary for the proper functioning of the premises. To ensure that all these various aspects are considered and incorporated into the scheme of design where possible, the brief for a restaurant design should, ideally, include advice on the following matters:
- planning the layout of the building; the relationships between the restaurant, bar, kitchen and ancillary areas;
- positions of doors and windows having regard to external aspects and to travel routes of customers and staff;
- interior construction of the restaurant areas; the types of linings and surface finishes;
- the scheme of decoration and special features of design;
- selection of carpets and other floor and wall coverings, furnishings and associated fittings;
- design and arrangement of tables, chairs, sideboards, trolleys and furniture generally;
- location and design of the food service areas, serving bars, cashier desks and other functional units;
- requirements for electrical and gas installations; positions of power, etc. outlets;
- system of lighting including the selection of light fittings
- methods of heating, ventilating and air-conditioning and the design of engineering services;

- control of noise by insulation and acoustic treatment;
- provisions for security and safety—including safety from fire;
- facilities for hygiene, cleaning and routine maintenance;
- design of signs, motifs, menu holders and other serving and table items;
- styling of staff uniforms;
- selection of tableware and inter-relationship of design with the style of meal service.

Where required the design brief may include the planning, construction and equipment for kitchens, stores, cloakrooms and other facilities associated with the restaurant. In addition, the design, construction and features must allow for the incorporation of engineering services—such as heating, air-conditioning, and electrical equipment—which will also need some provision for access and maintenance.

In practice, there is usually a distinct division of interests between the architect or designer responsible for the physical facilities and the catering consultant advising on food and commercial requirements, but the primary need in restaurant design, as in other working situations, is to ensure completeness of detail. Operating requirements must be integrated with the design, not implanted at a later stage, and functional and decorative features should be complementary.

Detail

2.02 The significance of accuracy of detail is revealed when there are glaring mistakes such as the use of modern Scandinavian cutlery in a mock-Tudor restaurant. Equally important, there should be a feeling of harmony and relationship between the interior design of the room, staff uniforms, furniture, linen and tableware, and even the way food is served. For instance, silver dishes—no matter how decorative—are not in keeping with plastic laminate table tops, whereas the same table items in a severe style of stainless steel or even earthenware would probably

1

The Barge Buttery, Post House, Leicester. Trust Houses Forte Ltd.
The buttery features a long mural by Mary Adshead depicting a typical long-boat scene and is decorated by boat rudders, horses' tails, brightly painted water cans, copper kettles and other features of barge life.

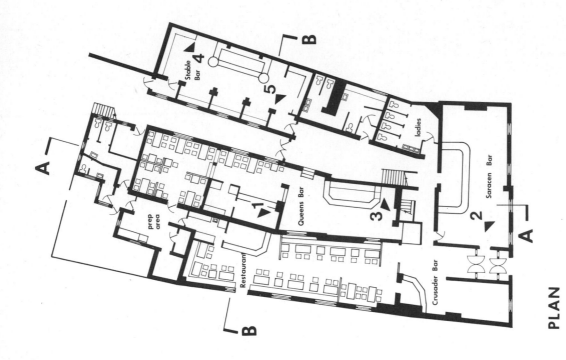

PLAN

- Stable Bar
- 4
- 5
- Queens Bar
- 1
- 3
- 2
- Crusader Bar
- Saracen Bar
- ladies
- prep area
- Restaurant
- B
- A

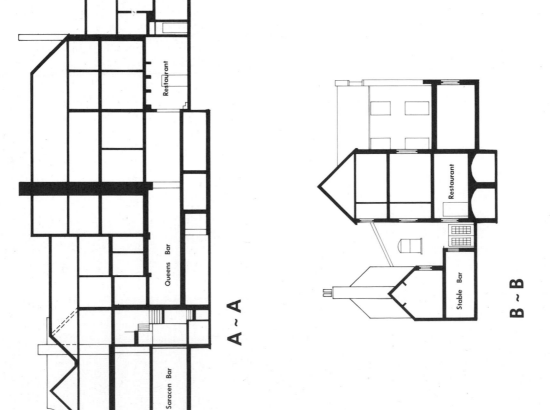

Restaurant

Queens Bar

Saracen Bar

A ~ A

Restaurant

Stable Bar

B ~ B

2

Details of restaurants and bars, etc, on the ground floor shown on plan and in sectional elevations. The latter indicate the difficulties of accommodating structural work when making alterations to existing buildings.

3

The Queens Hotel, Burton-on-Trent. Berni Inns Ltd, Property and Planning Department.

This hotel derives its name from three queens reputed to have stayed there over the years and the design of one of the bars develops this theme with wall pictures dramatised by lighting effects. From a practical viewpoint, the rear side of the bar shows how table wines are stored conveniently to hand in the canopy above the counter with wine glass storage—also housed in the canopy—forming a practical as well as decorative display effect.

The counter incorporates a double sink and other fittings as a standard unit.

4

Another bar based on the original use of the premises as a coaching inn.

5
Formula One restaurant, Post House, Hampstead. Trust Houses Forte Ltd.
The racing theme of this restaurant is based on the Vanwall Special racing car which was originally developed in a near-by garage. Designs of chairs and banquette seating simulate car *seats and pattern of the carpet gives the impression of car treads. Photographs of racing scenes form murals along the wall. Predominant colours are brown and dark gold with shades of brown in different areas of seating.*

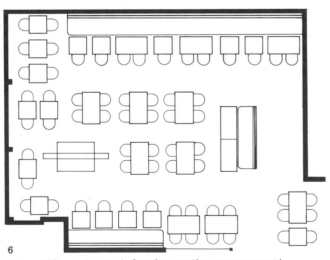

6
Plan of the restaurant showing seating arrangement.

harmonise well with this type of furniture. When there is any serious discord in design, part of the illusion is lost and there is a tendency to examine individual items—perhaps critically—rather than their overall effect.

2.03 Lack of order and arrangement also tends to suggest inefficiency. A sense of disorderliness can result from irregularity in patterns, distortion of horizontal lines, inconsistency in quality and insufficient care in clearing tables or setting places. It is also evidenced by bad arrangement of furniture causing congestion and disturbance of diners or difficulties in service.

The most serious effect of disorder is the type of untidiness which leads to low standards of hygiene and safety. Often operational failings of this nature derive from bad planning and design.

Identification

2.04 In the same way as there is a sense of association between the components of a particular scheme of design there is also an implied relationship between styles of catering and restaurant design. For example, the design treatment for a 'hamburger' type of operation must be different from that of, say a 'steak house'—mainly because they are catering for different markets.

Conversely, it should be possible for a customer to identify a particular type of catering from the style of the premises. A carpeted floor, for instance, may distinguish a restaurant from a café; self-service is associated with a cafeteria; quick light meals are identified with counter service, and the ranking of a restaurant is usually based on its elegance and degree of personal attention.

2.05 Perhaps the main distinction between restaurants lies in the method of serving meals and, apart from remote catering services, these can be generally grouped into ten types which broadly correspond to the extent of personal service and sophistication provided. In most cases there is also a correlation with the duration of meals involved, and the prices charged. A summary of the characteristics of different types of catering facilities is given in chapter 1, section 4 as a guide to design requirements.

3 PRINCIPLES OF DESIGN

Style

3.01 The basic theme in design may be to create or recreate a style which is recognisable. This may be expressed in several forms:

· mood—realism or escapism;

· period—futuristic, contemporary, reproduction;
· fashion—traditional, modern, ultra-modern;
· nationality—Chinese, Indian, Italian, Swiss, etc; and
· intensity—flamboyant, lavish, subdued, dignified.
In each case, the desired effect or illusion is achieved by introducing features into the design which have a familiar

association with the style represented and can thus be easily 'recognised'. To a large extent this is a question of careful research and interpretation of the original features since the end result must be a practical operation rather than a showpiece.

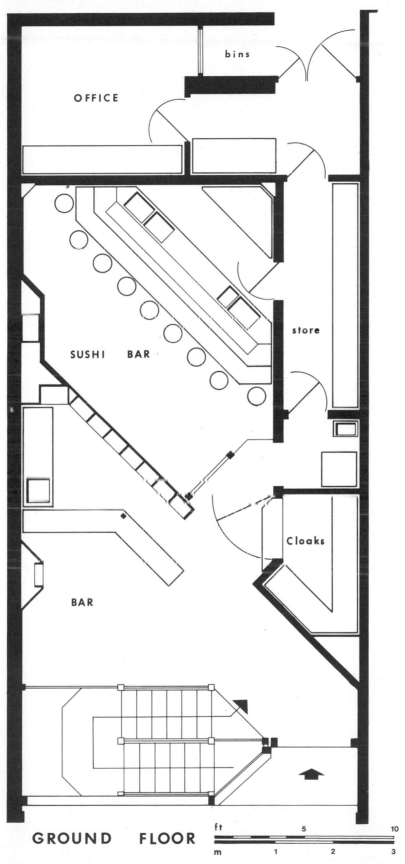

GROUND FLOOR

ft   5   10
m   1   2   3

7
Japanese Restaurant, London. Architects: W. H. McAlister & Partners.
Ground Floor plan showing the Sushi bar.

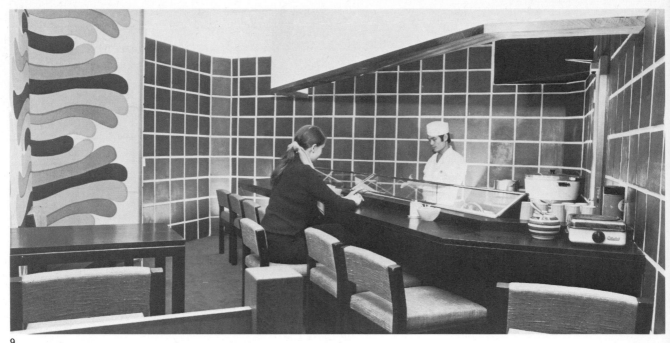

9
View of the Sushi bar.

BASEMENT

8
Basement plan of the restaurant and Tatami rooms. The basement area extends under adjacent premises and accommodates most of the dining space.

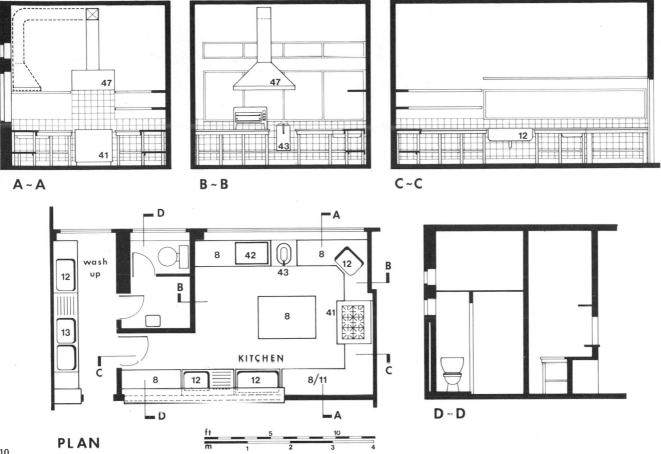

A ~ A   B ~ B   C ~ C

D ~ D

PLAN

ft   5   10
m   1   2   3   4

10
Details of the kitchen in which food is prepared mainly for cooking at the tables.

11
Tatami Room.
One of the private dining rooms designed in national style. Following Japanese custom cooking is mainly done at the table and hence kitchens for the restaurant are relatively small. Furniture is designed at a low level for squatting but floor mats around the tables lift up to reveal wells which can accommodate ordinary chairs for European guests.

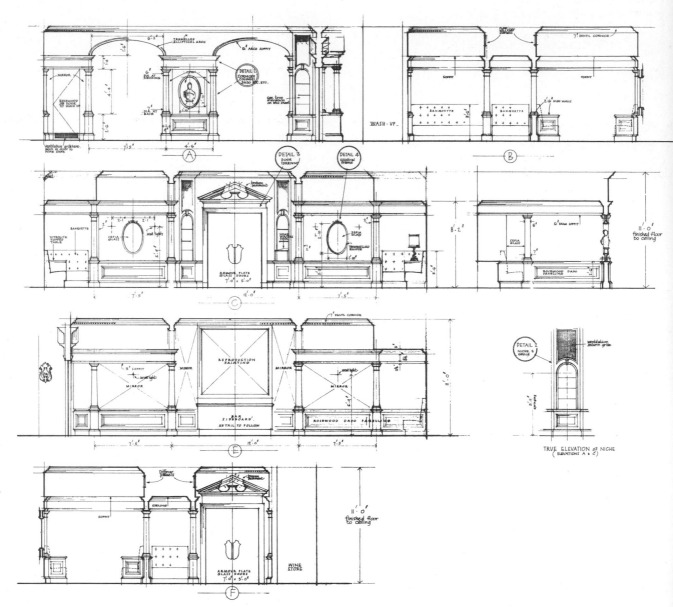

12
Draitone Manor restaurant, Excelsior Hotel, London Airport. Trust Houses Forte Ltd. Architects: Garnett, Cloughley, Blakemore & Associates.
Based on a Regency design, the restaurant has been accurately reproduced in a modern hotel with careful attention to detailing of the interior décor and furnishing. Elevations show the design of the interior panelling, alcoves, columns and other features employed in the styling.

There is, however, a need for care in detail if the created illusion is to be satisfactorily impressive. For instance, in the reproduction of historical settings it is important to maintain a reasonable degree of accuracy in combining correct period styles of furniture, décor and table items. Where possible, natural materials should be employed rather than obvious substitutes, and the whole effect is best designed around one or more authentic features which can withstand scrutiny as focal points of interest.

Authenticity is usually most difficult to achieve when it is in direct contrast with practical requirements as, for example, in staff uniforms—but the character of the surroundings can, in this case, be ingeniously represented by symbolic rather than factual styling.

Proportion

3.02 Interior design tends to have a greater impression on a person than the outside appearance partly because it encloses him physically and by doing so compels a greater awareness, and in part because of the closer observation which develops from longer contact in circumstances of restricted movement. For visual comfort, the composition of design must be suitably proportioned to be seen without distraction or strain. If the components are so widely separated that the repetition is outside the angle of view, or they lack balance, their full effect cannot be appreciated.

The scale of design must be proportionate to the size of the room and, in smaller intimate areas, attention to detail assumes increasing importance. Lighting can also be employed to alter shape, size and proportions by emphasising or obscuring certain features. This is particularly useful in disguising the excessive height of a room or passageway by creating the impression of a lower ceiling at the plane of lighting.

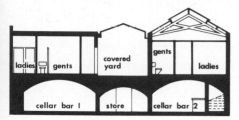

SECTION A–A

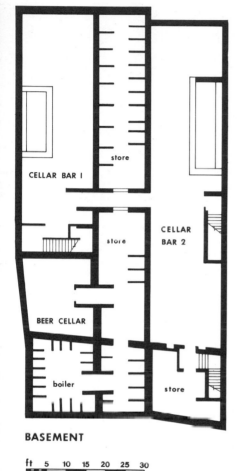

CELLAR BAR 1

store

CELLAR BAR 2

store

BEER CELLAR

boiler

store

BASEMENT

ft 5 10 15 20 25 30
m 1 2 3 4 5 6 7 8 9

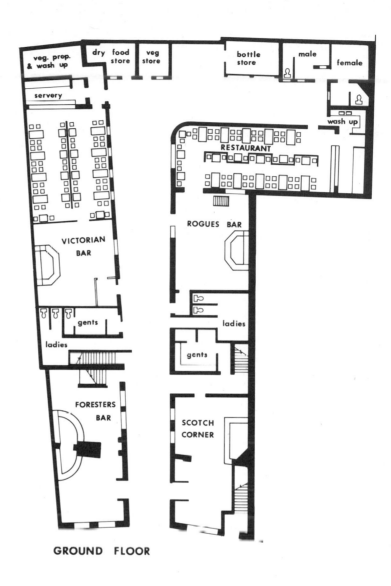

GROUND FLOOR

veg. prep. & wash up

dry food store

veg store

bottle store

male

female

servery

wash up

RESTAURANT

VICTORIAN BAR

ROGUES BAR

gents

ladies

ladies

gents

FORESTERS BAR

SCOTCH CORNER

13

Irongates Tavern, Derby. Berni Inns Ltd. Architects: Eberlin & Partners.

This plan illustrates the use of a courtyard layout with restaurant units grouped around a central accessway. Two of the original cellars have been converted to bars and the vaulted ceilings are emphasised by concealed lighting[14]. In

the background are barrel stillage displays[15].

Photographs of the restaurant show the tables, which have iron underframes, separated by decorative glass screens[16]. A lived-in atmosphere is created by the use of oil lamps, Victorian hats hanging on stands and other features[17].

14

16

Form

3.03 To be fully effective, design should provide a sense of unity within each part, and relate the various parts to the whole area of the restaurant. This may be achieved by some form of continuity in the space and design, by repeating certain patterns or features or by adopting a similar basic style throughout the whole room.

On the other hand, the large open spaces which are associated with traditional restaurants must not be allowed to become impersonal or monotonous. A long continuous wall may be divided up by the construction of alcoves or piers or by the introduction of panels of different colour and texture. Open rooms can be divided by perforated or low height partitions into smaller and more intimate

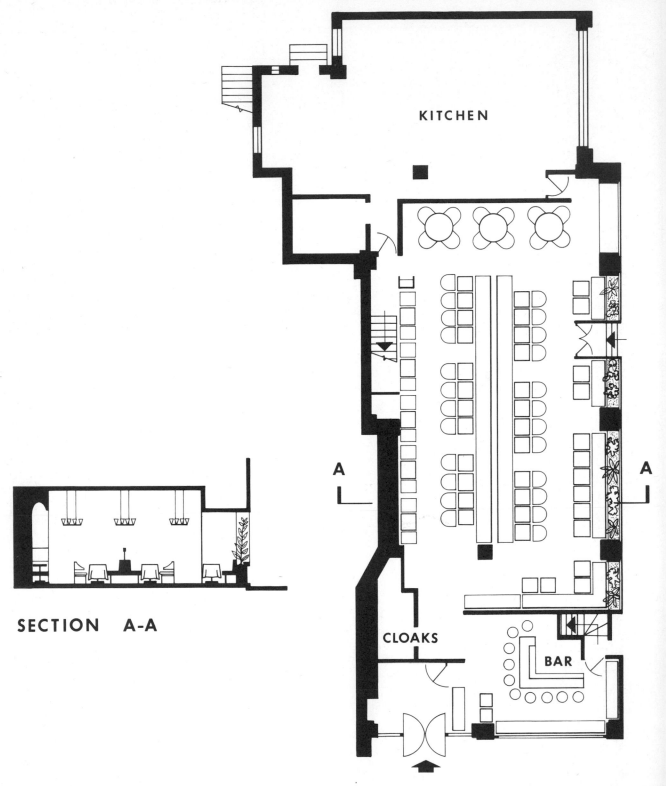

KITCHEN

SECTION A-A

A   A

CLOAKS

BAR

PLAN

18

La Napoule, North Audley Street. Architects: Lucas Mellinger Associated with L. Otton.
Specialising in French cuisine, the restaurant has seating designed in traditional banquettes and elevated vaulted niches *arranged so that all patrons can see and be seen*[19]. *Purpose-made turned perspex balusters, lighting fittings and decorative mirrors by Roy Bradley add sparkle to the restrained colour scheme*[20].

19

20

areas, and a similar effect is obtained when banquette seating is arranged in booths. To a lesser extent, the appearance and effect of separation can be provided by grouping tables and furniture into different combinations of size and shape, and by introducing variety of form such as plants and decorative features.

Stable horizontal proportions in a room tend to induce a feeling of ease and relaxation although, without relief, this is also a negative effect because the eye cannot, at one glance, take in the full extent of line. Vertically emphasised features in most instances have the opposite effect of imparting dynamism and interest and can most usefully be incorporated into the styling of the entrance foyer.

In terms of dynamic interest, one of the most impressive arrangements in a large room is the provision of a circle or oval surrounded by smaller linked areas each creating an individual compartment of space. This has the effect of a stage arena for dining or entertaining yet also provides the relative seclusion of a gallery, thus catering for all personalities and needs.

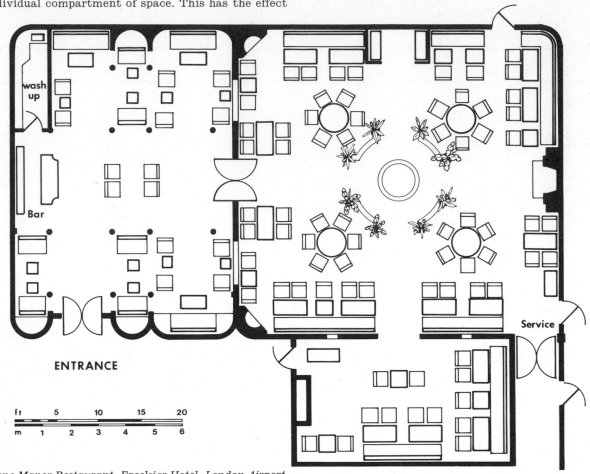

21
Draitone Manor Restaurant, Excelsior Hotel, London Airport. Trust Houses Forte Ltd. Architects: Garnett, Cloughley, Blakemore & Associates.
Plan of the Draitone Manor Restaurant.

22

01

*Views of the interior showing the entrance to the restaurant[22]
and bar area[23], the library which forms part of the restaurant
area and the central circular area used to display food dishes[24].*

Enlargement and combination

3.04 The enlargement of an area may be achieved by
combining two or more rooms together; incorporating
circulation space; or providing a mezzanine floor or
gallery.

Combination of rooms presents difficulties in unifying the
whole area and may involve changes in levels and ceiling
heights. One solution may well be to treat each area as a
separate entity linked only by the continuity of space
through an archway or corridor. An alternative may be to
continue the flooring and ceiling through and use related
wall coverings but to vary the styling of the furniture.

The use of open areas which embrace circulation space is
common in lounges and foyers in which maximum use
must be made of the area for a variety of purposes such as
waiting and assembling. By extending the corridor width
an impression of spaciousness is created and greater
flexibility is allowed in its use.

Mezzanine or gallery construction is a practicable way of
utilising tall spaces which may be uneconomic in area and
difficult to light and heat efficiently. An intermediate
floor may be provided over the whole or part of the area
with the effect of greatly increasing the usable space, but

this benefit must be judged against the cost and difficulties involved both in construction and in operating the
restaurant at two levels.

To ensure adequate height in both areas, it is usually
necessary to use a thin section floor construction of steel
sheeting or reinforced concrete slabs with steel joists and
columns for support and stiffening. Possible problems of
access, fire resistance, noise transmission and engineering
services have to be considered in the planning stage and
also the time factor involved in construction. In existing
buildings it may be possible to gain extra headroom by
removing part of the original ceiling and reconstructing
at a higher level—if necessary by repositioning ventilation ducts and other services.

The unconventional shapes which result from building
extensions may be used, with advantage, to create interest
and variety by applying different surface treatments and
colour contrasts. In addition, the difficulties of operating
at two levels may be ameliorated to some extent by introducing different styles of eating at each level or by providing a lounge and bar at one level and the dining area
proper at the second.

25
Main restaurant, Europa Hotel, Belfast. Architects: Sidney Kaye, Firmin & Partners associated with W. H. McAlister & Partners.
A view of the main restaurant showing the elegance of furnishings. The floor of the central area has been raised to provide a better view.

26
The Main Foyer and Bar.
The foyer leading to the restaurant on the first floor is approached from a circular staircase and forms the perimeter to the bar and to a lounge area in which tea and light refreshments are served, being separated from these by a colonnade of pillars.

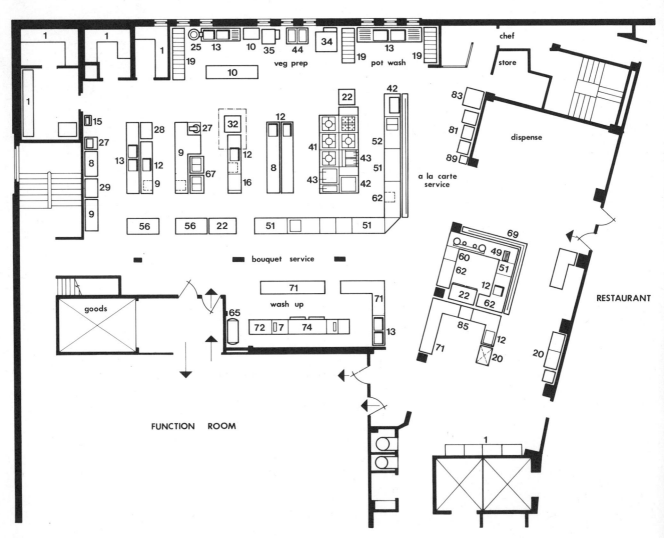

28
The kitchen layout.

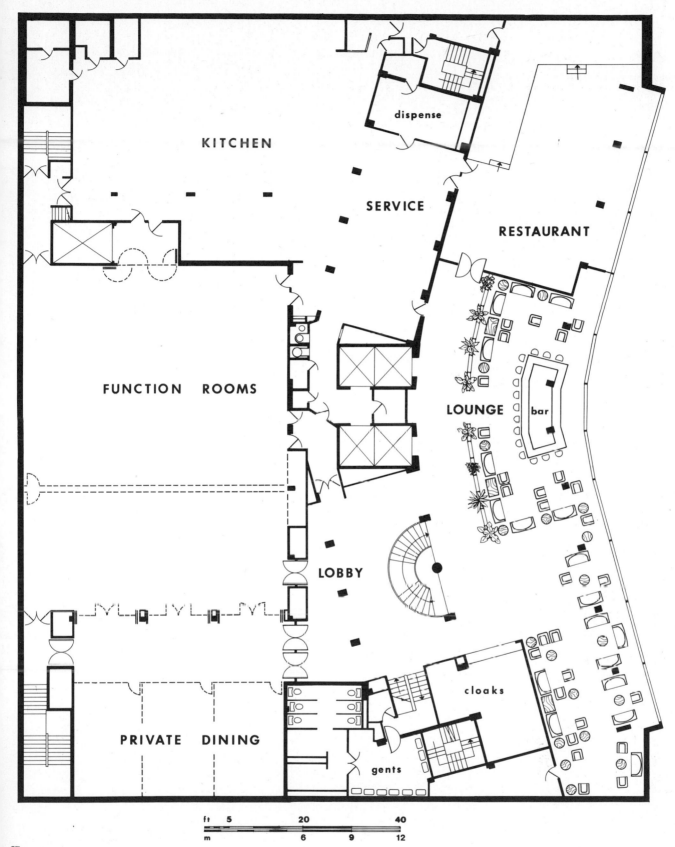

KITCHEN

dispense

SERVICE

RESTAURANT

FUNCTION ROOMS

LOUNGE

bar

LOBBY

cloaks

PRIVATE DINING

gents

ft 5   20   40
m   6 9 12

27
Plan of the restaurant and adjacent lounge areas.

Changes in floor level and ceiling heights

3.05 Any difference in the level of the floor is liable to give rise to difficulties such as the risk of accidents and the restriction on use of trolleys. On the other hand, floor changes may be unavoidable in practice because of differences in buildings and ground levels and suitably designed steps can provide a dignified impressive approach to an area. Sunken floors may also provide an added dimension of interest.

3.06 To avoid a sense of oppression the height of the ceiling of a room should be proportionate to the room size and when this height is restricted for any reason it is better to reduce the apparent size of the area. In some instances extra height can be gained by exposing the constructional elements, such as beams and ventilation ducting and by incorporating these forms into the design with appropriate treatment.

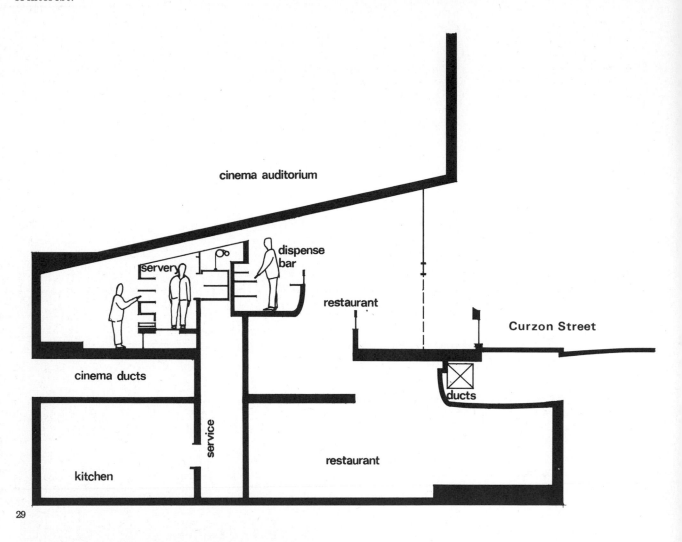

29

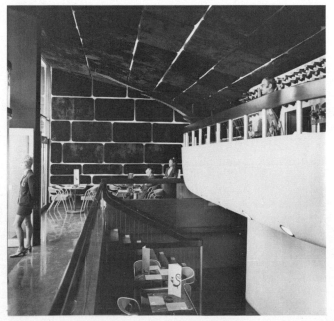

102

30
Day and Night of the Chimera, Curzon Street, London. Architect: Lucas Mellinger Associated with L. Otton.
A central service core links the basement kitchen with the ground floor servery which forms an island and is elevated to utilise the high ceiling space.
The air ducts are faced with mosaic surfaced anodised aluminium and left exposed as a decorative feature to obviate suspended ceilings. To reduce noise, the walls are lined with imitation fur clad acoustic panels which are illuminated from the rear.

Restriction of the height of the entrance lobby and lounge may be deliberately used to give an impression of loftier space in the restaurant.

Excessively high ceilings in rooms which are relatively small can be disguised by providing the illusion of a ceiling at a lower level using open joists or mesh and accurately spaced directional lighting. Open ceilings are, however, liable to present ventilation, condensation, heating and cleaning difficulties. They are generally not desirable for restaurant use and are quite unsuitable over the servery or kitchen areas.

Pattern

3.07 The present practice is to minimise or even abandon architectural features—such as mouldings and carvings—as a basis for interior design, and to place a greater reliance on added patterns, textures and colours to create the desired atmosphere. To a certain extent—particularly in the recreation of period styles—this is offset by the versatility of glass fibre and plastic mouldings but the trend is, in general, towards economical simplicity in constructional work.

Patterns and textures, however, offer increasing scope for interest and variety in design with the introduction of new materials and the use of others in new situations. A benefit from their use in interior linings is the ease by which designs can be changed without structural alterations—a factor of importance when one considers the average design life of a restaurant is only five years and may be as little as three.

Patterns tend to create flickers of movement in the eyes and must be used with care to avoid visual fatigue and irritation. This is particularly important when the total effect of lighting and the various shapes of and reflections from tableware are taken into account. Large sharp patterns, especially, need to be carefully located and spaced to avoid a confused picture emerging. This is less difficult with small patterns which tend to recede and merge into the background. The overall effect of a pattern is generally to make the surface appear nearer. Hence patterns may be employed to correct the scale and proportions of a room.

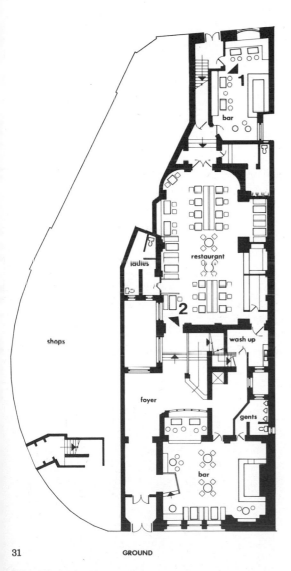

31   GROUND

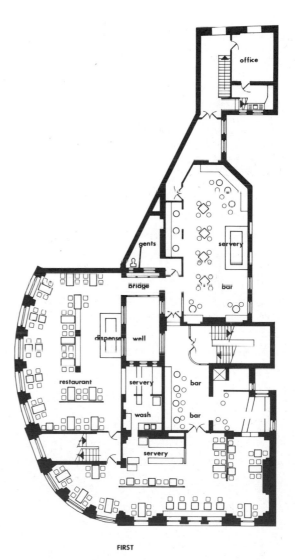

FIRST

The Tredegar Arms, Newport. Berni Inns Ltd. Architects: Alexander Beckingsale and Partners.

The design brief for Berni Inns is to provide an intimate comfortable atmosphere with some standard layout for functional purposes. Because of rapid expansion most branches have been adapted from existing properties and the Tredegar Arms is typical. The premises include three restaurants, one at ground floor and two at first floor level. There are two entrances each served by a small aperitif bar[32] and a third bar is located on the upper level.

Based on reproduction styling, the furniture is of polished wood with wheelback chairs, divided into small groupings by screens. Old lamps and bric-à-brac are used to create atmosphere and the tall ceilings have been reduced to more comfortable proportions by the construction of a mock gallery housing a plough and imitation sacks of grain[33].

32

33

Types of Patterns

3.08 As a broad classification, patterns may be grouped into five types:

· simple geometric forms;
· asymmetric groupings of geometric shapes;
· irregular patterns formally arranged;
· free-flowing patterns of indefinite shapes; and
· abstract designs.

Geometric patterns include lines, circles, squares, triangles and other identifiable shapes which tend to produce strong subjective effects. For instance, horizontal and diagonal lines appear to extend the width and can be used to adjust the proportions of a long narrow room which is a common feature of a restricted restaurant frontage. Circles and squares closely repeated in a pattern tend to produce a disconcerting flickering effect and should preferably be brought together in a more interlaced design as used, for example, in oriental scroll work.

An all-over pattern is liable to produce a feeling of oppression and visual fatigue unless the pattern design is small and delicate, and to obtain the best effect the spacing between patterns should be carefully proportioned to give balance and clarity. In most cases the full effect of a bold distinctive pattern can be appreciated only when it is used on a large expanse of wall and with suitable treatment this may be adopted as a feature of interest especially in lounge and bar areas.

The basis for a pattern may be any formal or decorative shape. In particular the selective use of a motif design which is also repeated on the menus and uniforms may help to establish this identity in the minds of the customers. Alternatively, a representation of the scenes commonly associated with the type of food served or other characteristics of the restaurant may be adopted in order to emphasise these aspects and create the appropriate atmosphere.

Free-flowing effects can be achieved by draperies and curtains and provide a balance to plain muted surfaces. As more emphasis is placed on the high quality of food and service, the design tends to recede into a background of elegant simplicity.

Abstract patterns are a compromise between art and design introducing a sense of movement and creativity into the field of view. The abstract may have its origins in the symbolic representation of food or the theme around which the whole design of the restaurant has been framed. A wide range of media and materials may be used including tapestries, and three-dimensional effects with surface relief or with solid objects help to project the design and compel interest.

Abstract drawings or compositions must be mounted in a place where they can be seen throughout the room and, preferably, viewed from a distance as an entity. A whole wall should be devoted to this purpose providing, as it

34

Dining Room, Galway Ryan Hotel, Galway, Ireland. Architects: Stephenson Gibney & Associates.
The ceiling of the dining room is designed on an open cellular

construction incorporating lighting. This area is designed to be flexible to allow for fluctuations in number of visitors.

35
The Shuttle Buttery, Post House, Leeds/Bradford. Trust Houses Forte Ltd.
The simple natural beech furniture and slate floor of the Buttery are complemented by soft wall hung tapestry depicting a weaving scene which represents the industry of the area.

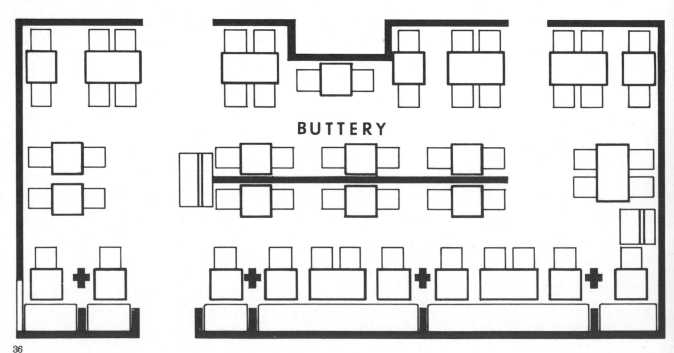

BUTTERY

36
Plan of seating layout in the Buttery.

were, a frame and mounting for the work. To obtain the best effect, the surroundings should be insignificant—that is to say, carefully neutrally balanced—and balance is also important in the arrangement of the tables and furniture.

Applications of pattern

3.09 In modern building forms, patterns are normally applied as woven, printed, engraved or embossed finishes. On walls, excessive use of pattern tends to make a room appear smaller and a more impressive effect may be achieved by focal points of pattern on a relatively plain background. With textiles bold patterns can often be employed, for example in curtaining, because of the softening effect of draping.

Pattern, to meet specific design requirements, can also be incorporated during manufacture of such items as lamp shades and table tops as an integral part of a theme design. To a limited extent contrasting patterns can be combined into a common design but careful balance of scale and prominence is necessary. On a large square expanse of ceiling it is unwise to use a repeated pattern because of the distortion which appears as the angle of view decreases. In this situation, radial patterns will probably produce a better impression. The same considerations may apply to the floor covering in, say, a reception area, but in a restaurant the furniture and tables will normally modify the appearance presented, and all-over patterns are quite appropriate.

Texture

3.10 The use of texture as a major component of design is a relatively new concept and stems, in part, from the parallel introduction of greater sophistication in lighting schemes. Texture can be visualised in a number of ways—by the effects of light and shade, the roughness or smoothness, hardness and softness, and so on—and interpreted by its association with the feel of other known materials. Hence, the appreciation of texture is mainly a sensation of feeling and can be considered in four main groups of materials:

· soft rough   · hard rough
· soft smooth   · hard smooth

A soft rough texture presents a broken-up surface which absorbs light and tends to look darker than other equally illuminated areas. Because of this darkening effect the surface may appear closer to the viewer. The soft appearance tends to suggest warmth and, as a result of the shading, it is often practicable to combine this surface with strong dark colours—dark brown for instance.

Soft smooth textures cover a wide range of close pile fabrics such as velvets and carpeting, silks, satins, leather

37
The Queens Hotel, Burton-on-Trent. Berni Inns Ltd, Property and Planning Department.
Stable bar showing the use of 'natural' materials in the interior design—rustic bricks, stone paviors, wattle ceiling

and timber and rough plaster. Barrels have been built into the counter front and the rustic effect is emphasised with converted storm lamp light fittings and wheelbacked chairs.

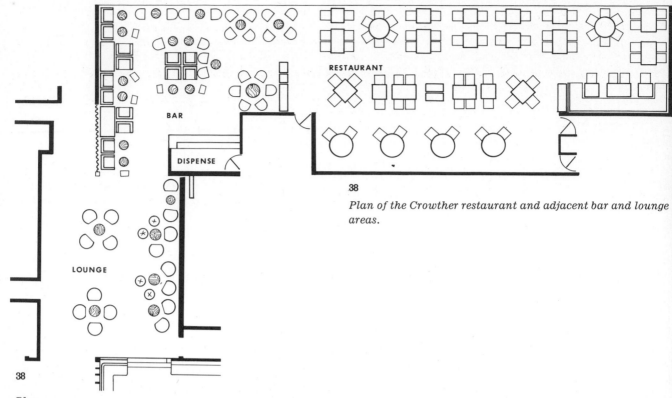

RESTAURANT

BAR

DISPENSE

LOUNGE

38

Plan of the Crowther restaurant and adjacent bar and lounge areas.

Plan

and vinyl and similar materials used in upholsteries and furnishings. They would also include fine white or coloured linen table cloths. To a large extent the rich quality appearance is produced by the sheens and shades of light reflection and the soft folds which may form. A wide range of pure or tinted colours may be used and materials of this character may be used to contrast with hard backgrounds.

In recent years there has been a considerable increase in the use of hard rough materials as interior finishes including, in particular, building construction materials such as exposed brickwork and stonework or concrete. Essentially, these textures produce strong, penetrating impressions and do not need any further emphasis in colour although the effect may be heightened by directional lighting. The area treated should be restricted to one

39

The Crowther restaurant, Post House, Leeds/Bradford. Trust Houses Forte Ltd.
Recessed and with a lowered ceiling, the back wall of the Crowther Restaurant is in reconstructed York stone hung with woven fabrics designed by Geraldine Brock. Chunky

modern chairs have arms and legs lacquered in milk chocolate colour and are upholstered in a coral and brown weave. The restaurant seats 100 and caters for both lunches and evening meals.

part—for example one wall—to show deliberation in design but may be complemented by the occasional use of soft rough materials—such as rugs—in other areas. Otherwise a smooth background is necessary to reduce the feeling of encroachment caused by the illusion of nearness which strong, prominent textures tend to create.

Most traditional finishes to buildings are hard and smooth —wall plaster, marble, glass, metallic surfaces and floor and wall tiles. Their effect is one of coldness and severity which must be softened by the addition of textiles, carpets and soft furnishings to provide a balance of sensation. In some cafeterias and restaurants designed for serviceability this may be difficult and a compromise may be obtained by the use of soft smooth materials such as leather and plastic and by rich warm colours—orange, red and brown—as a moderating effect.

Wood and leather are intermediate materials which can be modified to produce different effects depending on the surface treatment and can be combined with a very wide range of other rough and smooth textures. Similarly the use of matt finishes in paintwork reduces, to some extent, the effect of coldness and reflection glare.

3.11 In all aspects of restaurant design, regard must be given to the problems of cleaning and maintenance. Rough textured surfaces in relatively inaccessible positions are liable to become dusty and condensation stained, and the day-to-day cleaning of tables and furniture must be facilitated. For example, where there is a high turnover rate of use, it must be made possible for tables, chairs and other used items to be easily wiped clean. This becomes less important when the restaurant is used for longer meal intervals, as in formal and leisure dining, but, in any event, provision should be made for removal of fabrics which may require laundering or cleaning.

40
Entrance porch: Restaurant/night club, Berzelli Park, Stockholm, Sweden. Hans Asplund, architect.
Glass sheeting, glued together, used in the construction of an entrance porch. The dome rests on a rubber seating and is supported by eight stainless steel columns. The floor is of gold mosaic and marble.

41

42

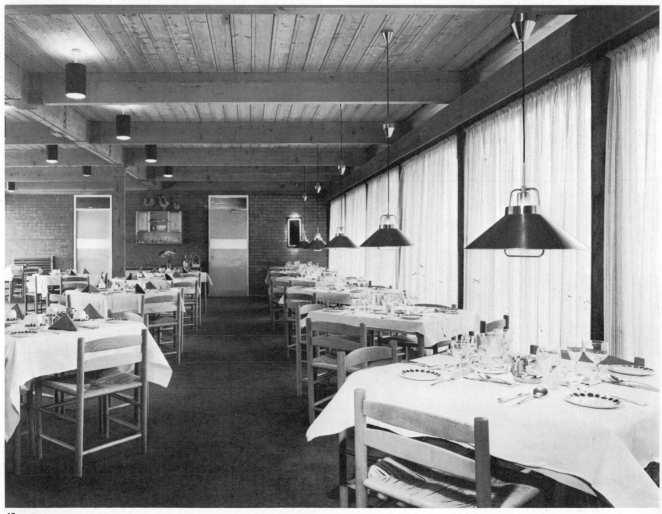

43

Motor Hotel, Nenagh, Ireland. Architect: R. F. Macdonnel.
Views of the entrance area[41], bar[42] and restaurant showing
the use of timber boarded ceilings and exposed brickwork to

contrast with the soft carpeting, curtains and table linen. The
restaurant and lounge chairs introduce wicker work into the
modern design[43].

4 COLOUR

Reflection of light

4.01 To a large extent the colours used in decoration and the lighting schemes must be interrelated since the reflection of light from various surfaces will affect the overall level of illumination in the room. This is of considerable importance in an area such as a kitchen or servery and counter where lighting is primarily considered as a functional requirement, but is often of less significance in a restaurant where the lighting is also used as an element of design.

Light reflection from a surface will depend on the

hue—colour in the sense of red, green, blue and so on;

value—lightness ranging from 0 (black) to 10 (white); and

chroma—saturation or intensity expressed from 0 (neutral) to 16 (strongest colour).

Under the Munsell system (BS 2660: 1955) each colour is given a designation based on these scales and the percentage reflectance of light from a surface can be determined from the Munsell value using the following formula:

$$\text{percentage reflection} = \text{value} \times (\text{value} - 1)$$

The way in which light is reflected from a surface will also be affected by the concentration and direction of light falling on it, and by its nature—ie whether a matt or gloss finish.

Sources of colour

4.02 Colour in a restaurant or lounge may be created by three main techniques:

· coloured lights illuminating a white or neutral screen, draperies or background;

· coloured lamp shades over tables and other areas; and

· colours in the decoration and furniture producing reflection effects.

The first method has limited application but provides the advantage of versatility since the positions of the lamps, the direction of the light, the colours used and the position and shape of the background curtains or draperies can all be modified. In addition the lights or curtains may be moving to create animation and interest and this principle can be applied with fascinating results on water fountains and waterfalls.

Coloured lamp shades are a useful way of producing local colour—for instance a pool of colour around a table, or over an alcove. However, this must be applied with caution and used only in local areas of neutral tones (black, grey and white). The effect of coloured light falling on a surface of another colour is to reflect only the chroma which are common to both. If the colours are in contrast the surface will simply appear black or grey.

This effect of lighting on colour is also important when a restaurant changes from the use of natural lighting in the day time to artificial illumination in the evening, particularly where fluorescent lighting is used.

Most of the colour and contrast in a room is introduced in the decoration of the walls and ceilings, and in the carpet, curtains and upholstery of chairs. Coloured table cloths and place mats will also provide splashes of local colour by reflection of light.

Colour combinations

4.03 The range of colours which forms the spectrum is composed of three types:

· primary colours—red, yellow and blue;

· secondary colours—produced by mixing two of the pigments of primary colours in equal proportions (orange = red plus yellow, green = yellow plus blue, purple = blue plus red); and

· tertiary colours—formed by mixing a primary and secondary colour, the effect depending on the proportions used (eg blue plus green = turquoise).

The intensity or chroma of a colour can be modified by adding black, grey, or white to produce different tones. Shades are colours mixed with black or grey and tints are colours lightened by white (ie pastels).

Colours can be represented as a circle to show their relationships and effects:

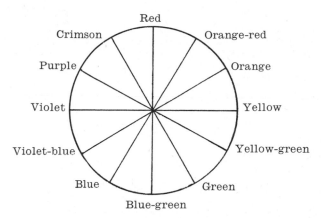

The colours to the left tend to be dark or heavy while those to the right are light with a high reflective value. Colours on opposite sides of the circle are contrasting or complementary while those adjoining each other are said to be in harmony. A strong pure colour—one with a high chroma—tends to dominate over larger areas of tinted pale or neutral colours, and can be used to highlight specific features of design or pattern. Similarly, metallic paints or films such as gilding can be used on prominent features to reflect light and sparkle.

Colour schemes

4.04 A wide range of colours and combinations of colours are used in decoration but there should be some form of association between the colours to produce a comprehensive scheme. The following are examples of the main colour schemes:

(a) *Monochromatic*

one colour in different shades and tints with a neutral background. This may be relieved by small areas of complementary colours, eg in flowers, paintings, or motifs.

(b) *Complementary*

two colours from directly opposite sides of the colour circle. The intensities and areas coloured must be unequal so that one colour predominates.

(c) *Split-complementary*

similar but with a colour complemented by either or both colours adjacent to the one opposite.

(d) *Analogous or harmonious*

adjacent colours used together. A limited amount of complementary colour may be used for features.

(e) *Triad*

three primary, three secondary or three tertiary colours used together. For detail one colour is used in intense tone while the others are subdued by shading or tinting.

Although a wide range of shades and tones can be grouped together with an impressive effect it is generally unsatisfactory to employ more than three hues or colours. Colours may, however, be used in conjunction with patterns and the light and dark effects of lighting produce similar shades and tones in the colouring. Colours on white tablecloths produce a variety of tints by reflection, and this will also have a similar effect on neutral backgrounds.

Effects of colour

4.05 Most colours tend to produce psychological responses mainly because of familiar associations with those colours in other areas and because of the effects of each particular stimulation on the sensory nerves of the eye.

Blues and greens form a natural background role (sky, grass, trees) and tend to be seen as cool, relaxing and soothing colours which make the surface recede. They are less quickly and easily discerned in detail, and should be used in pure or pastel tones rather than greyed shades. Dark blue is inclined to be oppressive (night) and should preferably be limited to small areas of detail. Having regard to the weather these colours are of limited application in restaurant design in northern climates and should not be used in rooms with a north aspect.

Oranges, reds and yellows (sunshine, heat, fire) are by contrast warm stimulating gay colours appropriate for a sociable environment. These colours tend also to advance surfaces, making a room appear smaller and more intimate. The reflection of red tints has a flattering effect and tends to emphasise the richness and freshness of meat. Brilliant hues of these colours, however, must be used with caution. Against a background of direct contrast, for example red against green, the prolonged effect may be to produce dazzle and flickering in the eye. The sensitivity of the eye to brilliant colours such as red tires quickly and this visual fatigue tends to distort the appearance of other colours by emphasising those in direct contrast. In a situation where there is a high turnover of occupancy—such as in snack bars—bright colours may be attractive but in other situations some toning down of the larger areas—by dilution into shades and tints—is often desirable without detracting from the other benefits.

Violet has almost the opposite effect of yellow, tending to produce an unreal sensation of withdrawal and escapism. On the other hand purple is a rich impressive colour (royalty) and is very effectively used in decorative features with gold.

A mixture of intense colours tends to heighten the tension.

Neutral shades such as cream and grey blend unnoticeably into the background. This effect is most desirable in a setting of elegance and simplicity where sufficient contrast is achieved by colours and patterns in the furnishings, paintings, flowers, etc, and food.

Black and white are employed mainly in the furniture and furnishings to contrast with other colours, and may be used to separate different areas of colour schemes. White tablecloths also emphasise the colour contrasts of food and wine.

Special effects may also be introduced to emphasise features and details or to provide focal points of interest and entertainment. Examples include stained glass and coloured mosaics which are often used in lounges and bars to add colour and sparkle, metallic colours or tints to impart sheen, and gilding carefully placed to reflect light.

6 ENVIRONMENT AND ENGINEERING SERVICES

1 LIGHTING

Functional requirements

1.01 One of the primary needs of a system of lighting is to provide adequate levels of illumination which will enable various functions to be performed accurately, efficiently and safely. In a working environment these considerations override other aspects and, in general, a uniformly high level of illumination—based on the demands of the visual tasks—is desirable. This also applies to local areas in a restaurant in which speed and accuracy are important—for instance the servery, bar, reception and cashier desks. Reasonably good lighting should also be provided in the circulation areas, and particularly over steps and stairs.

In the dining and lounge areas the desirable background level of lighting is largely a question of mood and tempo. For restaurants which provide fast service and quick convenient meals—such as cafeteria and counter service—a uniformly high level of illumination is generally preferred. In other restaurants and cafés a more moderate background lighting, which is increased over the tables, helps to provide an appropriate impression of personalisation, while for leisure and recreation dining the background level may be reduced dramatically and lighting used mainly to create atmosphere.

Table 6 (i) Typical levels of illumination based on the Code of the Illuminating Engineering Society

| Area | Illumination at table or counter height | |
	lux	lumens/sq ft
Reception desk	400	37
General office	300	28
Entrance hall	200	18
Stairs (tread level)	200	18
Lounges, bars	100	9
Dining tables	200	18
Background level*	50–100	5–9
Servery (cafeteria)	400	37

* Depending on type of restaurant

Adaptation

1.02 While the eye can adapt itself to different levels of lighting, this adjustment takes time. For an average person about thirty seconds is needed to adjust to a condition of relative darkness, and during this period of impaired vision he is particularly vulnerable to accidents. Stairs, steps or other obstructions must be avoided in the vicinity of any change in illumination—for example near the doors leading from a servery to a dimly lit restaurant, or from a bright entrance foyer into the restaurant or lounge.

The effects of a sudden change in lighting may be uncomplimentary in that the room may initially appear too gloomy—particularly in the daytime—or too bright at night. One solution is to graduate or vary the level of illumination within the room by separate controls to the various light sources or by dimming mechanisms. Another technique is to provide a separating area—entrance foyer, lounge, etc—of intermediate lighting.

It is also important to take into account the fact that at low levels of lighting people tend to be slow and clumsy in their reactions, and more generous allowances of space must be allowed in designing for these conditions.

Glare

1.03 While the eye can adapt to a wide range of conditions from the faintest light which can be seen (about 0·0001 lux) upwards by adjustment of the iris, it cannot cope with wide variations in brightness at any instant. It is possible, for example, to read large print in different lighting intensities ranging from about 0·2 lux to over 80,000 lux but the greatest variation in intensity which can be comfortably seen at once is only about 1000 to 1. If, at the same time, there are bright and dark areas visible together the former will produce a prominent glaring effect while the latter will recede into an even more obscured background. Such conditions produce temporary blindness, irritation and difficulties in orientation which may lead to over-reaction and accidents.

The degree of tolerance to glare depends to some extent on the circumstances and on the mood and need for concentration experienced by the person affected. With certain types of entertainment dining the momentary effects of glare may be desirable to heighten enjoyment, but in most work situations and areas for relaxation glare should be avoided.

Examples of sources of glare include:

· exposed light sources—inadequately shielded lamps particularly of highly concentrated brightness;

· sunlight—direct solar glare through a window (tall narrow windows emphasise the contrast); and

· reflected light—from mirrors, shiny metallic or white surfaces including exposed table tops (gloss finishes produce a mirror effect whereas matt finishes tend to diffuse the light).

113

Daylight

1.04 In most restaurants used for breakfast or mid-day meals some degree of daylighting is desirable on psychological grounds, but in most cases the variations of natural light in intensity, position and time necessitate supplementary artificial lighting.

The amount of light provided by the unobstructed sun during the daytime will vary from about 1000 lux under heavy clouded conditions to 10 000 lux or more when there is a bright sun shining under a clear sky. For purposes of assessing daylight availability, a standard sky condition must be assumed, which in the UK for instance is typically a bright overcast sky producing a light flow of 5000 lux (500 lumens/sq ft).

At any point within the room, the level of daylight available will depend on:

· the solid angle of sky visible from that point (direct component or sky factor), and

· the additional light provided by reflection from outside and within the room (indirect component).

These two components added together form the 'daylight factor' which expresses the percentage of daylight reaching that point. With a typical overcast or standard sky of 5000 lux, a daylight factor of, say, 2 per cent will represent a local internal illumination of 100 lux or 9 lumens/sq ft.

Levels of daylighting are usually determined at table height and will vary over the area of a room depending on the distance from the window and the effects of obstructions—both inside and outside. If there are any variations in the reflective properties of the interior—for instance in the flooring, wall decoration, or furniture arrangements— these will also produce differences in lighting.

To overcome the tendency for 'pools' of brighter lighting near the windows, the window area should extend over all or most of the length of the wall or, failing this, the windows should be arranged in a series so that the light overlaps. Greater daylight penetration into the room, without glare, may be provided by additional windows at a higher level—suitably screened—or by installing windows along adjacent or opposite walls. Daylight may also be supplemented by providing concealed and careful colour-balanced artificial lighting around the window opening to give the illusion of a brighter sky.

The recommended daylight factor percentages for restaurants and canteens serving meals during the daytime are: cashiers' desks, counters, offices and kitchens, 2; for stairs and the restaurant generally (over not less than 50 per cent of the area), 1; and for corridors, 0·5.

Where an existing area is inadequately illuminated the indirect component may be improved by providing decoration and flooring with higher reflective properties (Munsell values). In addition any external obstructions to light may be removed or modified in colour to increase reflection into the room. Conversely, to reduce solar glare and heat, screens, shutters, blinds or tinted reflective glass may be used.

Windows as an element of design

1.05 Windows assume increasing importance in design as they occupy a larger part of the enclosing area and may become an entire wall.

When the translucent or transparent surface extends down to the floor level it tends to draw attention to the flooring and to increase the horizontal spread of the area.

Large sheets of plate glass produce less directional emphasis than windows divided into smaller panes, and draped curtains tend to draw attention away from the size and placing of the window.

If screens and shutters are provided against the glare of the sun these become more prominent in terms of appearance than the window panes and form an important decorative feature in the interior and external design.

The view through the window of a restaurant or lounge is often an important aspect and should be emphasised by the planning and layout of the furniture and by the use of complementary colours in the interior decoration.

In addition to the use of framed transparent windows, consideration should be given to the contrast provided by translucent glass building blocks, and the animation created by light entering through stained glass screens.

Artificial lighting—functional needs

1.06 Artificial lighting is used in a variety of ways to meet functional requirements and as an element of design. So far as the determination of functional lighting is concerned, the necessary levels of illumination for various areas are set out in Table 6 (i). The light available at table or counter level will depend on a number of factors:

(a) *The installed flux*—light emitted from the lamps—will be given by:

$$\frac{\text{numbers of fittings} \times \text{lamps per fitting} \times \text{lumens per lamp}}{\text{area illuminated (metres)}}$$

Efficacies of lamps vary considerably and increase with higher wattages. Typical values are: 14 lumens/watt for incandescent; 68 for high-efficacy fluorescent; and 45 for de-luxe fluorescent lamps.

(b) *The utilisation factor* (UF)—the proportion of the installed light which will be available at table or counter level—will depend on the heights of the room and lamps; types of lamp fittings; and reflectance from ceiling and walls.

Table 6 (ii) Representative UF values for restaurant and lounge lighting

Condition	Type of fitting	UF
Wall lighting	Indirect	0·2 to 0·25
Subdued background	Indirect or semi-indirect	0·2 to 0·3
Overall lighting	General diffusing	0·3 to 0·5
Local service and access areas	Semi-direct	0·4 to 0·6
Local table lamps	Direct	0·6 to 0·8

(c) *The maintenance factor* (MF) is the obscuring effect due to dust and dirt on the lamps and shades. In restaurants, this loss is usually small (about 10 per cent) giving MF values of about 0·9.

Heat from lamps

1.07 The heat generated from lamps must be dissipated to avoid damage to fittings and shades, and in the vicinity of strongly concentrated light—such as over tables and serveries—the heat output may be a source of nuisance unless the lamps are carefully positioned and adequate ventilation is maintained. Integrated ceiling lighting and ventilation systems may be installed in canteen and kitchen areas to enable the heat to be extracted and recirculated for space warming.

Lighting as an aid to design

1.08 In restaurant design, lighting provides a valuable component which allows a wide degree of flexibility and control. Examples of the various ways in which lighting can be used are to:

· increase or reduce the impression of space;

· correct the proportions of the room;

· induce mood, tempo and atmosphere;

· reveal texture and heighten shape and form;

· emphasise features and display works of art;

· provide colour, animation and contrasts;

1
The Wyvern Grill, Post House, Leicester. Trust Houses Forte Ltd.
Traditional style restaurant showing use of various forms of general, local and spot lighting.

2
Tamarisk, Old Brompton Road, London. Architect: Lucas Mellinger Associated with P. Young.
The bar is indirectly illuminated from the rear and from lights directed through turned perspex balusters. The handrail of the stairs is covered by washable sueded vinyl.

· indicate directions and project information; and
· draw attention to dangers.

To a certain extent the lighting may be a compulsory need—such as in indicating exit and warning notices—while, in other forms, lighting may provide an aid to organisation and operation. High levels of illumination in the entrance help to attract passers-by by providing a 'shop window' effect, and in the entrance area a yellow or pink glow is possibly more inviting than the harsh white of high-efficacy fluorescent lighting.

Within the restaurant and associated areas, bright sources of light should be out of view, particularly if against a dark background. Downward directed wall lights may be used to illuminate perimeter tables and spotlights may be recessed into a low ceiling. With a tall ceiling, the true height may be concealed by providing screened lighting at a lower plane, while in other situations the ceiling itself may be formed from louvres or translucent panels to provide an illuminated surface.

Textures and shapes are best emphasised by lighting directed at an acute angle to show the surface in strong relief. Similarly, pictures and other features of interest need to be appropriately illuminated by directional lighting.

With evening dining in subdued light, the illumination should be concentrated over the tables and service areas. The fascination of flickering candlelight for creating mood and intense atmosphere is difficult to reproduce with artificial lighting. To avoid a flood of white light into the restaurant, serving doors from the kitchen must be carefully positioned and screened. This also applies to the cashier's desk.

Signs may be self-illuminated or displayed under directional lighting but it is important that these are not so numerous as to cause confusion and disorder.

3
Happy Casserole Restaurant, Bloomsbury Centre Hotel,
London. Centre Hotels Ltd.
Showing use of subdued background illumination to augment
the candle lighting of individual tables.

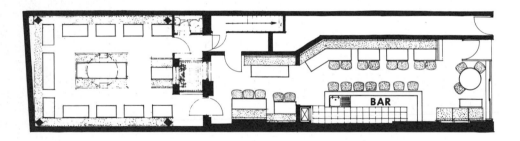

GROUND FLOOR

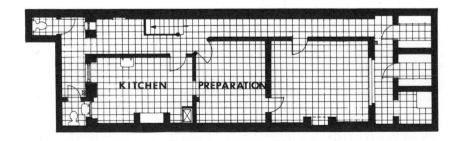

BASEMENT   **SECTION**

4
Wayang Restaurant, Earls Court Road, London. Architect:
Lucas Mellinger.
External and interior views of the Wayang cafe/restaurant
converted from a former wet fish shop and extending over the
original yard. The frontage is very narrow 3·90m (13ft 10in)—
and serves as a means of access for the public and goods[5].
Focal point of the coffee bar design is a canopy supporting
Javanese puppets[6] which are used to project silhouettes
on the wall opposite.
The restaurant at the rear is a self contained timber structure
constructed to avoid interference with adjacent party walls.
A decoration is suspended from the central skylight[7] and
the table below is sunken below the surrounding floor level
to accentuate the shape of the roof[8].

5

6

7

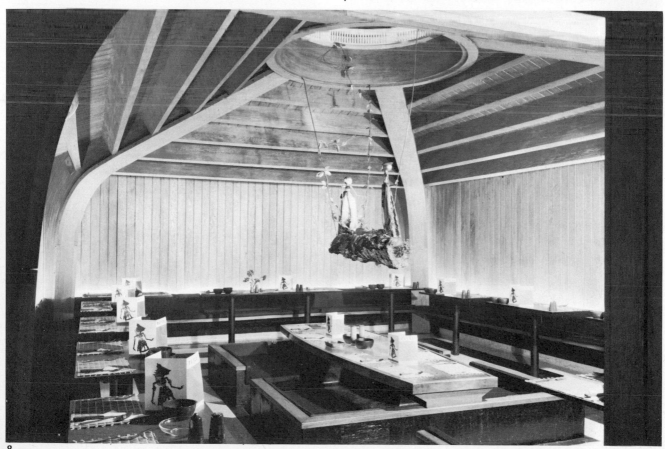

8

2 ENVIRONMENTAL COMFORT

Factors affecting comfort

2.01 An average person seated in a restaurant is normally most comfortable with the following conditions:
ambient temperature 18°C to 20°C (65°F to 68°F);
rate of air change 25m³/h (900 cu ft/h);
relative humidity of air 40 to 60 per cent.
Optimum conditions will, however, depend on the extent of activity involved and a lower temperature with increased air movement may be desirable for a club in which dancing is included.

Under sedentary conditions the amount of heat given off by the body is about 90 watts (300 Btu/h) of convection and radiant heat; and 30 watts (100 Btu/h) of latent heat in evaporated water vapour (perspiration).

Comfort may be affected by several aspects of environmental control and may be summarised into three main failings:

(a) *Too cold*—due to a low air temperature, excessive air movement or close proximity of cold surfaces.

(b) *Unbalanced*—excessive heat on head, cold feet, unsuitable flooring or draughts.

(c) *Too hot*—rarely due to air temperature alone but arising from high temperatures plus high humidity plus lack of air movement. May also be due to local intense radiation—eg sun shining through window or effects of heated counter units and equipment.

In considering the effects of heat and cold and of air movement, the variations on different people may be significant, for example:

Clothing—In winter indoor temperatures are appropriately lower than in summer. Women are more sensitive than men to draughts at a low level and to the radiation effects of cold windows.

Activity—Waiters, and waitresses in a confined area of fast service feel more comfortable with an increased rate of air movement.

Heating

2.02 The amount of heat required to provide a suitable temperature within the restaurant area will depend on the type of building construction and location of the room and also on frequency of use.

To maintain a steady temperature inside the room the heat input must balance the net loss of heat under the worst conditions regularly experienced each winter. For restaurant design purposes in Britain, the latter is usually assumed to be a prolonged outside temperature of −1°C (30°F), although this may depend on circumstances. In other countries, the design temperature will be determined by the weather conditions in the region.

The loss of heat will be compounded from the heat escaping mainly by conduction and radiation through the fabric of the building, and heat lost in ventilating the room. It is relatively easy to calculate fabric heat losses from the thermal transmittance (U-value) of each area of the building construction using the formula:

heat loss = area × U-value × difference in temperature

$$W = m^2 \times W/m^2°C \times °C$$

(or Btu/h = sq ft × Btu/sq ft °F × °F)

In restaurant construction two main problems are liable to arise which may affect the heating: A large area of glass is often used which will allow a high heat loss (due to the high U-value of glass) and to liable to produce condensation of moisture and misting; and many modern buildings, particularly canteens, are of lightweight construction, creating similar problems of wide temperature

fluctuation.

Standards for thermal insulation

2.03 In England, there are no legal standards for thermal insulation of restaurants and similar commercial premises as such although the Thermal Insulation (Industrial Buildings) Regulations 1958 prescribe a minimum standard for factory roofs which may, in certain circumstances, extend over an industrial canteen. In addition, the Building Regulations lay down the minimum standards which apply to residential buildings.

The advantages of thermal insulation lie in reduction of heat loss in winter, of entry of solar heat in summer, and of passage of heat from one part of the building to another. In the case of a single-storey building or a building of lightweight panel construction, a good standard of insulation will allow easier and more economical regulation of the internal temperature. This is of less importance in a restaurant which forms part of a larger building unless there are adjacent areas of extreme heat (boilers, calorifiers) or cold (refrigerators). Appropriate standards of thermal insulation of restaurant enclosures should be similar to those for residences.

Table 6 (iii) Thermal transmittance values

Area	Surface resistances (sum) taken as:		Maximum thermal transmittance value	
	m² °C/W	sq ft/h °F/Btu	W/m² °C	Btu/sq ft h °F
Wall with no windows	0·18	1·00	1·70	0·30
Wall with windows (average)	0·18	1·00	2·38	0·42
Roof with ceiling (average)	0·15	0·85	1·13	0·20
Roof with ceiling (minimum for industrial buildings)	0·15	0·85	1·70	0·30
Floor over open or ventilated area	0·18	1·00	1·13	0·20

The greatest heat loss through the building fabric is normally through the glass windows. Thermal transmittance values are about 5·67 W/m² °C (1·0 Btu/sq ft h °F) for single glazing and 2·14 W/m² °C (0·5 Btu/sq ft h °F) for double glazing with an average 15mm to 20mm gap.

While the use of double glazing reduces heat loss through the window by half, this saving has to be considered against the additional capital cost and practical difficulties of treating large expanses of plate glass windows in this way. In most restaurant constructions in the UK and countries with a similar temperate climate this will not be warranted on grounds of heat loss alone. However, where double glazing will also be useful against noise intrusion the dual benefit usually justifies the additional costs involved.

Selection of insulating materials

2.04 The appropriateness of a material for thermal insulation will depend on several factors, mainly:
· its heat resistivity or insulating properties;
· its physical properties with regard to support and fixing;
· its position in the building construction;
· the risk of damage by impact and moisture;
· the possibility of condensation within or behind the insulating layer;
· the potential fire hazard created; and
· relative costs taking account of installation and any protective treatment needed.

Warming up period

2.05 There is a delay in the warming-up of the mass of building structure which may give rise to difficulties and initial discomfort in a restaurant used intermittently. A sensation of chilling is produced when the surrounding surfaces are so relatively cold that the body loses heat to them by radiation, even though the air temperature may be high. This applies particularly to seating placed around the perimeter and is more likely to affect women than men because of clothing differences.

To overcome this variation the following arrangements may be used:

(a) The heating system should be designed to give an output two to three times greater than that required to maintain a steady temperature.

(b) The enclosing surfaces should be well insulated with the insulation placed either near to the inside of the structure in a building designed for infrequent intermittent use or near to the outside—in order to provide a thermal reservoir effect—where the building is intended to be used more continuously over longer periods.

Solar heat

2.06 The amount of radiant heat from the sun falling on an exposed horizontal surface in the UK increases to about 885 W/m² (285 Btu/sq ft h). Glass in common use is transparent to wavelengths over the spectrum 0·3 to 4·8 μm which includes most of the high temperature radiation from the sun but is opaque to the longer wavelength of radiation at lower temperatures (below about 230°C or 450°F). Hence the solar heat penetrating through restaurant windows and heating the interior cannot escape except by the normal processes of convection and conduction. This is the so called 'greenhouse' effect and can be reduced by the use of reflecting glass and louvred shutters or blinds.

Solar heat may also present problems of temperature regulation in lightweight building structures—such as the large expanse of roof over a single-storey restaurant—and this is most easily controlled by reducing the absorptivity of the exposed surface and by delaying heat penetration with insulation.

Ventilation

2.07 The rate of air replacement necessary in a restaurant will depend to a large extent on the number of occupants, since a small crowded café in which there is heavy cigarette smoking will require a greater rate of air change than a large expensive restaurant with a limited seating capacity. Against this, however, is the degree of tolerance of smoke and cooking smells which the customer would normally be expected to accept in the situation concerned. The more expensive the restaurant the greater the sophistication of environmental control expected.

As a guide to standards, the following rates of air-change are appropriate in most instances:

Table 6 (iv) Guide to air-change rates

Situation	°C	°F	Air changes/hour
Canteens	18	65	8 to 12
Coffee bars	18	65	8 to 12
Restaurants	18	65	10 to 15
Serveries	16	60	5 to 10
Bars	18	65	4 to 6
Lavatories	16	60	6 to 8
Offices (internal)	18	65	4 to 6
Dance halls	18	65	10 to 15

Based on IHVE Guide, Institution of Heating and Ventilating Engineers

Table 6 (v) Guide to fresh air standards

Air space/person		Minimum fresh air assuming smoking allowed	
m³	cu ft	m³/h	cu ft/h
2·8	100	51	1800
5·7	200	34	1200*
8·5	300	24	860†
11·3	400 and over	20	720‡

* Minimum for licensed premises 28·3m³/h (1000 cu ft/h) per person
† Recommended minimum standard for restaurants
‡ Minimum standard for canteens and coffee bars

Heating systems

2.08 Systems of heating used in catering premises comprise:

(a) *Low pressure hot water heating*
· exposed 'radiators' and skirting heaters,
· enclosed convection heaters,
· low temperature radiant panels.

(b) *High pressure hot water and steam heating*
· enclosed convection heaters,
· low temperature radiant panels.

(c) *Warm air heating*
· warm air heating systems,
· air-conditioning systems.

Low pressure hot water heating is the simplest and most commonly used method providing hot water at a temperature of about 82°C to 72°C (180°F to 160°F) for space heating and for heating calorifiers from which the domestic hot water for washing and cleaning is obtained.

Hot water is circulated by pumps (duplicated) to various types of fitting.

Radiators may be positioned under windows and other areas of high heat loss to balance temperature variations. Skirting or dado heaters form a continuous line of heating surface across windows, under fixed seating, and around the perimeter.

Convection heaters have hot water pipes or coils enclosed by panelling fitted with air grilles. They too may be at floor level or mounted higher on the wall as a fan-coil unit designed to force the warmed air downwards. The latter may be used in entrance areas as a form of warm air curtain.

Low temperature radiant panels are embedded in the ceiling or floor. With floor heating the surface temperature must not rise above 25°C (77°F) to avoid discomfort and this system is not rapid enough to heat a restaurant but may be used for draughty entrance areas or as background heating. For comfortable ceiling heating, the height of the ceiling must be at least 2400mm (8ft) and preferably 3000 mm (10ft) high. Embedded ceiling panels are generally restricted by the need to provide access to ventilation and electrical equipment in the ceiling space.

High pressure water and steam at both medium or low pressures are used in larger premises where the restaurant forms part of a larger complex—eg in a hospital, hotel or industrial premises. With the higher temperatures involved, the circulation is more sophisticated and protected from damage or danger. As with other methods, domestic hot water supplies for the kitchen and cloakroom facilities are provided through calorifiers.

Warm air heating includes local self-contained heating units; central warm air heating systems with hot air ducted to various parts of the restaurant; and combined air heating and ventilation systems in which the air may also be conditioned before distribution.

Local heating units may be used for entrance areas to supplement background heating and also in those parts of the kitchen—eg vegetable preparation—which may require local heating. They may be mounted at a high level to avoid obstruction or occupying floor space.

Central warm air heating systems are appropriate for small cafés, snack bars and other premises of limited capacity. Warm air is ducted to grilles (or registers) positioned around the perimeter, below windows and above the entrance to form an air curtain. The system provides for part recirculation of the warm air intermixed with fresh air admitted for ventilation. In summer, the heat exchanger may be by-passed enabling unheated air to be circulated.

With all ducted systems provision should be made for access for cleaning and maintenance and the size of the ducting and registers must be sufficient to allow reasonably low velocities which minimise the generation and transmission of noise.

Combined heating and ventilating systems are outlined in table 6 (vii).

Boilers and heat-exchangers

2.09 Space for engineering plant is often limited in small commercial establishments and where heating is operated independently the boilers or heat exchangers are frequently sited in a basement área. Under these restricted conditions, gas or electric heating is most convenient and allows wide flexibility in the type of plant used and economy of space and installation costs.

With larger premises, gas or oil burning boilers of sectional or shell construction may be selected with an appropriate heat output or rating to meet the total heating load. The latter is calculated from the normal space heating requirements under winter conditions; plus the additional heat input required during the period of warming-up if the building is to be used intermittently, or, in other cases, with a margin to avoid overloading and allow for extreme conditions. An additional allowance must be made for heating domestic hot water required in the kitchen, staff rooms, toilets and for cleaning.

The closeness of the boiler in relation to the restaurant and kitchen areas, and to the air-conditioning plant, is important in order to reduce distribution costs and heat losses from the mains. However, the boiler may be in a basement, at ground level or at roof level depending on the relative value of the area for other purposes.

Important considerations to be taken into account in location and construction of boiler houses include: access for maintenance and replacement; facilities for oil delivery storage and pumping; ventilation, lighting and fire precautions; safety and security; and requirements for the flues and chimney.

Examples of the range of boiler outputs and their approximate dimensions are given in table 6 (vi). While an accurate assessment of heating requirements can be obtained only from an analysis of the construction and operating needs, an approximate indication of fabric heat losses based on the total volume of a building is 30 to 40 W/m^3 (3 to 4 Btu/h cu ft) for a multi-storey building or 40 to 60 W/m^3 (4 to 6 Btu/h cu ft) for a single-storey structure. (This is not applicable to restaurants which form only part of a larger building.)

Loss of heat through ventilation in a restaurant in winter may be about 20 W/m^3 (2 Btu/h cu ft) depending on the extent of recirculation.

Table 6 (vi) Examples of boiler output, size and fuel consumption

Type of boiler and percentage efficiency	Heat output range kW	Btu/h	Approximate dimensions height × depth × width	Fuel consumption	
Gas				m^3/h	cu ft/h
Domestic range; 75 to 80		45 000	33 × 26 × 15 in		120
	15		850 × 650 × 400 mm	3·0	
		100 000	42 × 29 × 25 in		265
	30		1050 × 750 × 650 mm	7·5	
Sectional and fabricated boilers; 75 to 80		100 000	49 × 21 × 21 in		265
	30		1250 × 550 × 550 mm	7·5	
		500 000	44 × 69 × 31 in		1350
	150		1100 × 1750 × 800 mm	38	
		1000 000	64 × 92 × 50 in		2600
	300		1650 × 2350 × 1250 mm	73	
		1500 000	70 × 115 × 50 in		4000
	450		1750 × 2900 × 1250 mm	113	
Oil				litres/h	gal/h
Domestic range; 80		45 000	38 × 20 × 33 in		0·3
	15		950 × 500 × 850 mm	1·4	
		170 000	62 × 28 × 62 in		1·2
	50		1550 × 700 × 1550 mm	5·4	
Medium range Sectional boilers; 75 to 80		200 000	55 × 45 × 80 in		1·2
	60		1400 × 1150 × 2050 mm	5·4	
		1000 000	75 × 51 × 70 in		7·2
	300		1900 × 1300 × 1800 mm	32·7	
		2000 000	75 × 51 × 106 in		14·4
	600		1900 × 1300 × 2700 mm	65·4	

Table 6 (vi) Examples of boiler output, size and fuel consumption

Type of boiler and percentage efficiency	Heat output range kW	Btu/h	Approximate dimensions height × depth × width	Fuel consumption	
				m³/h	cu ft/h
Packaged steam boilers		1 200 000	58 × 42 × 69 in		9·2
	350		1500 × 1050 × 1750 mm	41·8	
Large range; 80 to 82		5 250 000	88 × 56 × 76 in		41·4
	1550		2250 × 1550 × 1950 mm	188·2	

Natural ventilation

2.10 Natural ventilation is feasible only where the occupancy in a restaurant is limited and where there is, proportionately, a large area of external wall or roof surface to allow an adequate number and spacing of ventilator openings.

To ensure effective ventilation there should be separate inlet and outlet openings on opposite walls or at window and ceiling levels in order to promote through circulation of air. The main difficulties with natural means of ventilation are the:

· dependence on weather conditions;
· lack of control over quality of incoming air;
· tendency for draughts particularly with high rates of air extraction in kitchen and servery;
· difficulty of warming air uniformly;
· security hazards;
· entry of external noise; and
· hygiene problems due to entry of dust, fumes, insects, and vermin.

The compensating advantages of natural ventilation in terms of cost, simplicity and ease of maintenance, and the psychological benefit of 'fresh air' may offset the difficulties listed but this largely depends on the situation and plan of the building. All natural ventilator openings should be provided with some means of adjustable control as in windows—or with provision for baffling to deflect wind and rain, for example by louvres. Unless the inlet is above seated head level—1500 to 1800mm (5ft to 6ft), high—the incoming air should be circulated through a heated radiator or convector to reduce the effects of draughts.

Mechanical ventilation

2.11 In kitchens and serving areas ventilation is normally carried out by extracting the air contaminated with steam and fumes, using mechanical extraction fans connected to ducting and hoods over the equipment areas. Extraction of air may also be provided as a separate system to the staff and customers' toilets. Within the area of the restaurant it is frequently necessary to provide mechanical extraction to remove smoke, heat, evaporated moisture and odours, and this is compulsory in internal rooms and basements which do not have means of natural ventilation.

To balance the considerable quantities of air being removed from these areas, the inflow of fresh air may be regulated by means of a plenum system. The plenum arrangement may consist of one or more fans blowing air direct, or through a system of ducting, into various parts of the building. It may include equipment for:

· filtering the incoming air;
· heating or cooling the air as required;
· adding or condensing out moisture (humidification or dehumidification);
· elimination of surplus water droplets;
· readjusting the temperature to optimum room conditions;

· sterilising the air using physical methods or bactericidal agents in the sprays; and
· part recirculation of air from the room.

These processes are described as air-conditioning, and the plant installed in a restaurant building may provide for complete or—more usually—partial air treatment.

Ventilation is not only the means by which fresh air is supplied and vitiated air removed but it is also important in maintaining a comfortable temperature and humidity. While heat can be supplied easily by hot surfaces such as radiators within the room, the only practicable way of removing heat from a dining room on a hot day—or from a crowded basement restaurant at any time—is by circulating air which has been deliberately cooled. Similarly, humidity control can be effective only if the air which is near saturation is replaced by fresh or recirculated air at a lower relative humidity.

Table 6 (vii) Air-conditioning equipment

Type	Components	Main uses
Unit air-conditioners		
Window and cabinet air-conditioning units	Self-contained fan and reversible refrigeration/heating unit sited in room under window or against outside wall	Small restaurants, wine stores and other individual rooms for temperature, etc control
Split system	Similar but with mechanical compressor, fan and condenser mounted outside room allowing greater flexibility, less noise	
Fan coil units	Similar but with heating/chilling water supplied from central plant	Entrance areas, air curtains
Ducted systems		
Ducted air-conditioning systems	Central air-conditioning plant with ducts conveying air to outlet grilles or ceiling diffusers at moderate velocities. Return duct for part recirculation of air to central plant	Most large restaurants and banquet halls
High velocity induction systems	Fresh air supplied from central plant through high velocity ducts. Mixed with air recirculated in room through induction units fitted with warm/chilled water coils	Private dining rooms in hotels, etc, where part of larger installations. Provide individual control
Dual duct system	Heated and cooled air supplied separately through high velocity ducts to mixing boxes in rooms. Return air duct (low velocity) for part recirculation of air	

Air distribution

2.13 Air ducts are designed to convey air at specified velocities or with limited pressure losses and are streamlined to minimise turbulence and noise. Further noise attenuation is usually required, particularly in high velocity

121

systems, and it may be necessary to provide thermal insulation if the temperature of the supply air is widely different from that of the surroundings.

The ducting is normally incorporated in the ceiling space with access to filters, sound attenuators and other equipment. Air is distributed from ducting or apparatus through a variety of grilles, registers or diffusers selected to suit the particular conditions, such as the velocity of air and whether it is required to be diffused generally into the room, deflected in a particular direction, be projected a long distance or over a wide arc.

Table 6 (viii) Air distribution

Direction of air flow	Installation	Applications
Upwards	Air intake through side wall grilles or registers; extracted through ceiling outlets	Liable to cause draughts unless velocity is controlled
Downwards	Air diffusers in ceiling and extract grilles near floor; separate smoke extract in ceiling	High velocity air flow; refreshing sensation. Control facilitated
Crosswise	Inlet grilles or registers high in wall at one end with extracts opposite	Suitable for long, low rooms
Mixed	Directional inlets in wall, canopy or ceiling with screened outlets in ceiling or wall	Used in servery, counter and mezzanine areas

Controlled recirculation of used air is a necessary requirement to enable rapid initial heating, allow fuel economy and provide flexibility to meet different occupation requirements. The air ventilating the wc areas and that extracted from the kitchen must not be recirculated. Air flows are regulated by dampers and the movement of air throughout the building must be carefully balanced by correct sizing and control:

· In restaurants, bars, lounges and offices the inflow must be greater than the extract, giving positive pressure.
· In kitchens, wcs, serving counters and back-bar equipment the extract must be greater than the inflow, creating negative pressure.

Extraction methods

2.14 The extraction of steam, fumes and heat from kitchen equipment, back-bar cooking equipment and/or serving counters may be facilitated by the use of canopies, high velocity slots or ceiling grilles.

(a) *Canopies* concentrate extraction in the areas immediately above equipment. They may be of galvanised or stainless steel, polished anodised aluminium or wired glass, and the sides may be vertical or angled. They are used extensively in kitchens and for grouped back-bar cooking equipment.

(b) *High velocity slots* are narrow horizontal openings connected to extract ducts. They form an integral part of equipment, positioned about 150mm (6in) above a working surface and produce a high velocity air flow across the surface to remove steam and fumes. This arrangement is most suitable for individual units of frying and grilling equipment used, for example, in visual cooking.

(c) *Ceiling grilles* are neat and unobtrusive and are often installed above cooking areas and serving counters which are in view of the customers. The ceiling in this vicinity may be lowered but, compared with other methods, larger volumes of air need to be extracted to effect control over fumes and steam.

British Standards for engineering services and related subjects include

BSCP 3/1: 1950 Ventilation
BSCP 3/2: 1970 Thermal insulation in relation to the control of the environment
BSCP 7: 1950 Engineering and utility services
BSCP 352: 1958 Mechanical ventilation and air conditioning in buildings
BSCP 406: 1952 Mechanical refrigeration
BSCP 413: 1951 Design and construction of ducts for services
BSCP 407, 101: 1951 Electric lifts for passengers and service.

7 INTERIOR CONSTRUCTION

WALLS AND PARTITIONS

1.01 Interior walls and partitions may be classified under various groupings.

Table 7 (i) Interior walls and partitions

Type and construction	Usual surfaces	Comments
Loadbearing walls		
Brick, block or monolithic concrete construction	Gypsum or lime plaster applied direct to surface. Sheeting materials fixed to battens and supports	Limited scope for alteration without providing alternative means of support (lintel, beam, etc) to building structure
Non-loadbearing partitions		
Fixed: lightweight blocks or slabs. alternative—studding or framework with or without solid infill	As above	Modifications involve substantial building work and making good
Demountable: Framework or studding screwed or bolted together	Sheeting materials secured direct to frame	Can be dismounted into components for alterations and reassembled
Movable: self-supporting panels mounted on rails or tracks—folding or hinged; side or vertical sliding; double or single	As above	Allow frequent easy removal for modifying room size and use. Must be suitably balanced and suspended

1.02 Lightweight partitions used within a frame building have several advantages in restaurant design:
(a) *Flexibility* in operation—spaces can be modified to allow larger or smaller rooms for banquets, private dining parties and so on.
(b) *Adaptability* to meet changing needs—variations in function and design; modifications to kitchens and storage areas to meet trends in practice.
(c) *Economy* in structural alterations.
(d) *Large open-plan areas* may be formed for cafeteria service.
(e) *Hollow* fixed partitions may enclose engineering services—electrical wiring, water and waste pipes and other components.

Table 7 (ii) Main problems associated with lightweight constructions

Defect, etc	Cause	Prevention
Cracking, particularly at junctions	Unequal dry shrinkage, thermal movement and vibration	Reinforcement or deliberate provision of flexible joints
Structural damage	Vibration due to door slamming or movement	Stiffening and securing
Surface damage	Impact—eg by trolleys, chairs, furniture, mobile equipment	Provision of fenders, skirtings and stronger sheeting in areas affected
Inadequate support	For wall-mounted appliances, shelving, fittings and equipment, eg in kitchen, counter area, cloakroom, etc	Strong framework where required. Pre-planned layout to position supports
Noise penetration and resonance	Limited weight and rigidity and difficulty of sealing joints	Special treatment applied—resilient linings and packing. Noise absorption may be provided

1.03 Interior wall finishes are selected to meet functional and/or decorative requirements, which will vary in emphasis according to the situation.

Table 7 (iii) Considerations in selecting interior wall finishes for catering premises

Consideration	Requirement
Ease of decoration and cleaning	Smooth and even
Hygiene	Non-porous; suitable for washing and cleaning
Appearance	Decorative features and retention of appearance in use over reasonable period
Maintenance	Ease of replacement or repair
Cost	Materials and labour of application or fixing
Time	Time taken for completion and availability for use
Security and damage	Strength of surfaces, framework and fixings
Adaptability	Ease of modification or changeover

The various types of surface finish include:
· exposed structural or decorative wall construction;
· plastered surfaces applied as a wet mixture in two or three layers;
· mechanically sprayed surfaces;
· dry lining with sheet, boarding or slab materials; and
· combined methods with sheets, slabs or tiles applied to plaster or cement rendering.

1.04 Exposed structural walling is occasionally used in restaurants as a decorative finish. The facing brickwork

The Buttery Grill, Europa Hotel, Belfast. Architects: Sidney Kaye, Firmin & Partners associated with W. H. McAlister & Partners.
Situated adjacent to the main railway station, the design of the buttery grill on the ground floor simulates that of railway engineering construction. *Walls are of exposed engineering brickwork, imitation railway sleepers provide a screen and decorative items of lamps and other fittings are hung on the walls. This theme is repeated in the place mats and menu folders.*

3
The Fleece Bar, Post House, Leeds/Bradford. Trust Houses Forte Ltd.
A mixture of modern and old prints and paintings showing different types of sheep hang on York stone walls in this bar, together with modern tapestries by Geraldine Brock to provide contrast in texture. The wooden tables, chairs and stools are stained bright green with peat brown and natural coloured tweed upholstery.

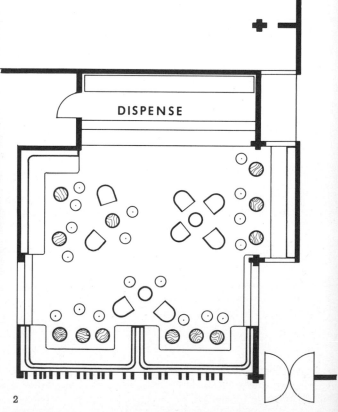

DISPENSE

2

or stonework must be carefully selected and constructed. The pointing is usually either flush or deeply recessed—to emphasise the texture of the surface. This treatment is usually most impressive when applied only to one wall. On a large expanse of brickwork the surface may be relieved by decorative features—such as patterns or projections. Natural and artificial stones and similar materials may be used as interior wall linings, flooring and in similar constructions.

Table 7 (iv) Exposed structural and decorative walling and flooring

Material	Characteristics	Uses
Natural stone		
Quartzite	Green, grey-green and brown variations. Close grained micaceous composition with slightly irregular surfaces. Resistant to stains—except oils	Decorative walling and surrounds
Slate	Grey, blue-grey (Wales), green (Westmorland), grey-brown (Cornwall). Split, sawn or polished surfaces. Impermeable but stained by oil	Cladding to external walls. Internal walls—decorative effects
Sandstone	Grey (York), blue (Forest of Dean), red (Mansfield). Sawn finish normally used. Hard wearing although stained by oils and usually damaged by acids	Paving and floor slabs, steps, surrounds. May be alone or with contrasts, eg pebble paving
Limestone	Grey, cream, brown. Sawn finish similar to sandstone but has a less uniform structure and an irregular grain which tends to wear unevenly	Similar to above. Also external walling. Water-worn limestone is used in rockeries
Marble	Wide range of colours and contrasts of veining supplied in slabs or tiles with highly polished surfaces. May be inlaid. Marble pieces may also be used in walling with broken edges exposed. Hard wearing and impressive but noisy, and liable to be slippery if wet. Damaged by acids	Conspicuous wall and floor surfaces—stairs, entrances, door openings, lift entrances
Granite	Grey or red. May have dressed or polished finish. Very hard wearing and resistant to damage but hard and cold	Limited uses. Paving (setts) or external decorative features
Artificial stone		
Reconstructed stone	Grey or coloured. Similar in appearance to sandstone but with smooth surface and even texture. Moderately hard wearing	Ornamental moulded work, cornices, lintels, sills, steps, stairs, surrounds, floor paving
Terrazzo	Reconstructed marble. Similar polished appearance to marble but with greater regularity of marking. Similar properties. Fixed as slabs or tiles	Used extensively for wall cladding in corridors and entrances and for flooring in these areas
Other materials		
Quarry tiles	Dense tiles of natural clays—blue, red, brown, buff—with natural semi-polished surface. Hard wearing, cold and noisy, highly resistant to water, acids, fats	Flooring in kitchens, entrances, serving areas. Occasionally as a decorative and durable wall surface
Glazed ceramic tiles	Tiles made of refined clays fired and glazed. May have moulded and decorative surface patterns in wide range of colours. Metallic sheens also available	Plain white or coloured glazed tiles—in kitchens, stores, wc's. Decorative tiles—wide range of uses in corridors, entrances, cloak-rooms, serving and dining areas
Mosaics	Similar to above but in plain or mottled colouring. Small squares and shapes used to form patterns	As above—primarily decorative. Also in flooring
Concrete tiles and slabs	Selected aggregate and coloured cement which may be exposed by polishing or provided with textured finish	Mainly external applications but can be used in decorative flooring and wall panels, eg in entrance areas and staircases
Glass tiles and mirrors	Coloured, transparent, opaque or obscured glass with polished reflecting surfaces which may be etched or sand blasted to produce textured effects. Edge lighting may be applied to emphasise colours and designs. Mirrors may be in framed sheets or wall tiles and be tinted, engraved or etched to produce patterns	Wide range of uses in lounges, bars, entrances, cloak-rooms, dining areas. Create illusion of space and provide mirror effects to the lighting, etc

The methods of fixing cladding materials will depend on such features as the unit size, thickness, surface roughness and weight. In general, small lightweight tiles are secured direct by adhesive or cement mortar to an even rendered surface. Larger sheet and slab materials are normally held in place with screws or cramps, and provision is made in the jointing for slight thermal or settlement movements.

Plastered surfaces

1.05 Use of plaster enables irregularities in wall construction to be levelled out to form a continuous smooth even surface for decoration, or as a foundation for covering. Lime or gypsum plaster may be used applied in two or three layers direct to the structural wall surface or to a foundation mesh or lathing.

In addition to smooth surfacing work, plaster may be finished with a variety of textures produced by spraying the surface or by stippling, brushing or impressing textured materials or rollers into the almost set finishing coat. Raised decoration and surface mouldings may also be applied. The use of patterned or moulded finishes limits the subsequent decorative treatment to painting.

As an alternative to hand work, plasters may be applied by pump and spray. The materials are similar to those used in general plasterwork but greater control must be exercised over the grading, plasticity and water retentivity to produce a uniformly even finish.

1.06 Almost all decorative finishes applied to wall plaster are damaged by moisture, efflorescence and alkali leaching. It is therefore essential that the underlying wall surface is dry and decoration should not be applied to a newly plastered surface until the constructional water has had an opportunity to dry out. Persistent dampness due to inherent defects in the building structure or to condensation—a common fault in poorly ventilated restaurants—is liable to produce mould and decomposition in addition to possible staining.

Examples of decorative treatments which may be applied to the walls of restaurants and associated areas are summarised in para 2.01 to 2.05.
Standards for plaster work are summarised in BSCP 211: 1966: *Internal Plastering*.

4

5

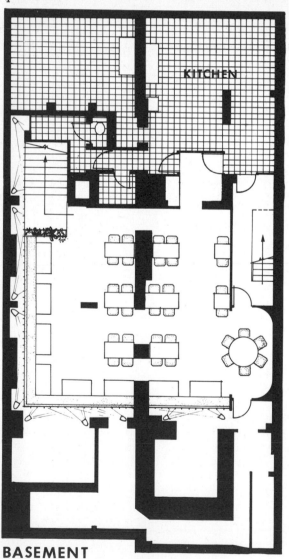

BASEMENT
6

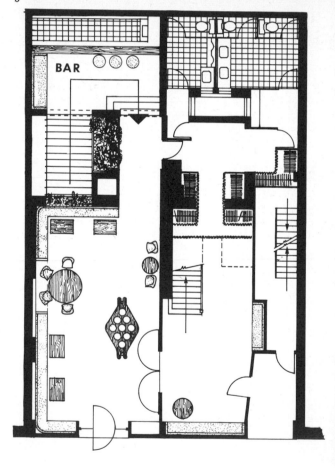

GROUND FLOOR

Shores and Tamarisk, Old Brompton Road, London. Architect: Lucas Mellinger Associated with Peter Young.
Converted from a car showroom, the premises incorporate two restaurants which have separate entrances, bars and kitchens but may share a common ground floor lounge and

cloakroom area as required.
Shores, which occupies the basement[4] is a fish restaurant with glazed walls and white mineral sprayed curtains. The ceiling is also mineral sprayed and incorporates sculptured air inlets. Tables are glass topped on sculptured bases[5].

7
Ground floor lounge with the Shores bar in the background. At the centre is a replica sculpture made by the British Museum casting department which has been modified to incorporate a holder for ferns. Purpose made wrought iron lighting fittings on chains are designed to harmonise with the staircase balustrade leading to the restaurant.

Board, sheet and slab materials

1.07 Sheeting materials of various compositions are used extensively in interior construction work as wall linings and finishes, ceilings and canopies, partitions and screens, doors, counter units (shelving, benching, panelling), and built-in and freestanding furniture surfaces.

In constructional work, there are three main advantages of using sheeting and similar materials. First, it is 'dry' work requiring no introduction of water nor the consequential changes from excess humidity and dampness during the drying out involved with 'wet' plaster applications. Second, the sheets are quickly assembled in position and may be fitted in a way which allows easy removal for alteration—a facility which is often advantageous in restaurant design. Third, the range of surfaces available is extensive, allowing a wide selection of special features such as resistance to scratching, ease of cleaning, sound absorption, decorative appearance and so on for particular situations within the restaurant and its associated areas.

Methods of fixing board, sheet and slab materials vary. Provided the underlying surface is sound, dry and flat, certain materials—eg plastic laminates—may be fixed direct by contact adhesives applied all over the back or to 'stick pads'. This method is also used in the manufacture of composite boards and slabs.

In most structural situations, because of the unevenness and differential movement, the wall and ceiling linings are secured to a framework of timber, steel or aluminium, eg battens secured to a wall face; studding forming the framework of a partition; the underside of ceiling joists; or a framework of steel or aluminium forming a suspended ceiling.

To allow for possible movement arising from changes in moisture, temperature or flexural stresses, and for future removal, it is usually necessary to provide open joints between adjacent sheets. These spaces may be:
· permanently left open and even emphasised as a feature, eg with V-grooves or painted with contrasting dark colours;
· partly filled by projections of the framework or inserted strips;
· covered by decorative mouldings, eg extruded plastic or aluminium, to separate the sheeting into distinct panels; or
· in the case of plaster board and similar materials, the surface may be skimmed over with a layer of 'wet' plaster reinforced with wire or scrim over the joints, thus forming a jointless surface.

1.08 *Composite boards and slabs* are usually supplied preformed and are composed of a core, which provides the structural strength rigidity, insulation, fire resistance, or other requirements; and a surface or veneer, which is selected to present a good appearance and/or to meet certain functional needs such as toughness and resistance to damage.

Most of the materials used in shop fittings and interior constructional work in restaurants are of composite forms extending from veneers and surfacing used on fibre board, plywood, particle board and asbestos wall board, to the hollow core constructions forming partitions and doors.

1.09 Examples of the more common sheet, slab and board materials used in the interior construction of restaurants and their associated areas are summarised in table 7 (v). The range of both foundation materials and surfacing is

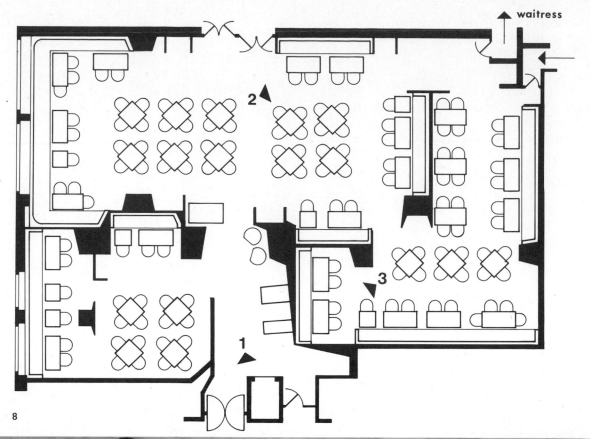

8

9
Main dining room. Queen's Hotel, Bournemouth. Architects: Mountford Pigott Partnership.
To allow flexibility in catering for long stay guests and the seasonal demand in this resort hotel, the dining room has been divided into a series of bays by screens. This arrangement also allows for private parties and dining in groups. The screens which almost come up to eye height are of Lebanese Cedar with reinforced edges.

considerable and, in selecting a material for any particular situation, regard should be given to its physical properties including such features as:

(a) *Strength*—tensile and flexural strength for suspended sheets; impact strength for wall linings and counter surfaces, etc; modulus of elasticity.

(b) *Abrasion resistance*—to scratching and scraping (eg by trays) and effect on appearance—this applies to surfaces of walls, partitions, counters, tables.

(c) *Dimensional stability*—coefficient of thermal expansion, dry shrinkage movement and effects of moisture and humidity change. Most important in kitchen, servery and toilet areas.

(d) *Resistance to oils, water and chemicals*—in all areas exposed to contact with food and requiring frequent cleaning. Includes the possibility of absorption, staining, erosion, decomposition or decay, corrosion and retention of dirt.

(e) *Resistance to heat and fire*—in proximity to cooking, holding or heating appliances; fire resistance may be of critical importance in separating walls and ceilings, corridors and staircases. The rate of surface flame spread requires special consideration.

(f) *Insulation*—thermal or sound insulation may be of primary significance, for instance, in partition and ceiling constructions.

Table 7 (v) Board, sheet and slab materials

Material	Features	Typical uses
Plywood		
3-ply 5-ply Multi-ply Blockboard Laminboard	Composed of crossed plies or a combination of plies and strips of wood, bonded with adhesive. May be faced with selected hardwood veneers or with	Wall surfaces, panelling and furniture
	laminated plastic or polyvinyl chloride	Surfaces and tables, counters
	or metal surfaces (aluminium, steel, copper or alloys)	wcs, etc
	The plywood, bonded with resin, may be bent or shaped under pressure	Furniture and cabinet work
Composite boards	Plywood lined with asbestos	Fire doors
	Plywood enclosing a layer of cork, or other insulation, with or without a facing of metal	Partitions, cold stores, telephone booths
Particle boards		
Chipboard	Wood chips or shavings of controlled size and formation, bonded with thermosetting resin glue and pressed into panels. Faced with wood or plastic impregnated paper veneers, metal or enamel finishes	Panelling, sheeting, counters, table tops
Fibre boards		
Wall boards— laminated or homogeneous	Wood and vegetable fibre pulped, felted and compressed into sheets. In three grades depending on density and tempering. Surfaced or decorative hardboards may be enamelled, plastic faced, veneered, moulded or embossed	Decorative panels
	Perforated hardboard may be used alone or with sound absorbent linings	Displays, wall/ceiling
Insulating board	Lightly compressed fibre board which is used for thermal or sound insulation. Must normally be covered or treated to reduce surface flame spread	Insulation— ceilings, upper walls
Asbestos cement		
Semi-compressed sheets and wall board	Flat or ribbed sheets of compressed asbestos and cement having a coloured cement composition or a coated surface which may be finished with marbled, stippled, ripple patterns or be lightly glazed and polished in various colours	Roofing areas, internal wall and ceiling linings, partition boards
Insulating board	Less compressed and generally with a higher proportion of asbestos. Used as insulating linings which are non-combustible and provide a high degree of fire resistance	Insulation in areas of high fire risk
Plaster board		
Wall board	Core of gypsum plaster between sheets of heavy paper. Finished with plastered face	Ceilings, partition surfaces
Composite walling	Wall board sheets separated by core of cellular construction	Partition walling
Plastic sheets		
Plastic laminates	Sheets formed from a compressed core of phenolic resin impregnated paper and surfaced with melamine resin which may incorporate litho or screen prints, special designs, plain or patterned colours or impregnated wood veneers and be finished with gloss, matt, textured, satin or imitation grain surfaces. Used alone or bonded to a plywood, chipboard or hardboard, base in composite boards	Wall and ceiling linings and panels, counter, etc, surfaces, table tops, trays, trolleys, display boards, work surfaces, partitions, wcs and cloakrooms
Acrylic sheets (eg Perspex)	Transparent, translucent or self-coloured sheets of moulded plastic. Use may be limited by combustibility	Glass substitute— lighting fittings, bar fittings
Polyester/glass fibre sheeting	Can be formed into shapes with almost any desired surface finish to produce a tough, practically unbreakable replica. May be self-coloured or translucent	Sculptures and reproduction work, translucent panels
Polyvinyl chloride	Applied as surface coatings to fibre board, etc, or formed into sheets of rigid pvc which may be plain or wire reinforced; coloured, translucent or transparent	Wall, etc, finishes, roof lights and translucent ceiling panels
Plastic surface coatings	Surface treatments incorporated in paints and films including epoxy resins, polyurethane resins, vinyl emulsion, etc (see paints)	Surface designs and decoration

British Standard specifications relating to sheet, slab and board materials:

BS 565 : 1963 *Glossary of terms applicable to plywood*
BS 3493 : 1962 *Information about plywood*
BS 1455 : 1963 *Plywood manufactured from tropical hardwoods*
BS 3583 : 1963 *Information about block board and lamin board*
BS 3444 : 1961 *Blockboard and lamin board*
BS 3532 : 1962 *Fibre reinforced polyester resin systems*
BS 3290 : 1960 *Tough polystyrene extruded sheet*
BS 2552 : 1955 *Polystyrene tiles*
BS 2572 : 1955 *Phenolic laminated sheet*
BS 1755 : 1951/67 *Glossary of terms used in plastics industry*

2 INTERIOR PAINTWORK AND DECORATION

2.01 Paint is applied to building finishes for a variety of purposes, for example, to:
· enhance the appearance of the surface;
· produce desired colours and an appropriate scheme of decoration;

· protect the surface from damage by improving its resistance and durability;
· reduce moisture absorption or loss in the material and swelling, shrinkage, warping, decay or corrosion; and
· improve light reflection or reduction.

In the interior design of restaurants, painting provides an economical means of disguising faults such as unattractive woodwork, and of creating decorative colour schemes which can be easily modified or renewed at frequent intervals. The appearance of a finished painted surface will, however, depend to a large extent on the quality of the underlying surface and this is exaggerated when a large expanse of surface is involved. Thus, a wall or ceiling which is scaling, rough, or uneven is unlikely to be made satisfactory with ordinary painting and is probably better covered with wall paper or fabrics. Similarly, in the painting of woodwork it is necessary to ensure that the surface is properly cleaned off, rubbed down and filled before new paint is applied.

It is also important to specify the correct system of paint and method of application which is appropriate for the type of surface to be covered, the conditions under which the painting is to be carried out, and the type of finish required. Porosity and chemical reactivity of building materials vary widely and specific types of paint are produced to meet different requirements. In food premises the use of lead-free non-tainting paint which is resistant to moisture, grease, organic acids, mould, condensation and cleaning agents may be important considerations in certain areas.

Table 7 (vi) Paints most commonly used in catering buildings

Type of paint	Composition—summary	Uses
General		
Primer	Depends on surface and subsequent paint	To provide key and foundation. May inhibit rust and decay
Sealer	Oil, emulsion and alkali resistant types—for various situations	To reduce porosity, provide even suction and barrier against reaction
Filler and stopper	Depends on material—cellulose, chlorinated rubbers, water fillers	To make surface level and even
Undercoat	Similar to finishing coat but with dulled surface	To build up body, opacity and colour
Finishing coat	Natural, synthetic or oil modified alkyd resins with a solvent of drying oils, thinners, pigments and colouring	Durable, semi-flexible wearing surface with full gloss, matt, eggshell or semi-gloss finish
Special		
Metallic	Aluminium, bronze, copper, etc, with solutions of alkyd or oleo resins. May tend to tarnish	Used as decorative reflecting surfaces for lighting effects and emphasising features. Also used to reduce heat absorption and emission, eg for canopies and counter fronts
Bitumastic	Natural bitumen in drying solvent	Provides protection against rusting in damp situations for pipes, ductwork, etc
Cellulose finishes	Ester solutions forming a clear lacquer with stain pigments or/and colours	Rapidly drys to form glossy, hard surfaces. Spray applied; on metal surfaces such as cabinets
Chlorinated rubber	Rubber emulsified with plasticiser and solvents	Resistant to moisture, acids, fats, etc, and impervious to water. Used in food stores
Fire retardant	Decomposes under heat to prevent oxidation	Treatment of ceilings, etc, to reduce surface flame spread in public areas and corridors
Non-toxic	Complete system free from lead (Lead based paint must carry a declaration)	Used throughout in food areas for general decoration purposes
Insecticidal paints, lacquers	Impregnated with residual contact insecticides	Lacquers applied around perimeters of floors in kitchens and stores
Emulsion	Alkyd resin type or polyvinyl acetate or acrylate copolymer types with pigments and colouring, applied as an emulsion in water	Matt to gloss surfaces which are alkali resistant and will allow moderate washing. Used for ceilings and upper parts of walls in dining rooms, corridors, kitchens
Cement	White or coloured cement base. May have added texture	Porous cement, etc, walls to improve colour, freshness
Polyurethane, phenol and epoxy resins	Synthetic resin finishes, transparent or with added pigment and colouring	Extremely hard and durable. For doors, panels, etc, subject to heavy use
Multi-colour	Suspensions of paint globules in spray medium	Multi-colour speckled effect for cloakrooms, wcs, etc

BS specifications relating to paint:
BSCP 231:1966 *Painting of buildings*
BS 2660:1955/66 *Colours for building and decorative paints*
BS 2015:1965 *Glossary of paint terms*
BS 4310:1968 *Permissible limits for lead in low lead paints*

Surface effects
2.02 One of the main disadvantages of painting the walls of a restaurant arises from the cold harsh impression created by hard smooth surfaces. To some extent this may be softened by the introduction of texture in curtains and fabric covered chairs. As a general rule the coarser the fabric the warmer and closer this appears and careful balancing of these effects can result in the formation of intimate—almost personalised—areas of seating.

As an alternative the wall surface may itself be given a texture by exposing the natural building materials or by applying wall paper or wall fabrics. The treatment of wall surfaces in this way must be approached with caution in view of the variety of contrast already provided by counters, carpeting, chairs, tables and the items on the tables. In general, a sharply textured or contrasted surface should be used only on one wall and countered by a reduction in surface features elsewhere.

In addition to considering appearance, regard must be given to cleaning and maintenance. A textured surface must, where possible, be located where there is no risk of splashing or soiling with steam or grease, and would be quite unsuitable in the areas of food preparation or service—in addition to being an offence under the food hygiene regulations in Britain and their counterparts in other countries.

Exposed structural materials include brickwork, concrete and stone, and may be extended to cover the solid natural stones and slabs applied as a permanent cladding to a wall. The use of the walling materials as an exposed finish achieves no real saving in cost. Bricks must be specially selected and pointed to give an attractive fair face and exposed concrete surfaces must normally be formed in special moulds. A serious disadvantage, so far as restaurant design is concerned, is the permanency of this type of feature.

Wall papers and surface fabrics
2.03 The range of choice available in colours, patterns, and surface effects using wall coverings is so extensive that the scope for variety in their use in interior design is virtually unlimited. In addition, the cost of these surface coverings compared with, say, wood panels or stone facings is so low it is practicable to plan for a relatively short period of use, thereby facilitating flexibility and change in the restaurant décor.

The choice of patterns must not be made in isolation but balanced against the effects of other surfaces and the contents of the room. Where possible contrasts should be created to draw interest and attention such as a patterned background against smooth uniformly coloured seating and curtains. If used together, patterns should be complementary in design, but one surface must be dominant while the other recedes into a subdued supporting role.

Wall paper and many fabrics are liable to be damaged by excessive wetting or rubbing and scratching. Hence, the areas subject to this damage must be covered in more durable materials. This would apply to the lower parts of walls up to, say, the shoulder height of a person seated at a table—1030mm (3 ft 5 in)—and in the entrance areas and corridors to shoulder height of a person standing (1420mm (4 ft 8 in)). Protection to walls from damage by moving furniture and shoes is also provided by skirting boards and by dados at a height corresponding to the chair backs.

Wallpapers
2.04 The standard dimensions of British wall papers complying with BS 1248: 1954 are: length of roll 10m (33 ft); width of printing 0·54m (21 in); giving a superficial area coverage of 5·4m² (57½ sq ft).

Surfaces to which wall paper is to be applied should be dry, chemically inactive, free from large cracks and surface blemishes, and have a slight degree of porosity or suction for adhesion of the paste. Thick papers should be applied on top of lining paper fixed horizontally around the room. In determining the coverage of a wall paper, allowances must be made for wastage and pattern matching. It is generally more economical to use a plain, grained or striped paper than one having a large pattern with a long repeat.

The range of wallpapers available includes
· ordinary surface printed papers;
· spongeable papers with treated surfaces;
· raised and textured papers (Anaglypta, oatmeal and flock papers, Lincrusta);

10
Dining room, Mount Brandon Hotel, Tralee, Ireland. Architects: Stephenson Gibney & Associates
Combination of textures of boarded ceiling, leather upholstery and fabrics contrasting with plain walls.

- woodgrain papers produced by photogravure and wood veneers mounted on paper;
- metallic papers printed in gold and metallic powders;
- silk, fabrics, woven grass and cork mounted on paper; and
- polyvinyl chloride and other plastics bonded to paper.

Other finishes

2.05 Wall coverings in fabric or other materials may be commissioned specifically or adapted to form a feature of the restaurant design. Examples of fabric wall coverings used for this purpose extend from traditional materials such as tapestries, damasks and brocades to modern designs with canvas, stabilised hessian and plain open-weave scrim cloths. The soft luxurious appearance of fabric surfaces can be enhanced by appropriate lighting. By using a series of coloured lights directed on to semi-transparent open-weave materials it is possible to produce a wide variety of surface effects which can easily be changed to suit the circumstances.

Fabrics may be fixed permanently to a frame or screen, or hang loosely from tracks, the latter allowing rooms to be divided into smaller areas by curtaining thus providing considerable flexibility in the layout of the area.

One of the main drawbacks to the use of wall fabrics in restaurant design is the difficulty of cleaning and keeping them free from dust. To some extent this can be eased by the use of easily washable materials such as glass fibre and plastic coated fibres—or by treating the surface of a fabric to make it less absorbent.

Other materials used in decorative work include mattings of raffia, rush, grass and woven bamboo materials. These are often employed to give atmosphere in restaurants offering speciality dishes.

In adopting fabric coverings as a mode of decoration, consideration must be given to the risk of fire and surface spread of flame and, if necessary, the materials must be treated with fire retardant solution.

Wood boarding or panelling in natural colours and grain, and real or imitation leather may also be used to line walls and partitions. Such materials are intermediate in 'feel' between hard and soft surfaces and provide a contrast which will harmonise well with most other forms of construction in addition to being relatively easy to maintain. Leather and woodwork are used particularly in those areas subject to contact with people—for example, bar counters and built-in furniture—because of their inherent durability combined with a degree of flexibility and warmth. Leather and polyvinyl chloride simulated leather when suitably padded are an acceptable substitute for the softer and less serviceable fabric materials, and are particularly suitable in situations where the covering material cannot be easily removed for washing. In selecting natural materials, however, it is important to make provision for the frequent treatment which is usually necessary to maintain the surface in an attractive condition.

3 FEATURES

3.01 A distinctive feature of art or architecture introduced into a restaurant design scheme can provide a focal point of interest and attraction, a subject for debate and publicity and a nucleus around which the theme of design may be created. Traditionally, features were provided by sculptures in such materials as stone, marble, bronze or lead, and modern equivalents can be produced inexpensively in plaster cast or moulded glass fibre work. This also applies to the reproduction of characterised rooms with imitation armour, oak beams and timber panelling.

132

11
The Boston Bar, Mayflower Post House, Plymouth. Trust Houses Forte Ltd.
Based on the Boston Tea Party, this bar is designed to re-create the atmosphere of that period. Grey brick walls provide a quiet background for a bright blue and green zigzag patterned carpet, orange curtains and blue and green seating. The curved timber ceiling resembles the hull of a ship and three portholes in the wall reveal model ships—made by John Clarke, DES. RCA—typical of the West Indiamen that carried tea to America. An early print of the Boston Tea Party has been blown up to provide a photo-mural.

13
Dukes, Duke Street, London. Architect: Lucas Mellinger, associated with Peter Young.
To advertise the large basement a fountain cascades from ground floor to the lower level and animated lighting displays attract attention from Oxford Street. The premises were originally a wine shop and store and the arched cellar character has been maintained. At one end of the basement a display is used to form a focal point of contrasting interest.

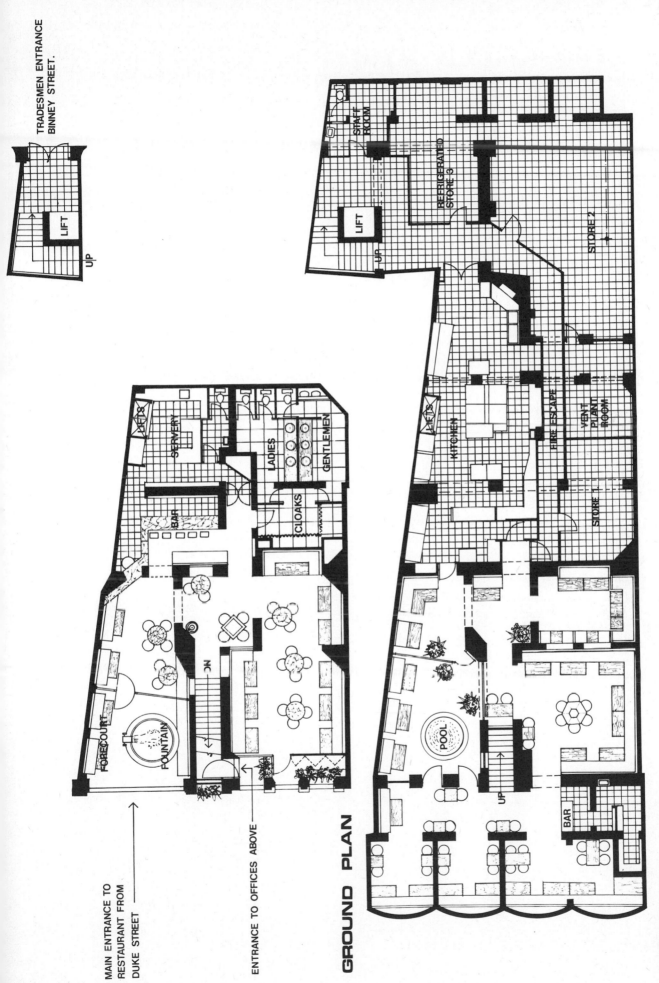

TRADESMEN ENTRANCE
BINNEY STREET.

UP

LIFT

MAIN ENTRANCE TO
RESTAURANT FROM
DUKE STREET

ENTRANCE TO OFFICES ABOVE

FORECOURT

FOUNTAIN

SERVERY

BAR

LADIES

CLOAKS

GENTLEMEN

LIFTS

UP

GROUND PLAN

STAFF ROOM

LIFT

UP

REFRIGERATED STORE 3

STORE 2

FIRE ESCAPE

VENT PLANT ROOM

KITCHEN

STORE 1

LIFTS

POOL

UP

BAR

BASEMENT PLAN

14

Anna's Kitchen, London. Equipment by Oliver Toms Ltd. Self-service counters and basement restaurant showing combination of functional and decorative features. Damage to walls is reduced by dado rails and the carpet is formed from squares. The dining area is divided by planted screens and functional severity is softened by use of pictures, ornaments and plants.

Modern features of art are much more versatile in expression, form and materials. Sculptures may be static or mobile, mounted on the floor or wall or suspended from the ceiling. Materials such as timber, wrought and welded iron, sheet metal, transparent or translucent plastics, and even simple articles like glass bottles may be used to create shapes and textures which can be emphasised by directional lighting and colour.

Paintings provide an interesting contrast in a room which is plainly decorated and furnished. The frames and mounts also have a decorative value. As a rule, the style of the painting should be in keeping with that of the room although this is not inflexible and depends also on the relative size and scale involved.

Engravings and lithographs using a restricted range of colours can produce striking austere effects while mosaics and enamelling provide lively colourful contrasts which require the minimum of maintenance even in areas of intensive use such as serveries. In the correct setting, fabric wall coverings and oriental rugs can create a sensation of soft rich luxury.

Plants

3.02 Perhaps the most common features now used in restaurant design are plants in containers of various sizes, shapes and arrangements. The infinite variety of textures provided by living plants and the cool, refreshing shades of green provide a relaxing contrast to the standard flat rectangular shapes which form the buildings of modern canteens and cafeterias. In addition, the increasing urbanisation of the external environment can be compensated to some extent by creating an indoor garden 'landscape'.

Plant containers and trellis screens may be employed to serve functional as well as decorative purposes by acting as physical barriers and divisions between different parts and by providing screening to unsightly areas.

3.03 At a local level small individual features may be provided on the tables or near each table grouping, thereby making them 'personalised'. This may simply take the form of a vase of flowers, a candle-holder or a lamp mounted on or over the table. Alternatively the menu can be distinctively designed as a feature of interest in itself, and the restaurant motif may be discreetly incorporated into table linen, serviettes, ashtrays and matchboxes as a decorative feature.

4 DOORS AND WINDOWS

Doors

4.01 The doors are an important feature of design of a restaurant since they form the first point of contact and

134

15
*The Day and Night of the Chimera, Curzon Street, London.
Architect: Lucas Mellinger associated with L. Olton.
Along the street frontage double glazed sliding folding doors
permit the terrace to be unified with the ground floor. The
main entrance is through a revolving door over which is
mounted an illuminated revolving sign.*

the customer has a close view of their appearance and
direct experience of the door function. A door or its framework which is scuffed or marked, or which is too small or
too difficult to open and close, creates an immediate
impression of bad management. The same applies to the
inner doors within the premises including doors leading
to the cloakrooms and wcs which must be selected to
withstand heavy usage, including frequent washing down.
Similarly, the doors used by serving staff will be subjected
to considerable wear with repeated impact and scraping
damage, and must be protected and appropriately hung
for this purpose

In general terms the type of doorway and main entrance to
a restaurant should be considered in relation to the following:

(a) *Appearance*—from both external and internal aspects,
having regard to the type of restaurant and its main
periods of use.

(b) *Protection from weather* where the entrance is exposed
and this is warranted by the numbers of people using the
premises.

(c) *Intensity of use*—related to (b) and other features. The
numbers of people entering and leaving during the peak
periods bearing in mind any joint use, for example as an
hotel or store.

(d) *Effect on customers entering or leaving*—ease of opening
and closure, width, appearance and impression created.

(e) *Effect on persons in the room*—risk of disturbance and
annoyance; prominence; noise and draughts created and
admitted.

(f) *Effect on heating and ventilation*—loss of heat and im-
balance of temperature and ventilation; compensating
arrangements and their effects.

(g) *Safety*—in terms of the normal use of the door and as a
means of escape in case of fire, including provision of
adequate fire resistance.

(h) *Security*—methods of fastening and securing against
unauthorised entry.

(i) *Maintenance*—durability and strength; retention of
appearance; reliability of operation; replacement of
damaged or worn part.

Table 7 (vii) Types of doors for restaurants

Situation	Features
Entrance Revolving doors	Usually of armour plate glass framed in stainless steel with satin or polished finish, or in anodised or polished aluminium. Create their own draught proof lobby. In hotels and department stores should have auxiliary swinging doors adjacent. Usually up to 1800mm (6ft) diameter. Steps should be 900mm (3ft) or at least 750mm (2ft 6in) clear of the door. For means of panic escape, the door leaves must be manually or automatically collapsible by folding clear. Secured by locking bolts or by collapsible gate, roller, or sliding shutters
Swing doors	Used for most entrances and in internal areas. Entrance doors may be hinged or pivoted and must be fitted with closure springs. For ease of movement the width of a single door is usually limited to 850mm (2ft 9in). Double doors are preferable for intensive peak traffic (cafeteria). The swing of the door should normally be inward and be clearly shown by the door furniture. Where a door swings in both directions (hotel entrances; inner doors) it should be provided with a glass viewing panel and check action springs.
Sliding doors	Of limited use in entrance or circulation areas. May be automatically operated (hotels, stores). Large sliding doors may be used to link and extend lounge and dining areas.
Restaurant	A door may be virtually concealed by reducing the surface framing. Doors may be panelled, glazed or flush. Flush doors may be faced with laminated plastics, linoleum, metal, imitation leather (pvc) composite veneer panels with contrasting veneers and profiled panels. Kicking plates and push plates may be fitted in doors exposed to heavy use. The position of entrance and exit doors must be considered in relation to the serving counters and seating areas. Screens may need to be provided. Door closure devices and stops should be included to reduce damage and noise.
Service	Separate 'in' and 'out' doors are essential with each door swinging in one direction. To reduce damage the doors must have metal kicking and finger plates. Flush faced easily cleanable surfaces are essential. To minimise noise the servery doors should be close fitting, screened or separated from the restaurant by a lobby. The clear opening size must allow for trolleys, trays, etc, and provision must be made for any carpet clearance
Cloakrooms, etc	Doors should be flush faced with simple furniture and fittings capable of being easily wiped down. Consideration should be given to noise reduction and risk of damage

Grilles

4.02 Grilles or shutters are necessary to close off bars outside the licensing hours and for security. In addition,
shutters may be employed as a means of regulating the
use of different sections of a cafeteria counter outside the
main meal periods.

The main types of grilles and shutters may be summarized
under three headings:

(a) *Rolling shutters* composed of slats of aluminium, steel,
wood or plastic which may be of interlocking sections or
connected by webbing or chain steel connectors. The
latter can be used in counter screens of up to 9·15m (30 ft)
length.

(b) *Rolling grilles* of open mesh formed from continuous bent
bars or horizontal steel rods connected by links. These
may be in plastic, aluminium, bronze or other decorative
forms and are appropriate for bar counters and openings
up to 4·90m (16 ft) wide.

(c) *Side folding* nylon grilles which are used in situations of
limited headroom and can follow the shape of any opening
up to 15·25m (50 ft) wide. The grilles move along tracks—
the lower of which can be removed when the grille is folded
back.

Windows

4.03 In many restaurants the window forms in effect a 'shop front' which provides a view of the interior and plays an important part in marketing the business. From the interior aspect, because of its size, a large window must have a significant influence on the layout and interior design. In addition, the effect of the windows must be considered in relation to practical requirements such as: natural light and ventilation; penetration of solar heat and glare; retention of space heat; entry of noise; cleaning and maintenance; security; and loss of privacy.

Table 7 (viii) Types of windows

Type	Uses
Casement	
Bottom hung	Inward opening hopper windows used in kitchens and naturally ventilated restaurants
Top hung	Top hung ventilators similar and also in toilets.
Side hung	May be used to supplement ventilation where security or danger are not involved
Sliding sash	
Vertical	Common in older premises of traditional design. Allow wide flexibility in size of opening without encroachment
Horizontal	Limited application except for high level ventilators provided to balance air movement
Pivoted	
Vertical	Use limited by draughts and extent of swing inwards
Pivoted hung	Pivot support off-centre allowing variation in openings. Used in kitchens and naturally ventilated restaurants to supplement cooling in summer
Horizontal	Similar uses providing better screening against wind and rain. All pivoted windows can be made to swivel through 180° for cleaning outside—with fixed stops for normal use
Louvred	Louvres may be fixed or adjustable. Used extensively in kitchens, stores and toilets as permanent means of ventilation providing screening and shielding against weather

4.04 The frames, casements and sashes of windows may be constructed from:
Wood—softwood, hardwood, teak, painted or with natural clear finish;
Steel—galvanised after manufacture and painted;
Aluminium—mill finish, anodised, colour anodised or polished anodised;
Polyvinyl chloride, and other plastics, including coated timber and steel frameworks;
Composite forms with subframes of wood or metal different from the window construction.
Window designs are made to standard forms and sizes for routine construction which offer economy in cost, simplicity in specifications and ordering and convenience in building since the dimensions are to module sizes. Such windows would be used in kitchens, stores, staff rooms, and, where possible, in the restaurant areas. For larger display or decorative windows, special designs are usually necessary and must be manufactured to order and/or assembled on site.

4.05 The type of glass used in windows will depend on: the situation—such as the need for screening, or privacy, or for good appearance; the size of the window—which will determine the thickness necessary to withstand wind pressure and other stresses; and special needs—in certain situations, fire resistance, toughening, reinforcement, reflection of solar heat, and other features may be required.

Table 7 (ix) Some uses of glazing in catering design

Situation	Typical requirements
Shop front windows and other large windows in restaurants	Plate glass; typically 6·4mm ($\frac{1}{4}$in) thick but may be increased to 9·5mm ($\frac{3}{8}$in) for large panes. The glass faces must be smooth and parallel to avoid distortion
Doors	Armourplate or toughened glass up to 12·7mm ($\frac{1}{2}$in) thick, with holes and grooves provided for fittings

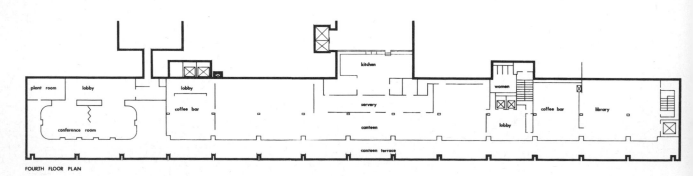

FOURTH FLOOR PLAN

16
Staff Catering, Electricity Supply Board, Dublin. Architects: Stephenson Gibney and Associates.
Outline plans of the canteen and dining facilities on the fourth and fifth floors. The canteen is designed to serve about 500 lunches each day with circulation from both sides of the self-service counter to check points in the centre. Teas are also provided. Of particular interest is the paved landscaped terrace which provides rooftop views over Dublin and is accessible from the canteen through the sliding doors of a floor-to-ceiling glazed screen.

17

Illustrations of the staff canteen[17] *and adjoining coffee shop*[18]. *Continuity is achieved by the extension of the carpet and ceiling design throughout the area. The carpet is in brown and beige and bright yellow has been used in the chairs and stools. Dining tables are in brown moulded glass fibre to the architect's specification.*

18

Situation	Typical requirements
Work surfaces and screens	Toughened glass which may be self-coloured. The exposed edges must be treated to remove roughness and sharpness. Vitrolite is an opaque coloured glass with brilliant finish used for wall linings and table tops
Kitchens and store rooms	Normal flat drawn sheet glass, depending on the situation. Wired glass may be needed for safety, security, or to increase fire resistance. Amber tinted glass is sometimes used in food stores as a fly deterrent
Cloakrooms, wcs and areas requiring privacy	Translucent or obscured glass—rolled glass with a specific texture or pattern. Graded according to degree of diffusion and obscuration, the light being reduced by 15 to 20 per cent
Walling	Glass bricks and hollow glass blocks built into wall or forming self-supporting partition. Various prismatic and patterned designs available in clear glass or coloured to give various tints. Small coloured glass mosaics may also be built into terra-cotta bricks or cast concrete frames
Basements	Pavement lights fitted into cast iron or reinforced concrete frames. The glass may be directionally prismatic
Roof lights for kitchens and restaurants	May be domed or shaped to fit over kerbs and surrounds. Usually in 9·5mm ($\frac{3}{8}$in) rough cast or 6·4mm ($\frac{1}{4}$in) wired cast glass. As an alternative plastic domes are available in Perspex, pvc or glass reinforced polyester resins treated to increase fire-resistance. For kitchen roof lighting, north lights inclined at 60° to the horizontal are advantageous to exclude direct sunlight. In restaurants, roof lighting is often combined with translucent ceiling panels
Fire resistance	Wired glass or small glass panes set in copper framework designed to reduce shattering under heat. Fire resisting glass may be required for fire escape routes and in situations of high fire risk
Decorative uses	In wall linings, screens, panels and decorated windows. Glass may be coloured—stained or flashed—composed into designs set in lead or other framework. Surface work on glass to produce decorative effects includes acid embossing, sand blasting, cutting and edging. For characterisation, antique glass panes may be introduced into suitably framed windows
Exposed situations	*Thermal insulation* Double sheets of glass separated by a dry air space of 19mm ($\frac{3}{4}$in) reduce heat transmission through a window to 2·84 W/m² °C (0·5 Btu/sq ft h °F)—about half that of a single sheet. Factory sealed units with 6·4mm ($\frac{1}{4}$in) spacing may be used giving about 3·34 W/m² °C (0·6 Btu/sq ft h °F) Double glazing is not normally practicable for large plate glass windows (cost) nor for kitchens—except to reduce condensation on roof windows *Noise insulation* Effective reduction of noise can be achieved only with a substantial space between double windows—minimum 100mm (4in); optimum for traffic noise 250mm (10in). The windows must also be tight fitting with the meeting surfaces preferably lined with absorbent material

BS specifications relating to doors and windows include:
BSCP 151: 1957 *Wooden doors*
BS 459: 1954/65 *Doors*
BS 1245: 1951 *Steel door frames*
BS 1567: 1953 *Wood door frames*
BS 664: 1951/58 *Wood windows*
BS 990: 1967 *Steel windows for domestic buildings*
BS 1787: 1951 *Steel windows for industrial buildings*
BS 1285: 1963 *Wood surrounds for steel windows and doors*
BSCP 152: 1966 *Glass and fixing of glass for buildings*
BSCP 153:1: 1969 *Cleaning and safety of windows*
BSCP 153:2: 1970 *Durability and maintenance of windows*

BS 3275: 1960 *Glass and glazing for signs*
BS 1207: 1961 *Hollow glass blocks*
BSCP 122:1: 1966 *Hollow glass blocks*

5 CEILINGS

5.01 Provided the room is reasonably proportioned in height, the ceiling is the least prominent of the interior surfaces in a restaurant. The view of a person entering a room or seated at a table is only occasionally elevated more than 10° to 15° above the horizontal and this is usually for a specific objective—for instance to examine an elevated menu or to speak to a waiter. Ceilings are therefore mainly functional in design and serve to house the engineering equipment and meet other functional needs.

Considerations which should be taken into account in determining the type of ceiling construction appropriate for a restaurant, kitchen or other parts of catering premises include:

the need to accommodate or integrate engineering services;
acoustic requirements—sound absorption and insulation;
fire resistance and rate of surface flame spread;
demountability and access;
thermal insulation;
condensation and effects of moisture:
constructional features—weight, support, finish;
decoration and maintenance; and
costs.

Types of ceilings

5.02 Ceilings may be broadly grouped into two main systems: those directly applied to the underside of the structural components of the building such as the structural floor or roof construction; and those suspended on a framework of ceiling joists or below the constructional floor—the void above may be used for services and other purposes.

Suspended ceilings are most frequently used in catering design, partly because of the heavy servicing requirements and partly to hide any irregularities in the structural work providing a level surface which can be easily maintained in a hygienic condition. The exception might apply in a basement restaurant or mezzanine construction in which headroom is severely restricted. In this case

19
Main Restaurant, Excelsior Hotel, London Airport. Trust Houses Forte Ltd.
Showing the restaurant reinstated after fire damage in 1971. Seating is provided for 180 arranged with a variety of circular and square tables. The ceiling is of an illuminated box grid design.

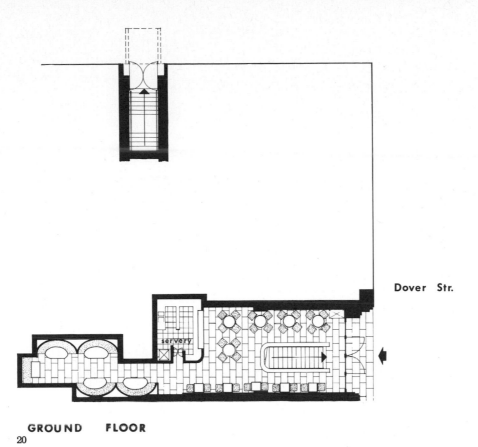

GROUND FLOOR

20

Dover Str.

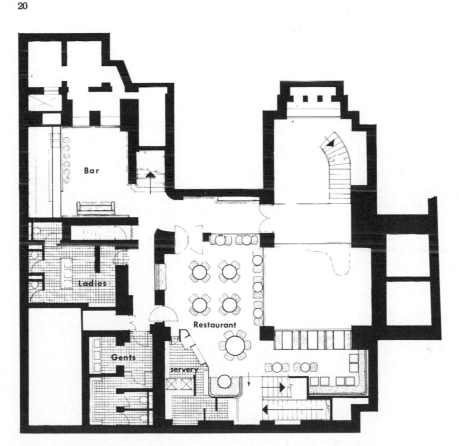

MEZZANINE FLOOR

21

Hatchetts, Piccadilly, London. Architect: Lucas Mellinger associated with G. Burns.
The Dover Street Bar, designed as an extension to the street, is lined with commercial advertisements[23] and forms one of the entrances to the main restaurant and Piccadilly Bar at mezzanine level[24]. The Playground discothèque, with a separate bar, and the kitchens occupy the whole of the base-ment. Surfaces of the walls and ceilings of the mezzanine restaurant have been lined with aluminium foil to reflect the colours and lighting effects[25]. Carpet tiles and leather panels provide contrasting texture. To meet fire resistance require-ments, the glass mosaic by Roy Bradley is mounted on both sides of georgian wired glass screens in metal frames.

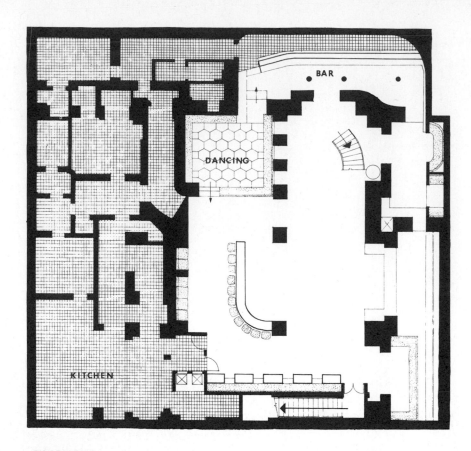

BASEMENT

22

23

24

the location—or re-location—of the engineering services must be taken into account in planning the layout of the area.

Ceilings may present a finish which is jointless; jointed or panelled; or comprised of strips. *Jointless ceilings* are usually formed by plastering over a foundation of lathing (such as expanded metal mesh) or plaster board. This type of ceiling is easy to decorate and provides an appropriate finish to a small room of traditional design. Decorative features such as architraves, mouldings and embossing may be applied to relieve the appearance of a continuous flat surface. For small restaurant areas, jointless ceilings may also be formed by stretching a membrane across the ceiling space.

Jointed or panelled ceilings provide convenient means of access to the ceiling space and the panels can be multi-purpose—for sound absorption, heat insulation and so on. In addition the ceiling construction may incorporate lighting fittings, ventilation openings, heating, and fire control components as an integral part of the design. To facilitate this, the panels and fittings must be to modular sizes and the most common module dimensions are 600mm (2 ft) and 300mm (1 ft).

25

Strip and boarded ceilings. As a third type, a ceiling may be formed from boards of treated timber and similar strip materials. This form of construction provides an interesting contrast over parts of the restaurant in which the ceiling may be sloping or curved.

Table 7 (x) Ceiling characteristics

Type of ceiling	Features
Jointless	Usually plaster based weighing about 49 to 59 kg/m² (10 to 12 lb/sq ft). May include membrane ceilings formed from stretched plastic membranes suspended across the areas
Panelled	Panels to modular dimensions. Average weight about 5 to 15 kg/m² (1 to 3 lb/sq ft). Panels may be of fibre board, asbestos or metal trays
Strip	Wood, metal or plastic strips. Weight about 2·5 to 5 kg/m² ($\frac{1}{2}$ to 1 lb/sq ft). Treated to reduce fire risk. Strips may be jointed as boarding or separated by spaces. Mostly used in tall rooms or over small local areas
Acoustic	Constructed of absorbent material or with an absorbent lining supported by perforated surface. Sound absorption in a restaurant used for music or formal speeches should be balanced over the full range of frequencies
Noise insulating	Additional weight (pugging) may be added to reduce noise penetration from or to overhead rooms. Air ducts and equipment must be properly supported and designed to avoid noise generation by vibration
Thermal insulating	Material or lining of low thermal conductivity or covered by aluminium foil as heat reflecting material. Important in cold rooms and in kitchens and dining areas in which the ceiling forms the underside of the roof
Damp resisting	To reduce effects of steam and possibility of moisture condensing within the structure (surface and interstitial condensation) a vapour barrier must be inserted below insulation layers and all voids sealed
Fire resisting	Ceiling constructions are important in terms of: (*a*) surface spread of flames and behaviour under fire; (*b*) fire resistance of the overall construction. The following recommendations are based on the standards laid down in British Standard Specification 476 Part 7 : 1971

Situation	Class—surface flame spread
Restaurants and public rooms	1 generally. Small areas up to 2·5 m² separated by 3·5 m may be class 2 or 3.. (see Chapter 8, para 2.06)
Staircases and corridors used as fire escape routes	0 or incombustible
Kitchens	0 or incombustible

The fire resistance will depend on the use of the space above

Type of ceiling	Features
Hygienic	In kitchens, serveries and food store areas, hygiene requirements include a ceiling which is free from inaccessible ledges or joints and easily cleaned and redecorated. The effects of steam and oily fumes (eg staining, condensation, heat, decay, rust) must be considered in selecting an appropriate finish

Integrated ceilings—designed to incorporate services

Illuminated	(*a*) Recessed lighting fittings built into ceiling either as modular units or individual fittings (*b*) Fully illuminated ceilings with translucent panels of pvc, etc, louvre egg-crate panels and other arrangements to diffuse light. May be supported by the ceiling or by a separate grid frame
Ventilated	Perforated and slotted ceiling panels to modular sizes ventilated by inverted V- or U-shaped ducts or direct to the ceiling void. Lighting fittings may also be ventilated to remove and/or utilise any heat which is generated
Heated	Low temperature radiant surfaces produced by heating pipes or electrical heating elements incorporated in the ceiling. Must be backed by insulation and enclosed to ensure even heat distribution over surface
Fire controlling	Sprinkler or spray outlets may be incorporated as a precaution against spread of fire, eg between kitchen and restaurant or other areas of high risk. Sprinkler systems usually operate automatically through thermostat controls

6 FLOORS

Floor finishes and coverings

6.01 The floor of a restaurant must be both functional and decorative and the choice of floor covering will have an important influence on the cleaning and maintenance programme. The floor finish must be generally in keeping with the character and quality of the walls, furniture and other features.

Appearance is of prime importance in a lounge or restaurant where an impression of comfort, warmth and quietness is expected and, in this situation, cleaning becomes a secondary consideration. These priorities would be reversed in a cafeteria with a high occupancy rate, particularly in those areas which are subjected to high traffic and risk of spillage or soiling. In all kitchens and food serving areas, durability and resistance to damage and disfigurement are important factors not only in maintaining a suitable appearance but also in promoting hygiene.

As a summary, the suitability of a floor finish for any particular use may be compared on the following points:

(a) *Subfloor*

6.02 The nature of the subfloor and other conditions will influence the choice of flooring. If imperfect, the supporting subfloor may damage the floor finish in several ways: a rough subfloor causes uneven wear; dampness leads to decay, swelling and loosening of the finish; uneven support may make it crack or crumble; and temperature variations encourage cracking and lifting.

To minimise these effects the subfloor is usually covered by a damp-proof membrane where in contact with the ground and a screed of fine concrete brought to a floated finish (minimum 38mm (1½ in) thick) on the surface of structural concrete. Alternatively, the flooring itself may provide for these variations and this is a feature of most jointless floorings such as granolithic toppings, mastic asphalt and Fleximer floorings. Suspended wood floors must also be protected against dampness and provide an even surface of properly seasoned, supported and jointed boards or sheeting.

(b) *Appearance, ease of cleaning* and *retention of appearance*

6.03 Appearance of the floor is a primary consideration in restaurant design but equally important is the ability of the floor finish or covering to retain a good appearance under operating conditions. For example, wool pile is still preferred to many tougher synthetic fibres in carpeting because the natural resilience of wool enables it to resist crushing and felting.

Similarly, the frequency, speed, and efficiency of routine cleaning must be taken into account since this will have a direct influence on the practicability of a flooring material, and its real cost in use. Cleaning would include vacuuming, washing, polishing and other routine work.

(c) Durability, maintenance and useful life

6.04 The wear and disfigurement of a floor surface will depend very much on its situation in the room and the intensity of traffic over that area. The wearing agents may be shoes, chair and table legs, trolleys or equipment, and their effect may be aggravated by the presence of grit, water, grease and food debris.

To a certain extent damage can be localised—for example by providing door mats, or carpet squares or strips which can be interchanged or replaced. The wear may be limited by providing protection such as a surface of wax, or camouflaged—for example by selecting tiles with mottled or marbled surfaces to disguise shoe polish and heel marks. Maintenance, beyond routine cleaning, is important because of the cost but also owing to the disturbance and possible interruption to the use of the restaurant. In selecting a floor covering or finish it is important to assess, in advance, the period over which it is likely to remain in use. With most 'permanent' floorings this is probably the full life of the concept while floor coverings such as carpets may have a replacement cycle which is relatively short—say three to five years.

(d) Noise reduction, warmth and comfort

6.05 These features also tend to be interrelated. A hard surface is liable to produce loud impact noise and reverberation of sound, and is also usually cold and uncomfortable whether in fact or in appearance. The more soft or resilient the floor, the less durable and able it is to withstand damage and, generally, less easy to clean thoroughly. Thus as a general rule hard durable floor surfaces are used in kitchens, floors of intermediate hardness in self-service areas, and soft floors in seating areas where the degree of soiling and wear is reduced.

(e) Slipperiness

6.06 This is an important consideration, particularly where different textures of flooring are used. The length of a person's stride is to a large extent related to the firmness of grip with the floor—which will depend on the frictional properties of the material, frequency of joints or/and the slight indentation produced by the resilience. In stepping from a 'firm' surface to one which is smooth, the stride may not be adjusted in time to prevent sliding and unbalance. Slipperiness may be aggravated by water and/or grease, wax carried over from other areas and water creating a smooth surface.

(f) Initial cost and cost-in-use

6.07 The initial cost of flooring, in particular, may be deceptive and a more realistic appraisal is the cost in-use which takes account of the total costs involved in providing an underlay and floor covering and laying and maintaining the floor compared with its useful life.

A valuation must also be put on appearance and the impression or atmosphere this creates, since this is a vital component of the catering operation. In this respect, appearance influences the customer's evaluation of the premises and may account for more income than the additional costs involved.

Table 7 (xi) Floor finishes

Type	Composition and main features	Main uses
Jointless		
Mastic asphalt	Asphalt, bitumen and fine aggregates laid hot. Available in dark colours. Impervious to water. May be treated to withstand oils and acids	Damp areas, basements, stores, wcs. May be covered by tiles, etc
Fleximer, plastic or rubber latex	Plasticised binder with fillers, pigment and setting agent. Semi-pliable. Permeable to moisture but unaffected by dampness	Canteens, offices
Granolithic topping	Selected aggregates and Portland cement producing a hard, tough but cold surface. May be reinforced to resist cracking and treated to reduce dust	Heavy traffic goods entrances, stores, corridors
Magnesium oxychloride	Burnt magnesia with wood fillers, sand and magnesium chloride. Light colour. Affected by damp—must be sealed and frequently waxed	Limited use
Terrazzo	Reconstituted marble, polished to smooth surface. Laid in sections—see table 7 (iv)	Entrances, corridors, stairs
Resilient tile and sheet floorings		
Cork	Compressed baked cork tiles, laid on dry floor and sealed. Resilient, warm, quiet	Offices, staff rooms
Linoleum	Cork, resin, fillers, colourings, etc, formed on hessian backing. Wide range of patterns and colours	As above, and canteens
Rubber	Rubber vulcanised with filling compounds. In many colours, marbled or mottled. May be affected by oils, fats, etc	Entrance areas, corridors
Flexible pvc sheets and tiles	Polyvinyl chloride binder with fillers and pigments. Sheets may be welded together. Flexible. Maximum temperature 27 °C (80 °F). Marked by cigarettes, etc	As above, and canteens, snack bars, serveries
Pvc asbestos tiles (vinyl tiles)	Similar but stiffened with asbestos fibre and mineral fillers. Wide range of colours and markings. Resist indentation, oil, water. Laid on dry floor with adhesive	Offices, staff rooms, wcs (with waterproof adhesive)
Thermoplastic tiles (asphalt tiles)	Thermoplastic binder (resin or bitumen) with asbestos, fillers, pigments, colouring, etc. Similar to above but special grease proof tiles required	
Hard tile and slab surfaces		
Quarry tiles	Natural clays, pressed to shape and hard burnt. Colours from red to buff. Durable, unaffected by water, etc. Easily cleaned but cold, hard, noisy surfaces	Kitchens, serveries, stores
Plain and vitreous clay tiles	Similar to above but with dense smooth surfaces which may be ribbed or studded. Wide variety of colours including white	As above, and entrances, passages
Ceramic mosaics	Small pieces of glazed tile set in acid resisting cement. Various colours and pattern effects. Decorative features	Entrances, serveries, features
Natural stones	As in wall cladding. Laid on suitable cement screed and pointed with flush joints	As above, and stairs
Wood flooring		
Board and strip flooring	Hardwood flooring may be used as a decorative feature. Sprung floors (maple, sapele) used for dancing. Frequent polishing required. Protected by carpets in dining areas	Banquet halls, clubs
Wood block	Blocks laid to decorative square and herringbone patterns, in bitumen latex adhesive. Must be sealed, waxed and periodically sanded	Entrances, dining areas
Parquet	Similar to above but with thinner sections and wider variety of patterns with smaller blocks in composite panels. Decorative but damaged by excessive wear	As surrounds to carpeted areas, etc

BS specifications relating to flooring materials:

BSCP 204: 1970 *In situ floor finishes*

BS 1076: 1956 *Mastic asphalt for flooring*

BS 1410: 1959 *Mastic asphalt flooring—natural rock containing bitumen*

BS 1451: 1956 *Coloured mastic asphalt flooring*

BS 3672: 1963 *Coloured pitch mastic flooring*

BS 1201: 1954 *Aggregate for granolithic topping*

BS 776: 1963 *Materials for magnesium oxychloride flooring*

BSCP 203: 1961 *Sheet and tile floorings*

BS 810: 1966 *Sheet linoleum, cork, carpet and linoleum tiles*

BS 1711: 1951 *Solid rubber flooring*

BS 3261: 1960 *Flexible pvc flooring*

BS 3260: 1960 *Pvc (vinyl) asbestos tiles*

BS 2592: 1955 *Thermoplastic flooring tiles*

BSCP 202: 1959 *Tile and slab flooring*

BS 1286: 1945 *Clay tiles for flooring*

BS 1197: 1955 *Concrete flooring tiles and fittings*

BSCP 201: 1951 *Timber flooring*

BS 1187: 1959 *Wood blocks (interlocking) for floors*

Floor coverings—carpets

6.08 Carpets are preferred as a floor covering in most restaurants because of their attractive appearance, texture, warmth, reduction of noise, and soft contact which create a sensation of comfort and luxury. In addition, the use of vacuum cleaners facilitates routine cleaning and, provided soiling is not excessive, may maintain the carpet in a suitable condition requiring only periodic shampoo and dry cleaning treatment.

The range of types of carpeting, colours, patterns, pile, fibres and qualities is considerable, but as a general rule quality is accurately indicated by price, and this is reflected in the way the carpet maintains its appearance.

In restaurant furnishing, carpets should be selected in widths or squares which will enable those aisle and entrance areas subjected to heavy traffic to be replaced or interchanged with the other sections. It is rarely possible to see the full effect of a large bold pattern because of the furniture and small repeat patterns are normally used. Uniformly plain colours tend to show up marks of soiling, wear and shading, and are not suitable. In most cases, a pile carpet will disguise soiling better than a plain woven cord type, but is liable to show shading—particularly over large areas of floor. Looped pile carpets tend to be snagged by chair and table legs.

To prevent grease drops and other minor spillage penetrating to the backing, the pile should be close. A deep pile with a resilient underlay creates a sensation of luxury but, if excessively deep, tends to be tiring for waiters and restrictive to trolleys. In lounge bars particularly, the carpets must be resistant to marking by spilt drinks and cigarette burns.

The main problems in carpeted corridors are liable to arise from shrinkage—which is more noticeable over a long length—and excessive wear in the centre compared with the edges. The main wear in stair carpeting is on the edges (nosings) of the treads and provision should be made for relocation to keep the wear even. To avoid accidents, bold patterns which camouflage the steps must not be used.

In banquet areas carpeting may need to be lifted and should be in sections for handling and storage. It must also be easily joined and be stable in dimensions to avoid distortion, particularly when cleaned.

The wear of a carpet will be affected to a large extent by: the way it is laid, stretched and secured; the resilience and stability of the underlay; and the joining or seaming of its sections.

Types of carpets

6.09 There are many variations in carpet manufacture but there are two main categories, namely: woven carpets—with the surface pile and backing woven together in one process, different weaves producing different types of carpet; and non-woven carpets—in which the backing is woven first and the pile subsequently inserted—eg by needles—and secured in place by pvc or rubber latex compound.

Carpet construction depends on two elements, backing and pile. Normally the backing or base is woven, with warp yarns (which run lengthwise, over and under); weft yarns (crosswise above and below) and stuffer yarns (lengthwise in the centre). The backing may be of jute, cotton, linen, polyester or polypropylene.

The surface fibres which project from the backing form the wearing face or pile of the carpet. These may be in the form of uncut loops or tufts. Pile yarns may be wool, hair, jute, cotton, viscose rayon, nylon, acrylic, polyester and polypropylene fibres used alone or in blends. The quality of a carpet is almost entirely determined by the pile and may be controlled in five ways:

· by the number of warp threads across with width (pitch);

· number of tufts per unit length (rows);

· height of pile;

· weight or thickness of pile yarn; and

· type of fibre or blend in yarn.

The total weight of pile per unit area is sometimes described as the pile density.

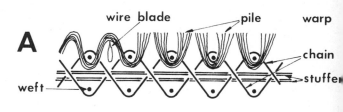

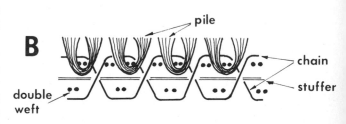

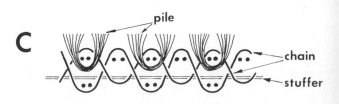

26

Diagrammatic sections of carpet weaves for

A—Plain Wilton

B—Spool Axminster

C—Gripper Axminster

27

The Lounge, Post House, Leicester. Trust Houses Forte Ltd.
Unusual features of design include a ceiling formed from
a series of vaulted arches which incorporate trough lighting
along the edges and a Roman mosaic patterned carpet, this
pattern being repeated on door handles and other fittings.

Table 7 (xii) Carpet characteristics

Type of carpet	Main characteristics
Woven	
Plain Wilton or velvet	Simple under-over weave with loops of pile drawn up and cut giving a close dense pile. Thickness of carpet body is usually increased with stuffing yarns
Cord	Similar in weave but pile remains uncut forming closely bound loops
Patterned Wilton	Pile threads in up to five colours are woven into back of carpet and raised where required to form pattern. Because of number of pile threads incorporated in thickness, elaborate patterning tends to be expensive
Brussels	Similar but with an uncut looped pile
Spool and gripper Axminsters	Individual pile threads are inserted into backing during weaving process allowing an extensive range of pattern and colour. Pile threads are longer but separated by two weft yarns as is shown by characteristic ribbed back
Chenille Axminster	Made in two stages by weaving surface on to backing using catch threads
Oriental	Persian, Turkish, Indian and similar carpets are hand woven each with a characteristic pile (wool, silk) secured to backing by knotting each thread. These are often used as screen or wall coverings for decoration.
Miscellaneous	
Tufted	Tufts inserted with needles into woven backing fabric and secured by pvc or rubber latex. May have foamed rubber back
Flocked	Flock pile is applied to backing material coated with adhesive by beater bars, spray or electrostatic processes
Knitted	Similar to weaving but pile and backing yarns are looped together on different sets of needles and bonded with latex. Cut and uncut pile versions are available
Tiles	Fibres implanted into solid base reinforced by backing of woven jute. Hair fibres are often used for this purpose and the shading effects can be used to form patterns

Table 7 (xiii) Pile fibre characteristics

Pile fibres	Characteristics
Wool	Natural fibre, highly resilient, moderately hard wearing and resistant to soiling. Does not readily ignite and burns are self-extinguishing. Static electricity is generated only in a very dry atmosphere (below 40 per cent RH). Good insulator of heat. Liable to be attacked by clothes moth and carpet beetle unless treated with residual insecticide. To improve wearing properties often blended 80/20 with nylon
Hair	Naturally coarse and stiff providing a tough hard wearing pile with distinct shading effects. Used mainly in corded carpeting and carpet squares
Nylon	Tough abrasion-resisting fibre with low moisture absorption. Tends to attract dust and stains but is relatively easy to clean. It has a high static generation even at relative humidities up to 60 per cent which may cause sparking and mild shocks. Low melting point and easily damaged by burns although unaffected by insects. Lacks the softness and resilience of wool. May be used alone or blended with wool and rayon to add to their toughness

Pile fibres	Characteristics
Polyester (Terylene)	Soft and strong although not so resilient as wool. Most commonly used in rugs. Liable to be damaged by heat and stained by oil
Acrylics (Acrilan, Courtelle)	Similar characteristics to wool but not so soft and liable to be damaged by burns. As with other synthetics, stain easily but are non-absorbent and easily cleaned. May be used alone or blended with other synthetics
Viscose rayon	Inexpensive, poor resilience and durability. Used in mixtures for economy carpeting
Polypropylene	Lightweight and durable, resists stains, cleans easily. Non-absorbent and rot-proof, may be used in damp situations—with appropriate backing. Low resilience, does not retain its texture well. Melts under heat

The Federation of British Carpet Manufacturers recommend the following grades of carpet for use in restaurants:
Medium contract grade—coffee bars, restaurants, lounges
Heavy contract grade—corridors, entrance halls, stairs
BS specifications relating to carpet construction and testing:
Colour fastness:
BS 1906: 1961 *Light fastness*
BS 2681: 1961 *Wet fastness*
BS 4088: 1966 *Shampoo fastness*
BS 2677: 1961 *Rubbing fastness*
Other qualities:
BS 4233 *Pile density and weight-methods of determination*
BS 4334 and BS 4052 *Resistance to crushing*
BS 4334 *Moth resistance of wool carpets*
BS 3638 *Sound absorption*
BS 2570 *Impact sound reduction*
BS 3655 *Labelling of carpets and rugs*
The wearability is measured by the tests carried out by the Wool Industry Research Association (WIRA) expressed in terms of the number of rubs—using a standard rubbing machine—which will wear out the carpet.

8 FUNCTIONAL REQUIREMENTS

1 NOISE AND ACOUSTICS

1.01 The control of noise in a restaurant and in other areas within a catering premises must be considered from four aspects:

· the reduction of noise generated within the room;
· prevention of excessive noise entering from outside;
· prevention of excessive noise being transmitted from other parts of the premises (eg from kitchen to restaurant); and
· acoustic values where the room is used for music, after-dinner speeches or social functions.

Each of these features will assume different degrees of importance depending on the type of restaurant, situation, and circumstances involved.

Reduction of noise levels within the room

1.02 In all situations, some background noise within the room is unavoidable—from movement of people and table utensils, conversation and so on—and this will also help to mask sounds intruding into the area. The level of the background sounds will depend mainly on four factors: the loudness of the noise; the extent to which this is absorbed by the surroundings; the volume of the room (tending to prolong the sound); and the additional intrusive noise contributing to the level of noise in the room.

To some extent, the level of noise in a large restaurant or canteen may be self-aggravating since the greater the background clatter of utensils and other sounds, the louder people tend to talk in order to be heard.

1.03 The sounds most likely to interfere with speech are within the three octave bands 600–1200Hz, 1200–2400Hz, and 2400–4800Hz. In order to be heard reasonably clearly, the level of speech needs to be about 6 decibels higher than the background sound within these frequencies.

Typical decibel levels of sound in speech over a distance of 1m are: whispers 20; quiet conversation 45; normal speech 65; raised voice 70; very loud voice 75.

Hence for very quiet conversation, the speech interference level (SIL) of background sounds should not exceed 39 to 40dB, while for normal speech a maximum background level of 59 to 60dB would be acceptable.

Other factors which affect the tolerance levels of background noise include the:
situation and area—town or country environment;
time factor—mid-day or evening;
character of noise—pure tone or mixed noise;
repetitiveness—frequency of repetition; and

conditioning—familiarity to sounds.

As a guide, the levels of background sound likely to be found acceptable in a dining room are:

Type of room	Level of noise decibels
Factory canteen	55
Average restaurant	50
Leisure dining	45
Banquet rooms—speeches	40

Absorption of sound

1.04 The sound waves within a room are to some extent absorbed as a coincidence of occupation by the clothing of people present, the furnishings, carpets and other contents. Sound reduction may also be arranged deliberately by the provision of suitable absorbing surfaces as part of the room construction. Loss of sound energy may be a result of several factors:
friction at the surface—eg fabric materials;
penetration into open porous materials;
molecular friction created in resilient materials;
molecular friction produced by resonance of the wave motion; and
conduction to other areas.

Soft, porous and resilient materials such as acoustic tiles and glass wool are most efficient in absorbing high and medium frequency sounds but do not appreciably reduce low frequency noise unless mounted over an air space. The damping effect on air resonating in a cavity—such as a panel cavity—can also be employed to reduce low frequency sounds over a specific range.

The absorption efficiency of a material may be expressed as a coefficient (1·0 corresponding to 100 per cent reduction) and is usually determined at three different frequencies to represent high, medium, and low pitched noises. This absorption coefficient will, however, depend on the: thickness of material; interconnection of voids and pores; method of mounting; and surface covering.

The last feature is particularly important in catering design since it is usually necessary to cover and protect a soft porous material in order to facilitate decoration, cleaning and hygiene. Provided the surface has holes totalling more than 10 to 15 per cent of the surface area, the reduction in absorption is not likely to be significant. However, the greatest loss of efficiency will be on those high frequency sounds which have a wave length shorter than the spacing between the holes and this must be

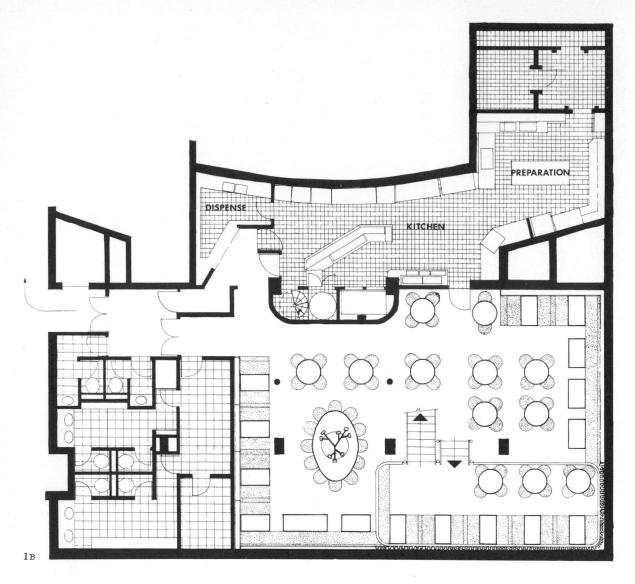

1B

BASEMENT

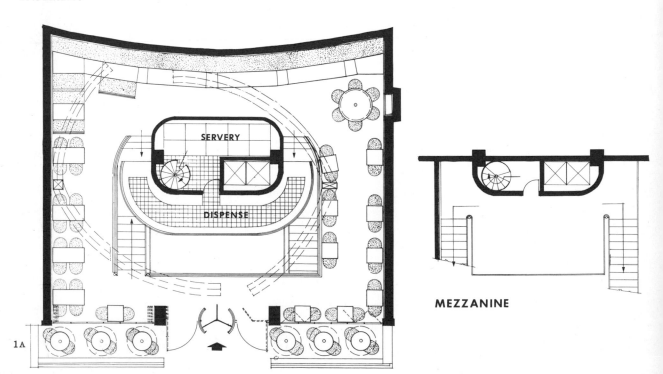

1A

GROUND FLOOR

MEZZANINE

148

3

The Day and Night of the Chimera, Curzon Street, London.
Architect: Lucas Mellinger associated with L. Otton.
Positioned below a cinema, the cafe/restaurant has an open
well staircase leading to the basement with an elevated servery
forming an island at ground level[2]. The ceiling, which forms
the structural floor of the cinema auditorium, is lined with fur-
clad acoustic panels and exposed ventilation ducts have been
disguised with anodised aluminium mosaic to create a decorative feature. All the furniture was specifically designed and an
illuminated mural painted on glass produces three dimensional
effects[3].

2

prevented by spacing the holes or perforations close together.

Table 8 (*i*) Examples of coefficients of absorption of common materials used in restaurant design

Material, etc	Coefficients of absorption at:		
	125Hz	500Hz	2000Hz
Asbestos 12mm thick sprayed on solid backing	0·10	0·40	0·60
Brickwork—dense	0·01	0·02	0·03
Carpet—thick on felt over solid floor	0·10	0·30	0·50
Concrete—smooth finish	0·01	0·02	0·02
Cork tiles, 12·5mm thick, sealed, on solid floor	0·05	0·07	0·09
Curtains medium weight, in folds on wall	0·07	0·35	0·50
Fibre board tiles, 1mm perforated over space	0·20	0·60	0·65
Glass in windows, 6·4mm (¼in) plate	0·10	0·05	0·02
Glass fibre 25mm behind perforated board	0·10	0·55	0·80
Linoleum on solid floor	0·05	0·05	0·10
Ventilation grilles—50 per cent voids	0·15	0·35	0·30
Marble on solid backing and terrazzo	0·01	0·01	0·02
Plaster on solid backing	0·02	0·02	0·04
Plaster, acoustic 1mm on solid backing	0·13	0·35	0·45
Plastic tiles 1mm expanded polystyrene	0·05	0·40	0·20
Seats—wooden chairs, each	0·15	0·17	0·20
leather or vinyl seats, each	0·20	1·60	1·90
upholstered chairs, each	2·00	3·00	3·00
Tiles—glazed	0·01	0·01	0·02
Wood blocks on solid floor	0·02	0·05	0·10
Wood panelling 3 ply over 2·5mm air space	0·30	0·15	0·10
Occupants—in wooden chairs, each	2·00	4·00	4·50
in upholstered seats, each	3·00	5·00	4·00

Prevention of excessive noise entering from outside

1.05 External noises vary considerably according to location and the extent to which the main source of noise is screened by other buildings and obstacles. As an indication of traffic noise climates, the average daytime decibel levels of noise measured at the kerbside 80 per cent of the time are: on arterial roads with many heavy vehicles 80 to 70; major roads with heavy traffic and buses 75 to 65; shopping areas with local traffic 70 to 60; and residential areas with local traffic 65 to 55.

These are average levels and do not indicate the peak noise output of individual vehicles. As an indication of the variations in different frequencies of traffic noise the following analysis shows the noise levels measured 5m from a main road at peak rush hour.

Table 8 (*ii*) Average noise levels at various frequencies near a main road

Octave band Hz	37·5– 75	75– 150	150– 300	300– 600	600– 1200	1200– 2400	2400– 4800	4800– 9600
Decibels	78	81	81	79	72	67	63	55

1.06 A reduction in outside noise levels can be obtained by screening from the main source of noise—whether this is road traffic or factory processes. Thus a restaurant or canteen can be kept relatively free from outside noise intrusion by: locating the building away from the main noise; screening with other buildings, trees, or blank walls or interposing cloakrooms, entrance foyers, storerooms, etc. between the main source of noise and the dining room.

1.07 External noises may enter the restaurant through: open windows, doors, ventilators; gaps in badly fitting windows and doors; the structural walls, window frames and panes; and doors and other building components.

The first two problems of noise intrusion through openings and gaps arise from sound which is airborne, ie travelling through the air, while the noise entering via the building structure is the result of resonance—vibrations set up in the building components which reproduce the sound inside.

Airborne noise can be reduced by minimising the various paths of entry and by providing baffling to prevent direct passage of sound. The use of well fitting windows and doors with deep rebates, and lining baffled openings with absorbent material, will appreciably reduce the level of noise entering. If necessary, natural ventilation openings may have to be replaced by mechanical means of ventilation and doorways may be enclosed by an entrance lobby to confine noise.

Noise transmitted by the structure can be reduced by insulation which is provided by three main techniques, namely:
· increasing the mass of the structure;
· separating the inner and outer components; or
· absorbing reverberation with a lining of resilient material.

As a broad rule, the sound transmitted through a solid building structure reduces by 5 decibels each time the mass—ie the thickness—is doubled. For any material there is an economic limit to thickness for this benefit and this, in practice, determines the maximum reduction in sound level which can be provided by this means.

Table 8 (*iii*) Examples of insulation values of building structures

Building structure	Thickness		Average noise level reduction
	mm	in	dB
Solid brick wall and plaster	115	4½	45
	230	9	50
Cavity brick wall and plaster	290	11½	55
Lightweight concrete and plaster	65	2½	40
Timber stud partition and plaster	50	2	30
Partly open window—up to			10
Closed window—edge gaps			15–20
Closed well fitting window			20–25
Heavy plate glass window	6·4	¼	25–30
Double glazed window with 200mm (8in) space and absorbent reveals			40

Separation of inner and outer components of the building fabric can further reduce the sound entering the building. This reduction is small and tends to be mainly in the higher frequency ranges if the space separating the components is small. To produce a more substantial reduction in low frequency traffic noises the space between the glass in double glazed windows must be at least 100mm (4 in), and preferably 200mm to 250mm (8 in to 10 in).

If this space—eg in a cavity wall—is bridged by rigid connections, its value as a noise insulating layer is greatly impaired. On the other hand the introduction of resilient linings into the space helps to damp down the vibrations and thereby improve insulation.

Noise penetration from other areas

1.08 Within the building there is the possibility of noise generated in one area penetrating into others either directly or indirectly through flanking paths. So far as restaurants are concerned the main sources of noise may be from the kitchen, servery and dish washing areas and from mechanical equipment generally.

In banquet and business functions similar noise problems are liable to arise from the food service and, in addition, sound may penetrate through dividing partitions from one part of the room to the next.

Kitchen noises arise from turbulence, vibration and impact and tend to be aggravated by reflection from the hard boundary surfaces prolonging reverberation within the large open space. To a great extent the level of noise will vary with the degree of activity from one time to the next but generally reaches a peak during the meal period with the maximum use of equipment and movement of utensils. Under these conditions the average noise levels are about 65 to 70 decibels in the kitchen and between 60 and 70 decibels in the servery and dishwashing areas. The noise level in the servery will depend very much on its size, shape and surfaces whilst the noise generated by a dishwashing machine generally increases with the size of the machine.

These values represent the averages only. Peak noise readings may be up to 20dB higher—eg when a dish is dropped. As an illustration of the range of levels of noise at different frequencies, the averages for a canteen servery with relatively hard surrounding walls are given in table 8 (iv).

Table 8 (iv) Average noise levels at various frequencies in a canteen servery

Octave band (Hz)	75–150	150–300	300–600	600–1200	1200–2400	2400–4800	4800–9600
Decibels	56	60	69	68	62	55	50

Methods of noise reduction

1.09 In each case the methods employed to reduce noise entering the restaurant are basically the same.

Method	Examples
Reduce noise at source	Use of nylon or rubber in moving parts of machinery. Damping vibration of benches, etc. by resilient linings. Selection of quiet machinery.
Isolate noisy areas	Isolation of plant in separate enclosures, eg dishwashing machines
Reduce direct entry of noise	Provision of double doors, baffle screens, pass-through units between kitchen-servery
Reduce indirect transmission	Provision of sound insulating panels and partitions. Sealing of flanking paths around edges

These rules also apply to partitions employed to divide up the space in a banquet hall. To achieve a reasonable standard of insulation while remaining sufficiently light in weight to allow removal, a partition must usually be in double layers lined with resilient material.

In mechanical plant, noise is most likely to arise from fan motors, air ducting, gas jets and burners, water pipes, and escaping steam. Where moving fluids are concerned, the main source of noise is turbulence caused by high velocities and poor design. Fan motors and other noise-producing equipment can be isolated from the vicinity of the restaurant and mounted in a way which will minimise sound transmission through the ducting.

Standards

1.10. The standard of sound insulation between the kitchen and restaurant will depend on the use of the latter. For most mid-day meals involving quick service and relatively short periods of occupation, a high proportion of the background level of noise is generated within the restaurant and noise separation of the kitchen, if required at all, can be met by light partitioning. A higher standard is necessary for restaurants used for business lunches, directors' dining rooms in industrial catering, or for leisure dining which involves a much longer occupation period. The highest insulation of all is required to separate kitchens from those dining rooms used for formal gatherings, involving after-dinner speeches, etc. Appropriate standards for noise insulation of a partition separating the kitchen and dining rooms are: for cafeteria 25dB; for business lunches or leisure dining with waiter/waitress service 35dB; and, to allow for formal parties or speeches, 45dB.

Details of sound insulation and reduction are given in BSCP 3: 1960.

Floors

1.12 When floors are constructed—particularly lightweight mezzanine floors—to provide additional floor space in existing buildings, difficulties may arise from the sounds of footsteps, moving chairs and other impact noise which is transmitted through the floor to the area below. Impact noise can be reduced by providing a thick resilient floor covering—such as a carpet on a sponge rubber underlay—but additional treatment to the floor construction is also usually necessary. This will include some means of separation to prevent sounds passing directly through the structure (eg floating floor and/or suspended ceiling) and also some additional weighting to reduce movement. (ceiling pugging).

2 SAFETY, SECURITY AND HYGIENE

2.01 As a functional aspect of design, provision must be made for the security of catering premises and the safety of occupants. The various steps taken to give this protection fall into a number of categories each involving different considerations.

Subject	Requirements
Employees	Safety; prevention of accidents during work or operating machinery. First Aid facilities. Fire control equipment and means of escape in event of fire. Washing facilities; training in hygiene. Efficient direction and supervision.
Customers	Safe and adequate entrances, stairs, exits—including fire escape routes. Precautions against accidents. Clear directions.
Premises	Secure against intruders. Design to minimise risk of deliberate damage and vandalism. Provision of reasonable resistance against fire spread and damage.

These requirements may be expressly stated in legal provisions or be implicit in general obligations. The terms of insurance may contain clauses which through limitations on indemnity, high premiums and penalty clauses may provide financial inducements to improve security or safety measures. A further factor is the standard of safety incorporated in engineering installations—both electrical and mechanical—against risk of danger or damage in use or in the event of failure.

Safety at work

2.02 The basic requirements for safety in kitchens and other areas where staff are engaged are contained, in Britain, in the Offices, Shops and Railway Premises Act 1963, and related legislation regulating the health, welfare and safety of employees. Similar legal protection is found in most countries. Accidents may arise through many different causes or combinations of circumstances but can be broadly identified into five groups:

Mental factors	such as ignorance, temper, haste, fatigue, confusion, carelessness, depression
Physical factors	failing senses, physical disease, disability, dizziness, lack of sensation in hands or feet
Design factors	bad positioning, congestion, inadequate support, exposed danger, poor environment
Maintenance factors	inefficient apparatus, unsecured parts, worn floors, maladjusted controls
Management factors	lack of supervision and instruction, disorganisation

Perhaps the most common types of accidents in kitchens are: burns and scalds in using cooking apparatus, often as a result of congestion or difficulties of access; collisions between employees carrying containers, etc. due mainly to poor layout and inadequate working space; cuts from knives, sharp edges of opened cans, blades, etc, and lacerations from moving machinery; and slipping-on wet greasy floors or steps. These dangers are increased by poor lighting and an environment which is either hot and humid or cold and humid.

Under the statutory provisions standards are laid down for first-aid equipment and training.

The safety of the customer

2.03 This may be, in part, regulated by requirements under the Licensing Acts as a condition of being granted a licence to sell alcoholic drink on the premises. In other instances, redress for accident and injury arising from negligence may be sought by the customer through legal action under Common Law, and the restaurant proprietor will normally indemnify himself against such liabilities—to the public or his employees—by taking out appropriate insurance policies. More specific provisions, relating to the safety of the employee and customer alike, are imposed by the Occupiers Liability Act, 1957. This places a direct obligation on the occupier to take reasonable steps to ensure and maintain the safety of his premises.

Accidents are most likely to arise when a customer changes his or her movements—for example: standing up from a seated position; lifting a tray from a counter or lowering it on to a table; stepping from a firm floor to one which is slippery; changing direction suddenly and causing a collision; or negotiating steps and stairs.

Safety from fire

2.04 Provisions to deal with outbreaks of fire include:
· active defence through detection and control;
· passive defence by selection and combination of building materials which will resist the spread of fire and its effects; and
· means of escape which are safe and appropriate for the numbers of occupants.

Requirements for fire precautions will vary from one premises to another depending on the particular circumstances and conditions. Whilst the following details apply generally, the views of the Building Control and Fire Authorities should be sought, in each instance, to obtain more specific directions.

4
Hatchetts, Piccadilly, London. Architect: Lucas Mellinger Associated with G. Burns.
Fire separation between the restaurant and Playground discothèque below is provided by glass mosaics mounted on both sides of georgian wired glass screens in metal frames.

Active defence

2.05 An outbreak of fire may be observed directly—by daytime employees or security checks at night—or detected automatically by apparatus which activates an alarm and/or control mechanisms. The latter may function by detecting gases, smoke, flames or excessive rise in temperature. Most of the simpler equipment used in catering operates by the last method either by melting special solders (eg fusible links) or expanding and releasing plugs or phials. This mechanism may release a damper to close off a duct—eg above frying appliances—or release a fine spray of water into the area—eg sprinkler valves over staircases.

The local equipment employed in bringing a fire under control may be based on: water—supplied through hydrants, hosereels and sprinklers; foam, carbon dioxide or vapourising liquids—usually generated in portable appliances; asbestos fire blankets—rolled into small containers. Water or foam cannot be used where there is 'live' electrical apparatus and hence are limited for use in kitchens. Carbon dioxide must also be used with caution in confined areas because of the danger of asphyxiation. The asbestos fire blanket is particularly useful in smothering the types of small fires which frequently break out in kitchens and the blanket containers should be located in a number of strategic points such as near the frying ranges.

All fire fighting appliances must be distinctly marked—the colour is not standardised but red and yellow are commonly used—and staff must be trained in their proper use. Clear concise instructions regarding fire control must be posted in the kitchen.

Structural protection against effects of fire

2.06 A building structure must be constructed to resist the effects of heat and flames for an adequate period without collapsing, allowing the flames to penetrate, or conducting an excessive amount of heat to ignite other areas. The period for this fire resistance will depend on several factors, such as the degree of hazard involved, but is intended primarily to ensure that the growth of the fire is restrained and that the building structure will remain intact long enough for the occupants to escape and for fire control measures to be brought into action.

Other structural precautions against the spread of fire in catering premises include:

(1) Protection of stairs, passenger lifts, food and goods lifts, chutes and ducts to prevent entry and escape of flames, etc.

(2) Use of smoke-stop swing doors in corridors to isolate dining rooms or kitchens from other areas of the building.

(3) Use of surface materials in the dining room and lounge which have a low rate of surface flame spread (class 1 over most of area). In the case of circulation areas, internal linings must be incombustible or of very low flame spread (class 0) and this should also apply in the kitchen because of the high degree of fire risk.

Means of escape in case of fire

2.07 These are legally controlled, in the interests of safety, under various statutory provisions.

Table 8 (v) Periods of fire resistance in hours related to heights, floor areas and capacities of catering establishments

Multi-storey buildings	Height m	ft	Floor area m² × 100	sq ft × 100	Capacity m³ × 100	cu ft × 100	Fire resistance above ground	below ground
Restaurants	7·5	25	1·50	15	No limit		0	1*
	7·5	25	5·00	50	No limit		½	1
	15·0	60	No limit		35·00	1250	1	1
	28·0	90	10·00	100	70·00	2500	1	2
	No limit		20·00	200	70·00	2500	2	4
Hotels	2 storeys		5·00	50	No limit		½	1
	3 storeys		2·50	25	No limit		1	1
	28·0	90	30·00	300	85·00	3000	1	1½
	No limit		20·00	200	55·00	2000	1½	2

* For basements under 50·0m² (500 sq ft) no fire resistance is specified

Single-storey (above ground) buildings	Floor area m² × 100	sq ft × 100	Fire resistance Above ground Elements of structure	Separating walls	External walls	Basement Elements below ground
Restaurants	20·0	200	½	1	½	1†
	30·0	300	1	1	1	2
	No limit		2	2	2	4
Hotels	30·00	300	½	1	½	1

Note: The figures for heights, floor areas, and capacities are the limits for each standard. For canteens forming part of an industrial or storage premises a higher standard may be required

† For basements under 50·0m² (500 sq ft) this is reduced to ½ hour

Source: Building Regulations 1972

Table 8 (vi) British requirements for means of escape in case of fire

Statutory control	Premises
Offices, Shops and Railway Premises Act 1963, and Regulations (SI 761 : 1964)	All restaurants—for the safety of employees—and employee catering facilities
Licensing Act 1964	Premises selling intoxicating liquor—licensing conditions
Public Health Act 1936	Entrances, exits, stairs, etc to new buildings
Building Regulations 1972 : 317	Fire resistance and protection of stairs and corridors, etc
London Building Acts (Amendment) Act 1939 GLC (General Powers) Acts 1966 and 1968	Requirements for fire escapes, etc in Inner London. Exhibitions and night cafés in the Great London area
Building (Scotland) Act 1970 and	Buildings, generally, in Scotland including shops and restaurants
Fire Precautions Act 1971	Institutions, hotels, residential clubs, assembly rooms, banquet halls, reception areas, etc
Education Act 1944 section 10 and Regulations (SI 890 : 1959) (SI 433 : 1969)	Standards for school premises including school canteens
Factories Act 1961 sections 40, 45, 46 and Regulations (SI 762 : 1964)	Canteens forming part of a factory premises (with exemptions for premises in which few people are employed)

BS specifications relating to fire precautions:
BSCP 3:4: 1949 *Fire precautions in buildings*
BSCP 3:4 (2): 1968 *Fire precautions in shops and stores*
BS 4422: 1969 *Glossary of terms associated with fire*
BS 476: 1953/71 *Fire tests on building materials and structures*
BSCP 402: 1952/64 *Fire fighting installations and equipment*
2.08 In order to serve as a means of escape in the event of fire a staircase must meet certain recommended standards. These are, in part, described in chapter 2, para 2.04, but the main design recommendations for dimensions and other features which meet most requirements are summarised in table 8 (vii).

Table 8 (vii) Staircase design recommendations

	Public staircase for premises having an occupancy of more than 100 persons		Other staircases and those for premises with a capacity of less than 100 persons	
	mm	in	mm	in
Height of riser* (maximum)	150	6	190	7·5
Width of tread (minimum)	280	11	250	10
Height of handrail from centre of pitchline	840 min 1000 max	33	As for public staircases	
Height of handrail over landings and open walls	1100	42		
Maximum gradient ramps	1 in 10			
Short ramps for disabled	1 in 12		Also for heavy food trolleys	
Ramps over 1·8m long for disabled	1 in 20			

* The maximum number of risers in one flight is 16, minimum 3

With the exception of small restaurants—of less than 50 people—regulated by the Greater London Council, spiral staircases are not normally allowed as a means of fire escape.

The doors on an escape route must open outwards to swing clear of the walking path at landings and be fitted with panic bolts for emergency use. All separating doors fitted in corridors must be self-closing.

2.09 The number and positions of escape routes which can be used in the event of fire will depend on a number of factors—particularly the layout of the catering premises—and should take account of the number of occupants, the risk of danger involved, and the distances to a fire escape. Potential numbers of occupants may be assessed from the layout of the restaurant and are usually based on average figures for floor areas. The total should include the kitchen and waiting staff unless separate exits are provided. For purposes of calculation, the occupancies of restaurants are normally assessed on a floor area of $0·9m^2$ (10 sq ft) per person, cafeterias on $1·0m^2$ (11 sq ft) per person and banquet halls with close seating or dance halls on $0·7m^2$ (8 sq ft) per person.

Catering establishments create a moderately high fire risk because of the high temperatures of equipment, hot fat, gas and other combustibles in kitchens and the high fire load in the dining areas due to combustible furniture and furnishings. The hazard is increased when there is a high concentration of occupants which, for example, may occur in banquet halls or industrial canteens. In addition, a greater element of risk may be involved in the case of high level restaurants (over four storeys), basement restaurants or kitchens, and restaurants in buildings constructed primarily of combustible materials—such as is the case in many old coaching inns and period properties.

8.21 The basis for calculating exit requirements is normally taken as a unit width of 530mm (21in) and the numbers of people who can pass through an exit per unit of width. This is often quoted as 40 persons per minute but under panic conditions in an unfamiliar building in which the doors will probably be closed, it is reasonable to allow a lower figure for commercial restaurants: 30 persons/minute/unit width (0·5 persons/second/unit width).

Complete vacation of the restaurant and its associated areas must be possible within a period of 2½ to 3 minutes, thus a single unit width should in theory be adequate for up to 100 persons. In practice, the minima given in table 8 (viii) are normally stipulated to ensure sufficient clearance:

Table 8 (viii) Minimum fire exit widths

Exit	Minimum widths	
	mm	ft in
Rooms		
Occupied by more than 5 and up to 100 persons at any one time	750	2 6
Occupied by 101 to 200 persons at any one time—main exit	1100	3 6
Occupied by 101 to 200 persons at any one time—secondary exits (each)	750	2 6
For wider exits, an increase for every additional 15 persons	75	3
Corridors		
Main, normally	1200	4 0
Secondary, normally	1100	3 6

The number and positions of exits from a room used by the public—such as a dining or reception room—and from any work room will depend on the size of the room and the degree of hazard involved to the occupants.

For a large banquet room, reception area, restaurant or canteen there will need to be at least two exits providing alternative means of escape, each leading by a separate route to a place of safety such as a protected staircase or the open air. To be suitable as alternatives, the exits must be positioned sufficiently far apart and will be appropriate only if the angle between lines from the exits to any point in the room is more than 45°.

Positions of exits will also be determined by the travel distance from the furthest part of the room served and limits to distances are summarised in table 8 (ix).

Table 8 (ix) *Limits of travel distances to fire exits*

Situation	Maximum travel distance	
	m	ft
Within the room		
Kitchens and rooms of high fire risk including dining areas having surfaces of rapid surface flame spead*, furniture and linen stores	6	20
Dining rooms and lounges with only one exit	9	30
Dining and other rooms with at least two alternative exits	18	60
Large banquet rooms with at least three alternative exits each adequate for the part served	30	100
From the room to a safe stairway or final exit from the building		
Where only one escape route is available	7·6	25
With at least two alternative routes of escape available	18	60
Ground floor rooms with an exit giving immediate access to a place of safety	No limit	

* Surface finishes of walls and ceilings are considered in paragraph 8.24

These travel distances should be regarded as the maxima and may have to be reduced where the premises present exceptional hazards because of their construction or use for other purposes. This might apply, for example, to a factory canteen forming part of a large storage building. The contents of a room, such as fixed tables, counters and furniture, should be so disposed that the actual distance travelled from any point in a room is not more than 1½ times the maximum linear distance quoted and must not obstruct any emergency exit.

Protection and lighting of fire escapes

2.12 To be suitable as a means of escape in the event of fire, a stairway must also be through fire-resisting self-closing doors and the route must lead directly to a safe exit from the building. In certain cases, alternative provision may be made with automatic fire detection, water sprinklers and other protective devices. Within the protected area all surfaces must be incombustible or have a class 0 standard of surface flame spread.

2.13 All escape routes must be clearly signposted and maintained in a suitable condition for use at any time when the restaurant is operating and whenever employees are working on the premises. Some form of emergency lighting should be provided for illuminating stairways, routes of exit and directional signs where and when the natural illumination is insufficient for this purpose. The emergency lighting system should be supplied with electricity from an independent source and come into operation automatically on failure of the mains supply. Normally, this equipment should be adequate to maintain the lighting for at least three hours but emergency lighting must be kept on continuously when large banquet and reception rooms and so on are in use.

Equipment for emergency lighting includes:

(1) Self-contained battery power lighting units incorporating their own chargers, and

(2) Lighting powered from a central source within the premises with battery and generating equipment.

2.14 In the early stages of a fire in a building the personal hazard to occupants can be severely affected by the internal linings and finishes of the walls and ceilings. The travel distances to exits quoted in the above tables are appropriate for materials with moderate surface flame spread, summarised in table 8 (x).

Table 8 (x) *Suitability of surface finishes with varying fire resistances*

Type	Examples	Conditions of use
Inorganic materials	Brickwork, blockwork, plaster, ceramic tiles, asbestos boards	Any situation including passageways and corridors
Materials of very low surface flame spread	Wood wool slabs, plaster board, thin paper and vinyl coverings on an inorganic base	
Cellulosic materials	Timber, hardboard, particle board, blockboard	In restaurants, lounges, bars if flame retardant type.
Thermosetting plastics	Decorative laminates	Mostly limited to small areas (2·5m²) at least 3·5m apart in ceilings. The aggregate area on walls should not exceed ½ floor area.
Heavy flock wall papers		
Thermoplastics	Expanded polystyrene Polyvinyl Chloride	Self-extinguishing type only. Used in separated small areas (4m²) of limited thickness in ceilings. Aggregate area not to exceed ½ floor area.

3 SECURITY

3.01 Many of the specific requirements relating to security are stipulated by insurance companies with the object of reducing the degree of risk involved in insurance. In a general sense, the main areas of security are concerned with the movements of people and goods, particularly in moving into and out of the premises. The extent to which control must be applied will depend, in practice, on the size of the catering operation and it will be particularly important, for example, when there is a large number of employees, particularly with shift work, or when large stocks of expensive food or drink are kept on the premises. As a summary, the following measures of control may be introduced in planning the physical facilities:

(a) *Control over the employees*

Changing areas—separate for the sexes—with lockable cupboards for outdoor clothing and working overalls should be available and provision for recording hours of work and for holding and storing records of employees. A separate staff entrance is warranted in larger premises.

(b) *Control over goods*

There must be a separate goods entrance, with a checking and weighing area, giving direct access to the stores. Bulk storage rooms must be properly designed and fitted with stout lockable doors. Issue stores for daily food requirements of the kitchen are used to simplify control. Separate locked cupboards or storage rooms should be provided for reserves of linen, silver, and china. Stocks of wines and spirits should also be kept in a separate store with special precautions against internal or external entry. This also applies to high cost items such as cigarettes.

The chef's office should be positioned and designed to facilitate supervision and control.

Provisions must be made for easy stock checking and for filing records including invoices and orders.

Control over the customers

The layout, entrances and exits must be planned to facilitate circulation, direction and supervision. In particular cashier points must be appropriately positioned and designed. There must be proper safe facilities provided for receipts and wages.

3.02 Measures to provide protection against unauthorised entry to the building include particular attention to those parts which are normally most vulnerable—such as doors and windows.

External doors of timber should be of solid hardwood at least 50mm (2 in) thick and flush doors must have a solid core. Doors to high risk areas such as wine stores should have a steel lining (2mm thick) screwed to the inside face. Glass plate doors are liable to shatter and should be used only in conspicuous positions such as street entrances. Folding metal lattice gates or rolling shutters may be provided for protection at night. Door frames must be firmly secured to walls by rag bolts.

Locks should be of good quality lever design, preferably with mortise fixing. If rim locks are used they must be secured to both the door edge and face. The performance of locks should comply with BS 2088: 1954. Typical uses include: dead locks for infrequent entry to stores, cellars, etc; two-bolt locks for entrances and internal doors with a latch for normal daytime use; and panic latches and bolts which are essential on public exits serving as fire escapes and must be fitted with locksets to prevent reverse entry. The release bar is normally fitted 1065mm (42in) above the floor.

Bolts provide additional protection to secure doors of buildings and yards from inside but must be securely fixed to be effective.

Windows must also be protected. At ground floor level they should normally be fixed but if opening lights and ventilators are used, the opening must be too small for accessibility. In other situations, casement, sliding, sash or pivoted windows must have fixing stops capable of being secured against outside entry.

To reduce risk of entry through window breakage, panes may be

(a) divided into metal frames of less than 0·05m² (0·5 sq ft) area;

(b) constructed of wired glass;

(c) protected by bars of minimum section 18mm spaced 100mm (4in) centres and welded to ties not more than 600 mm (24in) apart; or

(d) fitted externally or internally with collapsible or rolling metal grilles or shutters which can be removed during periods of use, eg to large front windows.

The *building structure* should also resist intrusion. External walls, particularly in areas screened from view, must be of substantial construction normally in brick or block cavity walling—minimum 280mm (11in) thick—or reinforced concrete slabs. Internal walls to store rooms should be in brick or block work—at least 100mm (4in) thick—or have metal face sheeting (eg cabinets) or wire mesh screens (eg partitioned-off wine or liquor stores).

Detecting systems

3.03 A number of alternative detecting systems are available, comprising:

· a detecting device;

· control equipment and relay network for power supply and signalling link; and

· alarm mechanisms—bells, alarms recorded message communication.

In catering premises it is usually impracticable to instal very sophisticated systems. The range of detection equipment includes:

(a) *Magnetic contacts*—eg recessed plungers and magnetic reed contacts, used to detect opening of doors and windows; which are relatively simple and easy to install.

(b) *Wiring systems* which can be used to show any break in a window, wall, ceiling, etc; but are of limited application in catering premises except for safes and wine stores.

(c) *Pressure mats*—simple strips which may be positioned in entrances, on landings, etc.

(d) *Infra-red beams* transmitted across an opening to a receiver. This system may also be used for opening doors, eg in hotels.

(e) *Vacuum systems, ultra-sonics, microwave* and *vibration detectors*—limited application due to distortion effects.

4 HYGIENE REQUIREMENTS

4.01 Strict observance of hygiene is essential in all areas of food service and handling not only in a restrictive sense but shown to be practised as a positive contribution to good management. No matter how well designed the premises, the impression instantly conveyed by a stained cloth, fingered cutlery or soiled glass—to name but a few complaints—will completely undermine confidence in the catering.

In Britain, standards have been laid down by the Food Hygiene (General) Regulations 1970. The catering premises and all surfaces, articles or equipment with which food is liable to come into contact must be kept clean and, to facilitate hygiene, must meet the following specific requirements:

Surfaces, articles and equipment must be constructed of such materials and kept in such good order, repair and condition as to enable thorough cleaning and prevent—so far as practicable—absorption and risk of contamination of food.

Food rooms, generally, must be of such construction, condition and situation; and kept in such good order, repair and condition as to avoid exposing food to any risk of contamination; enable effective cleaning; and prevent—so far as practicable—any risk of infestation by rats, mice, or insects.

In addition, all restaurants, cafés and other rooms in which food is handled must be provided with suitable and sufficient means of lighting and ventilation to enable the premises to operate with due regard for hygiene.

So far as handling of food is concerned, food must not be put in any place where it is liable to become contaminated and, if necessary, must be covered or screened from possible sources of contamination. In planning restaurants this would apply, for instance, to food exposed on a cafeteria counter and to the separation of returned soiled dishes from the counters where food is being served.

To minimise the risk of food poisoning organisms multiplying rapidly in foods containing meat, fish, gravy, imitation cream, or—with some exceptions—egg and milk, it is necessary that those foods should be kept until ready for immediate service at a temperature of above 62·7°C (145°F), eg in bains-marie or hot cupboards; or below 10°C (50°F), eg in chilled cabinets.

Facilities for personal hygiene

4.02 People handling food are required to keep themselves

5

6

Staff Catering, Kodak Head Office, Hemel Hempstead. Equipment by G. F. E. Bartlett and Son Ltd.

A modern L shaped service counter designed to facilitate easy cleaning and hygiene. Counter units are faced with stainless steel sheeting giving smooth impervious surfaces while the adjacent walls are ceramic tiled. A sneeze guard rail is provided over the section in which plated food is displayed.

All hot and refrigerated cupboards situated under the counter are arranged at waist level to avoid the need for excessive stooping and food is supplied to the servery via pass-through units in the rear walls[5]. The counter, which is 75ft (22·8m) long is arranged in an 'L' shape to reduce space and, to allow flexibility, the restaurant sections can be separated by screens[6].

clean, and suitable wash hand basins—with hot and cold water, soap or detergent, nail brushes and clean towels or drying facilities—must be provided in positions which are conveniently accessible.

Any exposed cuts or abrasions must be covered with appropriate waterproof dressings and, for this purpose, first aid materials must be provided and kept available for use.

Except for bartenders, waiters and waitresses—who must have clean clothing—people handling food are required to wear clean washable overalls and suitable accommodation must be provided for outdoor clothing and changing. If this is in a food room it must be in the form of lockers or cupboards.

In the interests of sanitation all food premises must be provided with:

1. an adequate clean and wholesome supply of both hot and cold water;

2. sinks and facilities for washing food and equipment;

3. suitable efficient sanitary conveniences, properly lighted and ventilated and kept clean, which must not communicate directly with a food room; and

4. adequate space and accommodation for separation of refuse and waste food.

In certain cases certificates of exemption may be allowed where it is not practicable to provide sanitary conveniences if these are readily available elsewhere in the building.

The provision of proper facilities forms a basis for good practice and the Food Hygiene (General) Regulations lay down a number of functional requirements which relate specifically to catering. However, the standards set in the initial design are fundamental in maintaining a high level of hygiene.

Methods of reducing risk of vermin infestation and dirt in buildings are specified in BSCP 3, Chapter 10: 1950—*Precautions against vermin and dirt.*

Table 8 (xi) Specific provisions for hygiene

Area	Considerations	Provisions
Walls	Areas exposed to risk of splashing soiling, smearing	Non-absorbent smooth easily washable surfaces
Floors	Subjected to heavy traffic— pedestrians and trolleys— possible spillage and soiling	Non-porous washable flooring, resistant to water, acids, grease and marking by shoes, etc
Ceilings	Risk of staining and condensation from steam, etc	Vapour sealed and insulated. Wipable surfaces easily redecorated
Tables	Frequent repeated use, difficulty of changing table cloths or maintaining clean cloths	Exposed table top—with or without place mats. Must be durable, scratch-resistant, free from cracks, impermeable, easily wiped clean and appear clean
Curtains	Difficulty of removal for washing or cleaning and rehanging	Designed to allow easy access and cleaning or substituted by blinds
Trolleys, serving counters	Frequent use, difficulty of washing with minimum of water in place	Smooth non-absorbent durable surfaces free from cracks and ledges. Shelves and tray inserts removable for washing
Trays	Continuous use with heavy soiling	Moulded in one piece of impermeable material. Designed to fit dish washing machine or sink
Crockery	As above	Sufficiently strong body to withstand heavy use. Heavily glazed non-porous base. Appropriate dish washing facilities and storage
Cutlery	As above	Stainless steel or heavily plated to withstand machine washing. Well designed cutlery trays provided for collection
Tableware	Difficulties of collection and washing	Disposable items may be used

9 TABLEWARE AND MENU DESIGN

1 TABLEWARE

1.01 Selection of tableware usually falls outside the scope of restaurant design and is, invariably, based on a different set of criteria. As a result the table items—which occupy the most conspicuous area in the customer's view—may be incompatible with the surroundings, producing an effect of disarray and confusion. The essence of good design is completeness of detail so that the impression created by the room is continued from one scale to the next and this should extend to influence the design of the set table.

As a subject, the selection of tableware is extensive, and covers ceramics, glassware, plastics and stainless steel, or 'plate' used for cutlery, flatware, and holloware. The following summary is, therefore, intended only as a guide to specifications.

Ceramics

1.02 Clay ware items are manufactured from refined clays blended with other ingredients, moulded or shaped and fired in a kiln at about 1200°C to produce the hard body of the article which, at this stage, is known as 'bisque' ware. A thin coating film of siliceous material is applied which, on refiring, fuses to form a hard glazed surface.

Decoration may be applied by hand, transfers or lithographs under a film of protective glaze (under-glazed) or on to the glazed surface (on-glazed). The latter is usually necessary for gold decoration and for certain colours, such as bright reds and yellows, which tend to be affected by the high temperature required for glazing and are reheated instead to a lower temperature—sufficient to allow the pattern to be absorbed into the glazed surface. On-glazed decoration may be damaged by strong detergents, very hot water or excessive abrasion, and generally requires more care in use.

1.03 The term 'china' is applied to all glazed tableware and will include the following types:

(a) *Glazed earthenware*—a mixture of flint and Cornish stone combined with a high proportion of ball clay which, on firing, produces a cream coloured porous body (about 15 per cent water absorption). Earthenware crockery is relatively weak and easily chipped. It is made in thick sections and relies on the glazing for impermeability.

(b) *Vitrified earthenware*—similar but contains more flint (as a flux) in the mixture and is fired at higher temperatures producing a stronger fused body which has a lower porosity and better resistance to chipping.

(c) *Vitreous hotelware* (*vitreous china*) has a similar composition but includes more flux enabling the permeability and strength to be improved.

(d) *Felspathic porcelain* is produced mainly on the Continent and is completely vitrified (fused) with a translucent cream or grey coloured body. Although non-porous it tends to be brittle and has relatively low impact resistance.

(e) *Bone china*—a clay composition which includes china clay (kaolin) and Cornish stone, and is intermixed with up to 50 per cent calcined bone to give great strength and fineness of moulding. Bone china is virtually impermeable, extremely strong, and can be produced in fine delicate shapes.

Metallised bone china is developed specifically for hotel and catering ware and contains added metallic oxides (barium and magnesium) which produce a more resilient bond giving greater impact strength.

(f) *Stoneware* is used for heavy articles which are impervious and resistant to damage. Stoneware cannot be produced in bright colours but is characterised by the dark brown, green, or blue used for the external surfaces of certain dishes, bowls, casseroles, jugs, and other kitchenware brought to the table.

1.04 Considerations in selecting tableware include:

(a) *Ceramic bodies*—the inherent properties of the clay bodies—usually of earthenware, vitrified earthenware or bone china, will largely determine the quality of the products and their cost. Bone china will normally be used only in the more expensive restaurants and high grade hotels. For most catering requirements, vitrified earthenware or vitreous hotelware will be suitable while, in some instances, a compromise may be more appropriate using, for example, bone china for the delicate shapes required for high tea or for the holloware generally and vitreous ware for dinner or for all the flatware (plates and shallow dishes).

BS 4034: 1966 specifies standards of resistance to crazing under conditions of changing temperature, and the porosity of an unglazed surface—which should not exceed 3 per cent.

(b) *Initial cost* must be related to the life of the tableware and replacement costs. As a general rule, damage during use is mainly the result of disorganisation, for example bad stacking.

(c) *Weight* is important in storage design and in limiting the number of articles—such as plates—which can be carried

1
Sands restaurant, London. Architect: Lucas Mellinger associated with K. A. Short.
Based on a Persian theme, furniture and table appointments of the Sands restaurant are purposely designed to create the correct atmosphere. Textured pattern carpet and wall covering blend with mosaic faced columns and table-tops. The menu holders portray a Persian warrior—copied from a relief in the Louvre—and this feature is also used in the illuminated flower holders.

by one person at once. Stacking is usually limited to 25 to 30 plates high.
(d) *Durability*—for example of the pattern, under conditions of heavy use and machine washing. This is improved by thickening or rolling the edges of plates to reduce cracks forming. Under-glazed designs are generally more durable than on-glazed patterns.
(e) *Hygiene*—resistance to chipping and crazing of the surface glaze is important and the toughness of the glaze to withstand repeated scratching, scouring, acids and alkalis while remaining non-absorbent and easy to clean.
(f) *Shape*—must be considered from a number of aspects—functional, visual, and operational—and the following features should be taken into account:

Table 9 (*i*) *Criteria for selecting tableware shapes*

Features	Examples
Interchangeability	To reduce the number of items, allow easier storage and flexibility in use, eg lids, plates
Replaceability	Standard designs with repeat production
Functional features including storage	Holloware: recognisable shapes, efficient pouring spouts, firm fitting lids, protection against chipping, shape and protection of handles, ease of cleaning, stability, simplicity of outline for easy washing Cups: design to avoid excessive cooling, allow nesting and fit machine baskets; handles—suitable strength of jointing, position, effectiveness Flatware: when stacked weight must be born by rims not the bases (scratching); rolled rims for strength
Appearance	Visual appeal of shape appropriate for restaurant

2
Dun An Oir Hotel, Co. Kerry, Ireland. Architects: Stephenson Gibney & Partners.
Traditional simplicity carefully reproduced in the design of the dining room is reflected in the tableware.

(g) *Decoration*—a wide range of stock patterns is available but the possibility of discontinuance must be investigated. Patterns may be specifically commissioned, the cost and production time depending on quantity ordered. Styles of patterns include: crests identified with the establishment—these are expensive and delay place setting due to the need for alignment; all-over patterns—of limited use because they tend to obscure the appearance of food and inside cups may appear to discolour drink by reflection; and rim patterns—in broad or narrow bands of continuous colour or decorative designs, which are most common in use.

(h) *Temperature range*—important in oven-to-table ware and in items which may need to be flameproof. The rate of temperature change is also critical, for example, in the use of containers for rapid freezing, thawing and heating of food.

(i) *Number of items*—depends on extent of standardisation and interchangeability, the trend being towards rationalisation of sizes and variations both for economy and for easier stock and portion control. As a rule, an additional $1\frac{1}{2}$ to 2 times the peak quantity of crockery needed for immediate use will be taken into reserve stock but this may have to be increased if there are likely to be delays in replacement such as with special designs. The range of tableware items needed will depend on the type of restaurant and the menu offered including provisions, where required, for speciality dishes and to allow for national variations in the types of crockery used.

Table 9 (ii) Range and sizes of tableware in general use

Type	Range	Size traditional	Metric*
Pots (related to cups and pint sizes)	Tea	15, 20, 30, 40oz	430, 570, 850, 1140ml
Jugs	Coffee, hot milk/water	10, 20, 30, 40oz	280, 570, 850, 1140ml
	Cream	1, 1½, 2½oz	30, 40, 70ml
	Milk	5, 10, 15oz	140, 280, 420ml
Cups	Tea	6, 7, 8oz	170, 200, 230ml
	Coffee (demi-tasse)	4oz	110ml
Saucers	Size related to cup but should be interchangeable		
Plates	Side	6½, 7in diam	165, 180mm
	Dessert	7½, 8in diam	190, 205mm
	Fish/dessert	8½, 9in diam	215, 230mm
	Meat	9½, 10in diam†	240, 255mm
	Oval meat	9½, 10in long	240, 255mm
Bowls	Cereal/fruit	6, 6½in diam	155, 165mm
	Sugar	3½in diam	90mm
	Soup	8½, 9in diam	215, 230mm

* Rounded to nearest 10ml and 5mm
† 10in is usually maximum size for a dish washing machine

Other items to be considered include salad dishes (often crescent shaped), egg cups, butter dishes, ash trays, and serving dishes with flat or raised covers (interchangeable), salad bowls, sauce boats, multi-purpose bowls and speciality dishes.

It is now probably exceptional to provide more than 20 different items of 'china', compared with ranges of up to 70 or more items which were at one time common in hotel use. Where a hotel or other establishment operates more than one restaurant it may be desirable, in terms of distinction, to have different designs and patterns of tableware for each, but against this must be balanced the costs and difficulties of regulating stocks of numerous items and a compromise may be to reduce each range.

(j) *Imperfections*—
Individual items must be checked for faults, for example:
crazing of the glaze—resulting from incorrect firing;
exposed dry edges—where glazing is incomplete;
uneven glaze thickness—caused when draining prior to firing;
voids and holes in the glaze surface;
distorted shapes and uneven rims;
irregularly or inadequately fixed handles; and
badly fitting lids.

Metalware

1.05 Metallic table ware items include: serving dishes and covers, beverage containers and table appointments such as cruets.

Compared with articles made from ceramics, metal based ware items are relatively strong and tough and thus better able to withstand the impacts and stresses arising from the frequent handling common with serving dishes and beverage containers. In addition the weight of a large metalware dish can be appreciably lighter than a 'china' one and a greater variety of shapes and embellishments is possible.

The choice of metal for food containers is restricted by the
(a) risk of tainting food, particularly by potentially poisonous metals or their compounds
(b) possibility of corrosion or chemical attack from acids, alkalis and other constituents of food etc.
(c) difficulties of washing and maintaining appearance.

As a result choice is limited to copper lined with tin, aluminium, stainless steel, silver and chrome plate.

1.06 Characteristics

Copper is attractive and an excellent conductor of heat and is thus used in cooking utensils which may also be brought to the table. Due to the high conductivity, the surface will also lose heat rapidly and tend to cool the contents quickly unless kept continuously heated. Copper must be lined with tin or silver to reduce the risk of contaminating food, but oxidation also tends to darken the external surface necessitating frequent cleaning. Compared with other materials, copper utensils are heavy and somewhat crude in appearance but may provide decorative attraction combined with functional value in an appropriate setting.

Aluminium is the most common material for kitchen utensils, being light in weight, non-tainting, reasonably resistant to acids and stain (although corroded by strong alkalis) and of good heat conductivity. As a table item, aluminium tends to lack visual appeal, being fairly soft and easily scratched and scruffed so that the surface appears dull. In addition, aluminium tends to mark glazed crockery surfaces and, having a lower elasticity than, say, stainless steel, is more easily indented. To some extent these properties can be modified by the use of alloys or by anodising the surface, and aluminium may be used in inexpensive holloware, plate dividers and covers, and for large containers where its low weight provides an advantage.

Stainless steel has about twice the strength of mild steel combined with an inherent resistance to corrosion. The latter results from the immediate formation of a natural invisible non-porous film produced by oxidation of chromium and iron. The composition of stainless steel depends on the properties required.

Table 9 (iii) Types of stainless steel used in catering

Type	Percentage (typical)		Chromium	British Standard	American ISI
	Carbon	Nickel			
18/8	0·08	8·0	18·0	EN58A	302
18/10	0·05	10·0	18·0	EN58B	304
Cutlery	0·30	Vanadium (optional)	13·0	EN56	420

18/8 and 18/10 chromium/nickel steels are unhardenable (austentic) but strong, hard, tough, abrasion-resisting, highly ductile and extremely resistant to corrosion. These materials can be welded and 18/8 stainless steel, in particular, is used in all forms of tableware and kitchen utensils. By contrast, cutlery steels can be hardened (martensic) but not welded, and are used for sharpened knife blades and cutting edges.

Stainless steel surfaces may be polished or produced in eggshell or satin lustre finishes which tend to show less marking. The surface cleans fairly easily and is resistant to staining by food or detergent contact. Marking of stainless steel may result from hard water scale, strong bleaches, and detergents, silver cleaners and overheating. The last two, in particular, may be difficult to remove without repolishing.

The main disadvantages of stainless steel lie in its dull grey colour—which may not be accepted in a traditional style restaurant—and the fact that the surface is not so water-repellent as, say, glazed ware. As a result water tends to form a semi-adherent film which does not readily drain and dry and, to some extent, this also applies to oil smears. In addition, the softer 18/8 steels, when used for cutlery blades, tend to produce marks on a glazed ware surface.

Silver plate is produced by depositing a film of silver by electrolysis on to a pressed and welded body—or blank— of nickel-silver (EPNS) or nickel-brass or stainless steel. The base alloy gives the article strength while the silver provides a rich lustre surface which may be supplied with a satin finish or a polished mirror finish.

The quality of the article is largely dependent on the thickness and evenness of the silver film which is difficult to measure precisely and is usually expressed in terms of the weight of the silver per single item of holloware—in the finished polished state—or per dozen items of flatware or cutlery. For A1 catering quality the following standards are typical and are quoted in traditional units of pennyworths (dwt) of silver per dozen items and the metric equivalent in grammes per 10 items. The silver deposit may not be uniform but may be deliberately thickened over points of wear or table contact—for example, on the backs of spoons. The film thickness can be measured by micrometer.

Table 9 (iv) Silver plate standards

Examples	Weight of silver plate					
	dwt/12 items		gm/12 items		gm/10 items	
	heavy	standard	heavy	standard	heavy	standard*
Main course spoons or forks	30	20	46	31	38	26
Dessert spoons or forks	20	14	31	22	26	18
Teaspoons	10	7	16	11	13	9

* With normal catering use, standard quality plate should have a life expectancy of about 20 years

Silver is a relatively soft metal and liable to be damaged by rough handling. In addition, the surface tends to tarnish by the formation of silver sulphide as a result of exposure to compounds of sulphur present in the air, and in many foodstuffs, eg sauces, eggs, onions. This tarnish may be removed by chemical action or mechanical burnishing, but represents extra cost of maintenance. In a large hotel where silver plate is to be extensively used, a separate room—a 'plate room'—should be provided for storage and care of the silver.

Chromium plated articles are limited in catering use mainly to fittings and items which are difficult to produce in stainless steel. Examples of chromium plating include tubular rails and counter fittings, table appointments and stands. The protective film of plating provides an attractive polished appearance and is fairly durable, but is less able to withstand repeated use and washing than stainless steel.

1.07 Uses of metalware

(1) *Cutlery*—
A wide range of manufacturers' cutlery patterns is available of which probably the best known is the traditional 'Old English' pattern. The number of different items will depend on the catering establishment but is normally about 12 for hotel use (excluding servers). Several features must be taken into account in selecting cutlery of which the most important are:
· quality—of plate or composition, etc;
· balance—in sizes, proportions and weights;
· design—in keeping with the character of the meal and surroundings;
· durability—having regard to use and methods of handling and washing; and
· stackability—nesting with minimum of scratching.
· knife edges—retention of sharpness, and serrations and
· handles—materials and method of fixing. Handles may be of nylon, xylonite, compressed wood (eg rosewood), solid steel or hollow plate and may be in one piece with the blade or fitted with a bolster or rivets.

(2) *Serving items* are generally grouped into:
holloware—tea and coffee sets, dishes and covers, tureens and bowls etc. and
flatware—shallow dishes, plates and trays.
Dishes and flatware may be round, oval or rectangular in shape and are in suitable ratios of size. If a lid is provided it must be well fitted and sufficiently tall, and preferably interchangeable to allow versatility in use. Edges of trays and dishes may be plain or wrapped for rigidity. Components may be sold separately or combined—eg tureen and cover, gravy boat and stand. It is also necessary to make generous provision for serving spoons, ladles and similar utensils.

(3) *Table appointments and accessories* extend over such items as condiment sets, finger bowls, stands, napkin rings, and menu holders.

Badging
1.08 To reduce pilfering tableware may be distinguished by badge marking with a name of symbol. Methods of badging include: etching—burning into steel electrically; stamping—impressing into the surface; and engraving— cutting into the surface. Engraving, which is usually done by hand, is more expensive than other processes and is generally limited to special presentation pieces.

Glassware
1.09 Glass is produced from sand (silicon dioxide) combined

3

The Library, Draitone Manor Restaurant, Excelsior Hotel, London Airport. Trust Houses Forte Ltd.
Based on reproduction of Regency style in a modern hotel building, the design of the Draitone Manor restaurant involved careful research and detailing of the furniture, glassware and silverware to ensure compatibility.

with other substances which produce characteristic properties, and heated to a very high temperature to form a molten mass. This may then be blown or moulded to shape and allowed to cool and solidify by carefully regulating the temperature (annealing). Handles and other parts are attached by welding during this process.

Types of glass

1.10 The various types of glass used for catering utensils and tableware include:

(a) *Soda lime glass*—contains sand, soda ash and limestone as the principal ingredients. Used for inexpensive glassware.

(b) *Lead crystal*—includes sand, red lead and potash which produces a slightly softer glass of high brilliance. The surface is usually cut to produce prismatic effects and sparkle.

(c) *Borosilicate glass*—addition of borax increases hardness and heat resistance and this glass is used for flameware.

(d) *Tempered and toughened glass*—by tempering glass can be made more resistant to the effects of heat and this is the normal treatment applied to ovenware glass and glassware generally which needs to withstand heavy usage.

1.11 Glass surfaces may be decorated by: cutting to produce sharp grooves, etc, which increase internal reflection; sand blasting to texture the surface; acid etching to produce obscuration and patterns or for badging; engraving by grinding wheels to provide patterns; or surface-printed with decorative patterns from transfers during annealing.

Selection and use of glassware

1.12 In selecting glassware the following features should

be considered:

(a) *Range of stocks*—multi-purpose use where possible.

(b) *Matching suites*—glassware items should be basically matching in design.

(c) *Functional aspects*—smooth simple robust shapes; width of opening for washing; efficiency of draining, drying, pouring and stacking.

(d) *Manufacture*—clarity of glass, freedom from cracks, faults, bubbles, distortion.

(e) *Replacement*—availability of supplies.

Storage requirements for glassware must be examined in the light of the large surface areas needed and the divergent use of glasses in bar and dining areas. Specially designed hanging racks and trays may be used for glasses to facilitate handling.

Consideration must also be given to glass washing facilities which may be kept separate from the main dish washing area to avoid heavy soiling. Marking by lime scale is more conspicuous on a glass surface than on other glazed ware, and care should be taken in selection of water softening apparatus.

The range of glasses used in hotels and licensed restaurants is usually extensive. Some—for example liqueur and brandy glasses—are specifically associated with particular drinks, while others may be interchangeable to some extent, particularly in certain sizes. The degree of sophistication in glassware will greatly depend on the type of restaurant, and variety of drinks sold, but rationalisation in glass shapes and sizes is desirable.

Table 9 (v) Typical sizes of glasses in common use

Purpose	Capacity millilitres*	Fluid ounces
Liqueurs	35	1¼
Port and sherry	70, 85	2½, 3
General wine and spirit	140, 190, 225	5, 6 , 8
Brandy	155, 340	6, 12
Beer and lager (½ pint)	285, 340	10, 12
Beer and lager (1 pint)	570	20
Tumblers (water, squash)	225, 285, 340	8, 10, 12

* Rounded to nearest 5ml

Plastics

1.13 The use of plastic tableware is still very limited in restaurant practice, partly because of unfavourable consumer reaction and, in part, due to the difficulties of maintaining a satisfactory appearance of a plastic surface which is liable to be damaged by scratching, scuffing and heat.

It is in the development of disposable cutlery and tableware that plastic materials have become widely used, being relatively cheap and easy to produce and having appropriate properties of strength, rigidity or flexibility as required, with light weight, adequate impermeability, low noise, good heat retention, stackability and good storage. In particular, plastics are suitable for vending machines including those providing food heated by microwaves.

9.13 Plastics employed in tableware include melamine and polystyrene.

Melamine is available in white and coloured mouldings for dishes, bowls, cups and similar items. It is extremely tough and resistant to abrasion, making it suitable for decorative place mats and as a surfacing to moulded laminated trays and bowls.

Polystyrene is the most common plastic material used for serving food. It is rigid, can be produced in various forms, and is used in lightweight 'glasses', jugs and other table items.

Table 9 (vi) Uses of polystyrene

Type	Use
Thin sections	Cups for vending machines, inserts for polypropylene holders, plates and trays in plain and compartmented shapes
Thick sections	Bowls, cutlery, dishes
Translucent	'Glasses' for cold drinks, jugs
White opaque	Normal appearance for plastic items
Coloured	Items in limited plain colours
Expanded	Stiffer mouldings, light in weight and with good insulation properties

2 TABLE LINEN

2.01 Table cloths, napkins, and similar items are traditionally made from linen—a natural fibre produced from flax—and this term is still applied, in a general sense, to all table fabrics although it is now common for linen to be substituted by other fibres. The main fibres used in the yarns of table fabrics are:

(a) *Linen*—natural fibre of flax which is long, smooth, straight and almost solid, giving good resistance to soiling and abrasion, high density, lustre, strength and weight, but has a poor resilience and easily creases. Used in high quality table cloths.

(b) *Cotton*—short natural fibres which are moderately strong and produce tight yarns with a slightly raised surface which easily soils, tends to leave a deposit of lint and has a low resilience producing creasing. Cotton is the most common fabric material in catering used alone, in 'union' with linen (typically 60/40) or blended with rayon.

(c) *Viscose rayon* is pure regenerated cellulose which is highly absorbent and has a relatively low wet strength and resilience. To provide greater strength rayon is normally blended with cotton for table fabrics.

(d) *nylon (polyamide fibre) and Terylene (polyester fibre)* are synthetic filaments which have high elasticity and strength, good durability and resistance to creasing, moisture and staining. Terylene is less affected by electrostatic dust attraction and sunlight than nylon, and may be combined with cotton (67/33) to give a more conventional appearance.

Properties of fibres may be modified by treatment such as mercerisation of cotton and linen to form smoother sheened fibres with increased strength and affinity for dyes.

Selection of fabrics for table use

2.02 Many features must be taken into account when selecting fabrics for table linen. To some extent these—such as colour, pattern, texture and closeness of weave—will be closely related to the style and décor of the restaurant. Other features requiring examination are concerned with the serviceability of the fabric and operational factors, for instance, the repair and replacement of the table

4
International Restaurant, London Hilton Hotel.
Situated on the second floor, the restaurant overlooks Park Lane and Hyde Park and reflects the culinary experience of Hiltons around the world. The table linen incorporates the Hilton motif.

cloths. As a summary, the factors include the following:
· appearance, weave, colour and pattern appropriate for décor;
· strength and durability to withstand use and laundering;
· resistance to soiling and fading;
· ease of repair, replacement and matching; and
· finish—quality of edging and stitching.

Coloured cloths

2.03 The introduction of coloured cloths may be partly functional, since they show less marking, and partly for reasons of decoration. Compared with white, coloured fabrics are more difficult to launder, repair and replace, and are often liable to fading. A compromise may be adopted using coarse coloured slips over white cloths or white slips—of cloth or paper—on a coloured cloth base. Often, where a décor requires colour contrast in the tables this may be more easily and economically achieved by exposing decorative table tops, or by using place mats and/or coloured serviettes with white table clothes.

Weaves

2.04 A fabric is woven by interlacing a weft yarn under and over parallel lines of warp yarn. The character of the fabric will depend on the types of fibres used, the thickness of the warp and weft yarns, and the variation and closeness of the weave. Standard weaves used in table

linen are: the plain weave and the figured or damask weave.

In *plain weave* the weft yarn passes alternately under and over the warp yarn to produce a smooth surface effect. Coloured cloths are sometimes loosely woven with thick yarns and, in other cases, the warp and weft threads may be made to look slightly thicker at intervals to give a more interesting surface to the cloth. Decorative effects can also be introduced by the use of threads dyed in different colours or by applying bands of contrasting colour to the edges.

Fancy weaves, such as twills and checks, are not widely used in table linen but are more common for furnishings and uniforms. The twill weave gives a very firm close fabric formed by the weft yarn crossing the warp at different intervals—for example, over one then under three yarns.

Damask is a patterned or figured cloth in which the ground is developed in warp satin weave and the pattern in weft satin weave. The range of patterns available extends from traditional flower designs, classical inspired themes and acanthus leaf motifs to modern designs such as the damask cloth woven with polka dots or sprigs or with a border of damask as a plain satin band. Matching serviettes and tray cloths are also available.

Patterns are produced—in a Jacquard loom—by varying the spacing of the weft yarns and linen damask is of two kinds. Single damask is usually woven in a five end satin

5
Parador nacional Carlos V. Spanish National Tourist Office.
Fine table linen in a traditional setting created within a
reconstructed palace now used as an hotel.

weave, each weft crossing over four then under one warp thread to form the design. The numbers of warp and weft threads are the same, with about 5·5 to 7 threads per mm² (140 to 175 per sq in) and a typical linen cloth weight is 0·19 to 0·20 kg/m² (5½ to 6 ounces/sq yd). Double damask is usually woven in an eight end satin weave, the weft thread crossing over seven then under one warp thread to give a pattern which is more distinct. Although not so tightly woven, the cloth is more fine than single damask. There are more weft threads than warp threads and the sum of threads should not be less than 7 per mm² (176 per sq in) and may be up to 9/mm² (220/sq in) or more. The double damask cloth is rarely produced nowadays.

Stocks

2.05 As a rule, for each table cloth or serviette in use, five others will be required to allow for collection, washing, return, resting and reserve. Hence the minimum requirements of table linen will be six times the number of tables and place settings, and the allowance for wear and replacement is usually based on 20 per cent per year (ie a five-year cycle).

To ensure proper stock control these articles should be marked for identification including an indication of the date of purchase. Motifs may be embroidered or woven into the cloth. Storage requirements will depend very much on the size of the establishment and the extent to which linen is used elsewhere. For example, in an hotel a linen room is normally essential with facilities for storage, sorting, checking, and repair work. A large hotel may have its own laundry while other large groups of hotels or restaurants may centralise this service. In most cases, however, laundry work is contracted out and in most restaurants linen storage is provided in cupboards.

The main essentials of storage are:

· easy access and adequate space and lighting to allow inspection, separation, and rotation of linen;
· warm, dry, ventilated areas to allow airing and prevent mildew and odour contamination;
· avoidance of stained wood, iron and other possible sources of marks and of risk of damage by tearing;
· access for cleaning and smooth interior surfaces which can be easily kept clean and free from rodent and insect infestation; and
· space for dirty linen hampers, for sorting and checking and—depending on the establishment—for repair and other work

To reduce capital outlay and the associated costs of storage and administration, the trend—particularly in small catering establishments—is towards hiring linen.

3 THE DESIGN OF THE MENU

3.01 A menu serves as a means of communication between kitchen, dining room and customer. It informs the customer what food is available and, depending on the establishment, facilitates his choice of meal by providing various balanced alternatives. In this capacity, a menu must measure up to the customer's expectations while, at the same time, arousing interest in the food items available.

6

The Happy Casserole restaurant, Portsmouth Centre Hotel. Centre Hotels Ltd.
This design illustrates the effective combination of contrasting patterns and shapes. One wall is entirely occupied by a window which is warmed by means of skirting heaters and fitted with a dado rail to allow tables to be positioned around the perimeter. The motif of the restaurant is represented in the menu holders.

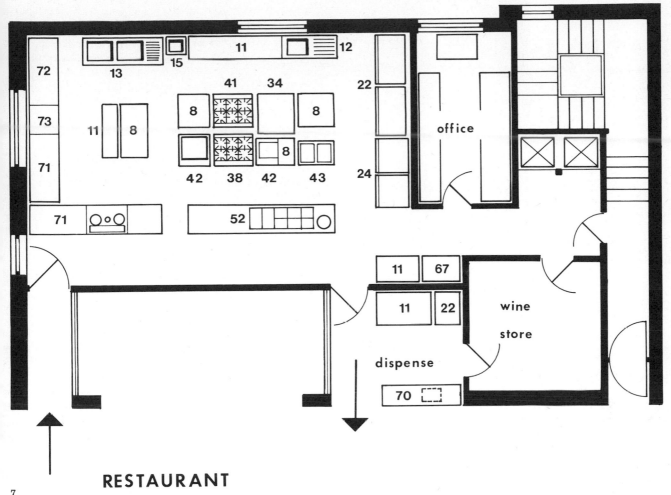

RESTAURANT

7
Kitchen equipment by Oliver Toms Ltd.
Plan showing the layout of kitchens to the restaurant.

In the same way as a self-service counter promotes impulse buying, the menu has a sales function through its appeal and descriptive persuasion. From the viewpoint of design, a menu must satisfy three main requirements:
· it must be easy to handle in terms of size and layout;
· easy to read with concise accurate descriptions and prices; and
· attractively designed, in keeping with the surroundings.
So far as the dining room and kitchen operations are concerned, the roles of the menu are more extensive and provide the basis for ordering raw materials and for pre-planning and sequencing the preparation, cooking, and service of the meal.

3.02 Compilation of suitable menus involves considerable expertise and must take into account numerous factors such as limitations of equipment and catering staff, costs of food, and balance of choice. These may be summarised as follows:

Preparation facilities	Scope of equipment and capabilities of staff. A simple but well produced meal is preferable to one which is over-elaborate.
Service facilities	Number of waiting staff, level of training, layout of dining room and tableware. Meals may be à la carte and/or table d'hôte.
Costs	Costs of food materials and the prices which must be charged. As a broad indication, raw food costs are normally about 30 to 40 per cent of the meal prices.
Occasion	The menu will normally vary with the time of the day (lunch, high tea, dinner, etc) or the occasion (functions).
Market	Numbers of people likely to use the restaurant at different times and for different types of meals.
Balance	Balance of choice in variety of food, sequence of dishes and preparation, balance of colour, quality, nutritional value and price.
Description	Descriptions must be clear, concise, accurate, in correct sequence and easily understood by the type of customer likely to use the restaurant.
Repeatability	Having established an appropriate menu, consideration must be given to the frequency of its use in order to ensure variety in the choice of meals.

Food research
3.03 No matter how well designed, the primary function of a restaurant is to sell food and while the facilities and décor play a valuable part in providing convenience, comfort and atmosphere, the ultimate success or failure of a catering enterprise or service will depend on the choice and quality of the food and whether this represents good value for money at the particular level of catering involved.

This last point is important since comparisons must not—as is so often done—be made between different levels of catering but only between catering establishments of the same type competing in the same market. The success of a fish and chip saloon will depend, not on whether its products compare with those of an expensive hotel restaurant,

8

9

The Mediterranean Cafe, Royal Lancaster Hotel, London W2.
The outdoor atmosphere of a Mediterranean scene has been
created by featuring the building structure as a component of
the interior design. The scenery is also represented in the
design of the carpet, furniture and decoration[8]. Positioned
adjacent to the bar, the entrance to the servery forms part of
the background[9].

10
Silver Table Coffee Shop, Centre Airport Hotel, Centre Hotels Ltd.
Displayed on a silver table, this attractive presentation of food and wine correctly forms a focal point of interest.

but on whether the food and service is better than those of other saloons and snack bars in the vicinity.

The first step towards producing good food is research. It is not enough to expect that traditional ingredients and methods can be used in modern catering without substantial modification, nor can catering requirements be translated from one level or scale to the next by simply altering the quality or quantities. Research into the most suitable ingredients and their preparation is just as vital as market research and this must not only be concerned with food science as it is practised on a large scale. It must include practical requirements at a local level such as:

· improved control over the quality and keeping properties of the ingredients;
· simplicity, speed and economy of preparation using the minimum of equipment and labour;
· retention of freshly cooked appearance and flavour of the food under operating conditions; and
· appearance and balance of taste, texture and colour when food is presented as a meal.

10 DESIGN BRIEFING GUIDE

1 DESIGN BRIEFING GUIDE

Considerations	Data required

1 PRELIMINARY SURVEYS

Market survey and feasibility studies — Establish market potential for various types of catering, patterns of trade, types of customers, expenditure likely on meals, preferences and other influences on trade.

Site location — May precede above—in a town centre site is usually predetermined and the need is to establish its best use and development.

Site considerations — Location should take account of convenience of access, local attractions and external influences, competition, restrictions to development and access for goods.

2 SITE DEVELOPMENT

Town and Country Planning Acts — Permission normally required for new development or material change in use of premises. For new sites, outline application should be submitted first to establish use before further investigation.

Demolition works — Approval for proposed building demolition work, safety measures, access to site, etc.

Licensing Acts — Proposal to apply for licence to sell alcoholic drink on the premises advertised. Advertisement—before planning application—and licence may also be required for music and entertainment.

3 ACCESS

Deliveries — Consider means of access for food delivery and collection of refuse. Vehicle turning space. Facilities for storage of refuse.

Unloading facilities — Ascertain delivery times and any restrictions on delivery, methods of unloading, checking and weighing goods.

Staff entry — Consider possible routes, secondary staff entrance or use of main entrance, control and security arrangements, suitability for fire escape requirements.

Customer entrance — Examine main modes of transport and requirements for main entrance from street, car parking and secondary entrances.

Employee catering — Consider relationship between canteen and work areas, travel distance, convenience and environmental surroundings. Similar considerations applied to other dining rooms.

Cloakrooms — Positions of cloakrooms, sanitary conveniences in relation to dining area and circulation routes. Numbers of units and size of rooms determined.

4 RESTAURANT POLICY

Character of restaurant(s) — Ascertain general character of restaurant(s) appropriate for customer needs, type of room, overall size—or number to be accommodated; possibility of dual service and separate restaurants at different levels.

Catering policy — Standards of size and design to be adopted based on policy of operating company.

Cost policy — Capital cost limitations on building and on fitting out. Leasehold restraints. Anticipated life of concept and estimated cost in use.

Menu — Type of meals to be offered, level of sophistication and choice.

5 SERVICE ARRANGEMENTS

Type of service — Determine type of service appropriate for number of customers, peak demand, meal range and price. Dual service or a choice of restaurants may be provided.

Arrangement — Decide position of service counter in relation to entrance, dining area and kitchen. Plan circulation routes.

Counter details — Determine details for service counters, speed of service needed, length and shape of counters, by-passing arrangements, duplicate and multiple service points, tray collection and return.

Waiter/waitress service — Establish numbers of covers and staff required, waiter or waitress service, positions of stations, standard of service, circulation routes.

Considerations	Data required
Cash payment	Method of payment to be used; location of cashier points, control system.
Dirty tableware	Examine alternative methods and assess suitability of points for disposal of dirty tableware relative to circulation routes and dishwashing area.
Self-clearance	Facilities for self-clearing of tableware, type of tray and utensils, method of use.
Trolley clearance	Trolley circulation routes, types of trolleys, parking areas for unloading and storage, cleaning facilities.

6 RESTAURANT DESIGN

Circulation	Consider the travel routes to be followed by customers and serving staff, the positions and other requirements for corridor and aisle spaces, entrances and exits.
Décor	Decide the basic scheme of interior design, its method of interpretation and constructional features to create the character and style of restaurant desired.
Table and seating arrangements	Having regard to access, service, windows and other features of the room, prepare preliminary interior layout plans showing the arrangement, grouping and sizes of tables and seats and determine the most appropriate seating densities and types of furniture.
Floor	Consider the construction of the flooring and select suitable floor coverings having regard to the décor of the room and other requirements, eg intensity of wear, degree of comfort, noise, ease of cleaning and comparable costs.
Walls	Examine the choice of alternative wall linings and coverings including the possibility of varying the surface finish to meet special needs—staining, rubbing, fingerings, etc.
Ceiling	Decide an appropriate construction and finish for the ceiling taking into account its height, the décor, fire risk, regulation of heating, ventilation and lighting and need to incorporate services.
Fixtures and fittings	Select and purposely design suitable fixtures and fittings for the restaurant including built-in furniture and other units and decorative features, in each case having due regard to functional needs.
Furniture	Specify details of the furniture—type, style, quality, quantity and the requirements as to design, manufacture and delivery.
Decoration	Decide a scheme of decoration including the main colours and contrasts, wall coverings and other methods of creating texture and variety.
Furnishings	Determine requirements and select materials for curtains, upholstery and other fabric coverings taking into account the difficulties of cleaning, replacement, etc.
Noise	Consider the need to reduce noise entry from outside and from the kitchen, etc., the internal noise climate, absorption of sounds, sound clarity and reverberation—particularly in large rooms intended for functions.
Ventilation and heating	Examine alternative arrangements for heating and ventilation suitable for the varying conditions, the use of air-conditioning, balancing of air flows and other aspects of planning for engineering services.
Lighting	Decide appropriate standards for functional and background levels of lighting, the extent of variation in lighting and means of regulation and select suitable lighting fittings.
Safety and security	Review the risk of fire, accidents and other hazards and consider the provisions for fire escape and security.
Control and management	Determine the location, design and servicing of cash desks, waiting stations and other units required for operation and control of the restaurant.

7 KITCHEN DESIGN

Catering policy	Consider policy of food buying, preparation and menu choice in relation to size of kitchen, staffing, equipment and capital costs.
Food storage	Examine method of food purchasing, availability of local supplies, areas of storage required for vegetables, dry goods, chilling and deep freeze stores.
Control	Stock control methods, checking and weighing of deliveries, secondary kitchen stores and refrigerators.
Preparation space	Consider policy with regard to centralisation, commissary arrangements and buying in of prepared foods. Determine space requirements for vegetables, meat and fish and pastry preparation.
Layout	Plan layout on flow routes of food, convenient access to stores cooking area and service, location and separation—if necessary—of work areas.
Preparation facilities	Locate positions of work benches, sinks, potato peeler, vegetable preparation, mixer and equipment for pastry preparation, etc.
Cooking areas	Decide type of equipment required in light of catering policy, menu choice and peak demand; unit sizes, possibility of dual use and flexibility.
Layout of equipment	Plan groupings of equipment aisle and working spaces in relationship to engineering services, preparation and service areas.
Engineering services	Decide requirements for ventilation, space heating, lighting, hot and cold water supplies, electrical and gas services, waste disposal and drainage. Plan layouts of engineering services and terminals having regard to positions of equipment, loadings and possible extensions.
Access and control to services	Locate access and control points, switchgear, meters, fans and motors, filters, interceptors and traps, inspection chambers, valves and other service points.
Maintenance	Consider maintenance requirements—

Considerations	Data required

access, working space, cleaning and replacements and storage requirements for cleaning equipment and materials.

Construction Decide materials for floors, walls and ceilings and needs for floor drainage, hygiene and cleaning, durability, noise reduction, light reflection, access to services.

Administration Provisions for supervision, office work and records made by partitioning off area in kitchen or elsewhere.

Food Hygiene Regulations Consult public health inspector regarding legal requirements and appropriate provisions.

Waste disposal Approval of local authority required for type of refuse storage and access for refuse vehicles and disposal of waste debris to public sewer.

8 FOOD SERVICE

Layout Plan facilities for service of food, positions of counters in relation to cooking area and dining room, means of transferring and holding food, use of pass-through units, refrigerated or heated trolleys and other equipment.

Supplementary dining areas Consider means of conveying food to other dining areas, banquet rooms, etc; provision of service lifts, food conveyors, insulated containers and multi-purpose trolleys.

Counter details Decide arrangement and sequence of food service, provision of display counters, heated and refrigerated cupboards, bains-marie, cold wells, ice cream conservators, beverage units.

Control and circulation Consider means of regulating movement and circulation, provision of barriers and screens, positions and types of menu boards, tray stands, cutlery, glasses and other table items.

9 CENTRAL KITCHENS

Feasibility Examine relative costs of installation and operation, and practical features of processing, storage and distribution.

Blast freezing and storage Determine preparation output and maximum loading for blast freezer and cold stores; layout in relation to kitchen and dispatch areas, and type of equipment required.

Transport Examine alternative means of distribution from central production kitchen to peripheral units, facilities for off-loading and recharging, etc.

Finishing kitchens Consider details of size, reheating equipment, facilities for supplementary preparation and methods of food service.

10 BAR SERVICE

Location Determine suitable location in relation to entrance, cloakrooms, restaurant, kitchen and wine storage areas.

Lounge Assess size required, seating and tables, waiting and circulation space. Consider

multi-purpose use—eg as coffee lounge, for light meals or as reception area.

Décor Determine the character of the lounge and bar style of furniture and fittings, colour scheme, use of patterns, introduction of motifs, selection of wall coverings, carpet and other features.

Bar Design bar details for construction, lighting, fittings, sinks and glass washing facilities, water, electricity and other services, access to lounge restaurant and wine stores.

Engineering services Allow for integration of appropriate heating, ventilation, lighting and other services into design. Decide lighting fittings and regulation of lighting. Consider noise reduction and insulation to adjacent areas.

Safety from fire Fire regulations must be taken into account and fire authority consulted during planning stage on all aspects.

Stores Examine position of stores and means of access for deliveries, return of empties and bar service. Detail constructional features to facilitate thermal insulation, hygiene and cleanliness, security. Decide method of air cooling/heating to regulate temperature and ventilation.

Security Consider general aspects of control and security of bar, stores and premises having regard to insurance requirements.

Licensing Acts Submit application to sell spirits, beer, cider and wine on the premises. Approval will depend on suitability of the premises with regard to safety, construction, sanitary accommodation, and other provisions.

Bar catering Decide whether to provide facilities for bar catering and examine requirements for installation of back-bar appliances, preparation and counter surfaces, local storage, washing and waste disposal facilities, engineering services, ventilation and other needs.

11 WASH-UP AREA

Layout Consider arrangements for collecting or depositing soiled tableware, transportation to dish washing machine, and return of clean tableware back to servery.

Equipment Examine details of dish washing machines suitable for quantities of tableware at peak periods of use and provision of supplementary sinks, benching, trolleys, waste disposal facilities.

Construction Determine constructional features with regard to extent of splashing, steam, damage, soiling, noise. Provisions to minimise noise entry to dining area.

Services Assess requirements and positions for engineering services including hot and cold water and water at sterilising temperature, softening plant, waste outlets, exhaust ventilation and lighting.

12 STAFF FACILITIES

Numbers Assess numbers of staff of each sex to be

Considerations	Data required

employed in kitchen, stores, servery, dining rooms.

Offices, Shops and Railway Premises Act Consider legal requirements in relation to wcs, washing facilities, first aid, accommodation for clothing, facilities for meals, safety and means of escape in event of fire from all areas.

Sanitary conveniences Decide locations of wcs etc., numbers, separation for each sex, screening, privacy, lighting, ventilation—including ventilation of intervening space between food room—constructional details, possibility of noise transmission to restaurant and engineering services requirements.

Control Consider facilities for time recording, records and office facilities.

13 PUBLIC CLOAKROOMS

Requirements Determine location, size, provisions for coats, hats, umbrellas, attendants, sanitary conveniences, washing facilities, powder room, mirrors, and other needs as appropriate.

14 OFFICE

Provision Consider need for manager's office and space necessary for working areas, desks, record files, safe, typing services and staff as necessary.

15 REFUSE

Requirements Determine appropriate storage for refuse facilities for washing down the area, means of access for collection. Approval of local authority sought to proposals.

16 HEATING, ETC

Boiler room Locate appropriate space for boiler room, if required, with provisions for oil storage if used, safety, ventilation, security, regulation and servicing, flues and disposal of gas products.

Ventilation Decide extent of sophistication in air-conditioning desirable and positions for fans, plant, intake and exhaust outlets.

17 LEGAL PROVISIONS

Building Regulations Obtain approval of local authority to proposed building works and installation of appliances and services.

Statutory water, gas and electricity undertakings Apply for connections and service supplies as necessary and comply with installation requirements.

18 TABLEWARE

Policy Consider type and range of items required for tableware, table appointments and serving dishes.

Quality, quantity Decide quality of china, metalware and other items, details of shapes, sizes, patterns and quantity of each required for use and stocks.

Linen On a question of policy, decide whether table cloths and linen serviettes are to be used and specify quantity, materials, weaves, colours and qualities required.

Stores Consider areas of storage needed for stocks of tableware and linen and detail storage conditions and their provision.

19 MAINTENANCE

Cleaning Having regard to cleaning requirements and equipment, provide space for cleaning materials, vacuum cleaners, brooms, floor polishers and other items.

Future maintenance Submit proposals for future maintenance needs including means of servicing equipment, cleaning filters, replacing components, redecoration of surfaces, and schedule of renovations and replacements based on life of concept.

2 CONVERSIONS

2.01 Most town centre restaurants are constructed in existing premises which may or may not have been previously used for a similar purpose. The conversion work usually involves modifying the internal space to provide suitable dining and kitchen areas and may include structural alterations to allow the removal of internal walls, enlargement of windows, provision of entrances, and staircases or lift shafts. The tendency in modern restaurants is for the revenue-producing space—the dining and drinking areas—to be made as large as possible with a proportionate reduction in the size of the kitchen. In many cases, when an existing restaurant undergoes modernisation, most of the space previously occupied by a kitchen of traditional proportions may be converted to form an additional dining area.

Much of the work in restaurant conversions is in the nature of shopfitting and, generally, the installation of new electrical and ventilation plant is also involved. The average life of a themed restaurant is only about five to seven years, after which alterations in style and services will normally be required in order to keep in line with contemporary standards.

2.02 Whilst the costs of constructional work, engineering services and furnishings vary widely, depending on such factors as the location, type and age of the building and also the commercial value of the premises, the following analyses—based on two of the schemes illustrated in this book—represent typical proportions of the costs incurred in converting existing property to restaurants.

Table 10 (i) Typical proportions of costs in restaurant conversions

Location	Dukes (Ref 712)	Day and night of the Chimera (Ref 801)
Type of work	Percentages of total costs	
Preliminaries	5	5
Structural work	17	7
Plumbing and drainage	6	9
Mechanical ventilation	8	10
Electrical installation and lifts	14	15
Carpentry and joinery work	19	7
Shopfront, metalwork and glazing	14	18
Seating and tables	5	6
Finishes and decor	19	23
	100	100

Notes

(a) The proportionate cost of mechanical ventilation in-

1

2

3

Mandy's Kitchen. Equipment by Oliver Toms Ltd.
Illustrations of the alterations to an office building during the construction of a restaurant. The entrance[1] is created from window space[2] and the interior design incorporates structural columns which have been extended by wrought iron work to reduce the apparent length of the room[3]. A suspended ceiling has been constructed to enclose the structural beams and engineering services[4]. The restaurant, which is in a basement, is mechanically ventilated through diffuser grills positioned along tops of the walls.

4

5

The entrance steps leading down into the restaurant.

175

male wc's

female wc's

staff wc's

female
staff
changing

male staff
changing

92

PLANT
ROOM

92

cold
room

29

12

11

81

13

8

2

13

25

15

27 16   10   24

41   42

43

19

42/48

38 35 46 32

KITCHEN

77 72 73 71 76

75

60

56

9

52

69

70

60 92

RESTAURANT

DRINKING
AREA

BAR

92

1

12

1

store

OFFICE

1

DRY
STORE

1

BEER
STORE

1

BASEMENT

6

Kitchen layout and plan of restaurant, Mandy's Kitchen.
A typical island grouping of cooking equipment surrounded
by the work tops, sinks and preparation facilities. This kitchen
is located in a basement necessitating complete mechanical
ventilation.

| ft | | 5 | | 10 | | 15 | | 20 |
| m | 1 | 2 | 3 | 4 | 5 | 6 |

creases where full air-conditioning plant is installed—for example, in basements.

(b) Catering equipment is normally supplied directly by the client and, therefore, is not included in these figures. For restaurant schemes the additional cost of installed equipment is about 6 to 8 per cent on the total costs of conversion.

2.03 Estimates of the actual costs for restaurant conversions change with situation and time in addition to depending on the extent and quality of the work involved. Unit costs are also liable to be distorted where, for example, the restaurant area includes space for reception, entertainment and other ancillary functions.

An analysis of schemes, based on 1972 prices, for internal reconstruction and conversion of a number of city centre premises ranging from snack bars to high quality restaurants indicated a scale of costs from £85 to £215 per m² (£8 to £20 per sq ft) and from £150 to £500 per seat. These figures, which include fittings and furniture, are representative but do not include the extremes of costs.

Standards to be adopted in the demolition of buildings are outlined in BSCP 94: 1971: *Demolition*.

3 LITERATURE

For general information and statistics relating to the hotel and catering industry, reference should be made to the following:

Hotel and Catering EDC, Economic Assessment to 1972. London 1969, National Economic Development Office.

Hotel and Catering EDC, Your market 1971. London 1971, National Economic Development Office.

Hotel and Catering EDC, Investment in hotels and catering. London, 1971, National Economic Development Office.

Food Manufacturing EDC, Food statistics. London, 1971, National Economic Development Office.

Industrial Society, Annual survey of canteen prices, costs and subsidies. London 1972, The Industrial Society.

Inter Unit Comparison Survey, Annual surveys of hotels, restaurants and holiday camps. Glasgow 1972, The Scottish Hotel School, University of Strathclyde.

Catering, Hotel and Institutional Managers Year Book 1972. London 1972, Kogan Page Ltd.

Medlik S, Profile of the Hotel and Catering Industry. London 1972. Heinemann.

Kotas, R, Labour costs in restaurants. London 1970, Intertext.

Bryn Jones M, Food services in Britain 1970 to 1980. London 1970, New University Education.

Directory of Products and Members, 1972. London 1972, Catering Equipment Manufacturers Association.

Advisory Committee on Hotels and Restaurants, Reports on tableware, restaurant tables and chairs and on food storage requirements. London 1965–1970, The Council of Industrial Design.

Architects Journal, Principles of hotel design. London 1970, The Architectural Press.

Fairweather L and Sliwa J A, AJ Metric Handbook. London 1969, The Architectural Press.

Cottam D J, Production kitchens, yes or no. Oldham 1969, Stotts of Oldham, Ltd.

The Gas Council, Gas in restaurants. London 1970, The Gas Council Commercial Gas Centre.

The Gas Council, Gas equipment data sheets. London 1972, The Gas Council Commercial Gas Centre.

The Electricity Council, Cater for profit. London 1970, The Electric Catering Centre.

National Catering Inquiry, The British eating out in pubs. London 1970, Smethursts Foods Ltd.

INDEX

Figures in italic refer to pages in which illustrations occur